Advance Praise for

Ideology and the Politics of (In)Exclusion

"Ideology and the Politics of (In)Exclusion is a refreshing volume that troubles the too-easy ethical positions around inclusive schooling. The volume makes apparent the exclusions accompanying popular inclusion rhetoric. In the effort to inspire continuous conversations within a more broadly conceived discursive community, the editor and contributors have provided turgid, new grounds for honoring the paradoxes of schooling and engaging the complexities of life. This is an overdue ice-breaker."

Bernadette Baker, Associate Professor,
University of Wisconsin, Madison

"Linda Ware and her colleagues embrace disability, listen to the politics of disability, and pose troubling questions about professional practice. At a time when disability is becoming ever more medicalized and personalized, the authors of *Ideology and the Politics of (In)Exclusion* remind us that prevailing, professional conceptions of disability always serve a regulatory function, rather than a liberatory one. The contributing authors for this volume, representing diverse international contexts, are at once provocative, critical, theoretical, and engaged in the everyday worlds of disability and education. This is the most clearly political analysis of special education and inclusion yet available in print."

Douglas Biklen, Professor,
University of Syracuse, Syracuse, New York

Ideology
and the Politics
of (In)Exclusion

Studies in the
Postmodern Theory of Education

Joe L. Kincheloe and Shirley R. Steinberg
General Editors

Vol. 270

PETER LANG
New York • Washington, D.C./Baltimore • Bern
Frankfurt am Main • Berlin • Brussels • Vienna • Oxford

Ideology
and the Politics
of (In)Exclusion

EDITED BY
Linda Ware

PETER LANG
New York • Washington, D.C./Baltimore • Bern
Frankfurt am Main • Berlin • Brussels • Vienna • Oxford

Library of Congress Cataloging-in-Publication Data

Ideology and the politics of (in)exclusion / edited by Linda Ware.
p. cm. — (Counterpoints; v. 270)
Includes bibliographical references and index.
1. Inclusive education—Social aspects—Cross-cultural studies.
2. Special education—Social aspects—Cross-cultural studies.
I. Ware, Linda P. II. Series: Counterpoints (New York, N.Y.); v. 270.
LC1200.I34   371.9'046—dc22   2003025199
ISBN 0-8204-7065-1
ISSN 1058-1634

Bibliographic information published by **Die Deutsche Bibliothek**.
Die Deutsche Bibliothek lists this publication in the "Deutsche
Nationalbibliografie"; detailed bibliographic data is available
on the Internet at http://dnb.ddb.de/.

Cover art by Chris Knauf
Cover design by Lisa Barfield

The paper in this book meets the guidelines for permanence and durability
of the Committee on Production Guidelines for Book Longevity
of the Council of Library Resources.

CONTENTS

ACKNOWLEDGMENTS

The contributors wish to thank the Spencer Foundation of Chicago, Illinois for their generous support in funding the original conference from which the chapters in this book are drawn, *Ideology and the Politics of Inclusion*. Their funding not only allowed for the participation of these scholars, but also for scholarships for students to present their own research and to be included in this rigorous critical exchange of ideas.

As the editor of this collection and the conference organizer, I want to acknowledge my former colleagues at the University of Rochester, Lisa Cartwright, Brian Goldfarb, and Lisa Lopez-Levers, who along with Nancy Chin, Stephanie Brown-Clark and David Marcus in the School of Medicine, Department of Medical Humanities, continue in an invaluable partnership. And to the teachers who participated in my research: Michael Occhino, Marianne Holtzberg, and Mary Stuckey—because they resist giving up on young people—they inform my own critical hope.

Finally, I wish to acknowledge *Ali Bey* for his generous presence and enduring joy in my life.

Permissions

"My Place" taken from a book of poetry by Sue Napolitano and reprinted with the permission of Greater Manchester Coalition of Disabled People, Manchester, England.

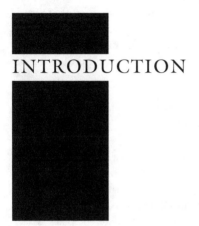

INTRODUCTION

There is no disability, no disabled, outside precise social and cultural constructions; there is no attitude toward disability outside a series of societal references and constructs.
HENRI-JACQUES STIKER

Inclusion, as it has come into *practice* in K12 educational settings, has been misleadingly simplified, if not disguised as an implementation strategy to support school restructuring, and as such it is assumed unencumbered by ideological and political influences. Inclusion dots the educational landscape as an adjective that serves in discussion of the "inclusion" child, the "inclusion" teacher, the "inclusion" classroom, the "inclusion" school, and "inclusion" policy. Its use as a synonym for *mainstreaming, integration* or *special education* further obscures the meaning of this multivalent educational term now common in many international contexts. As a consequence, it is easy to overlook the significance of the ideological distinctions among these terms and to minimize the political terrain unique to each era that shaped special education over time. *Ideology and the Politics of ~~In~~EXclusion* explores and exposes educational "inclusion" by unpacking the ideologies and politics that have come to shape this movement over time and across continents. Because underlying ideologies and politics are deeply embedded in special education their influence on inclusion remains unexamined; thus, this book provides a perspective that is long overdue in both general and special education. It is a timely offering as the United States Congress prepares for the reauthorization of the Individuals with Disabilities Education Act (IDEA), and in an international context as increasingly neoliberal policy agendas target all youth, and not just those in special education. The contributors to this book describe various geographic locales, recount multiple historical contexts, rely upon differing sources of evidence, and as a consequence, relate a more complex and varied notion of "inclusion" than that which is traditionally considered in education. Our efforts recognize and honor the evolving texts of "inclusion" and we take the issue seriously enough to examine closely its components, to see what it's made of, and to understand better what inclusion asks of educators.

Recovering Our History

Umberto Eco (2002) argues that history is always written from a contemporary lens reflective of the historian's obsessions and interests—he likens the process to looking at events from a balcony—the *point of view* depends *always* upon the balcony one occupies. The history of special education, like all histories, is better told across multiple registers that consider both origins and effects. Obviously, the place where one locates the origins of special education is significant, and for the purposes of this book, it is of greater importance to consider how we *continue* to write the story of special education. In the contemporary context, one well-known account is the continuous progress narrative of special education authored by scholars who minimize the field's discontinuities and the influence of ideological and political debates. Brantlinger (2003) faults this special education as *"peaceable kingdom"* narrative as deceptive and detrimental to understanding special education as anything but consensus and collaboration. In contrast, *Ideology and the Politics of InEXclusion* draws upon ideologies of cure, care, benevolence, charity, control, and professionalism in ways that are far more complex and nuanced. These ideologies and others, some of which date back several centuries and across various locales, have historic and continuing influence on educational and social inclusion.

The story so far offers the origin of special education as that which began with the creation of special schools for blind and deaf students abroad in the late 18th century, and soon thereafter in the United States. Safford and Safford (1996) retell this story and further suggest that it was even earlier that Enlightenment thinkers in pre-Revolutionary Paris first influenced special educational instructional pedagogy, approaches to assessment, and behaviorism. In a departure from the medico-pedagogic approach, Armstrong (2002) links special education to the late 18th-century workhouses in France and England, while Richardson (1999) recounts the influence of compulsory schooling in the late 19th century as he reconstructs the institutional shape of special education in America. Borrowing from Foucault's discussion of the institutionalization of disciplinary power, Richardson (1999) argues that the "expanded surveillance " of children sanctioned by special education and school psychology in the 20th century, coupled with the late 19th century mandate for compulsory schooling have calibrated "educability" criteria as natural and inevitable features of today's educational landscape. Others consider the link between institutions and special schools to explore contemporary special education (Trent, 1994; Ware, in press). In the account offered by Trent, parents, who made demands for "special" educational rights, are faulted for inadvertently reinforcing a vision of special education that went "back to the beginning of history" (243). Ware sieves through similar primary source documents, not to fault parents, but to instead fault the medico-pedagogic approach authorized by institutions centuries ago and still firmly entrenched in special education today. Among the various authors, most would agree that the ideological constraints on practice today are not unlike those that date back 100 years. It is more than ironic that, as Barton & Tomlinson (1981) point out, special education in the modern era is often cast as little more than a "historical accident"—an amalgamation of events *seemingly* divested of relationship to regular education. Rather than dismiss these competing perspectives as troublesome and contradictory, they merit debate and critical consideration within a more broadly defined discursive community because ultimately these multiple stories inform how we continue to conceptualize disability, special education, and inclusion.

Disagreements and ideological differences are not uncommon among special educators and inclusion has proven to be one of the more rancorous debates in the field (Brantlinger; 1997; Winzer & Mazurek, 2002). This book is not intended to fuel existing arguments. Instead, our dialogue seeks to engage an audience willing to recognize the broader context of social issues relative to educational inclusion. Obviously, inclusion does not exist in a vacuum—it is more significant than mere implementation strategies in pursuit of the romanticized realm of benign cultural space. Inclusion impacts and is informed by both general and special education and thus this book aims to engage a broad audience of readers, including teachers, administrators, counselors, parents, and educational researchers and scholars who recognize the inextricable link between educational and social inclusion. *Ideology and the Politics of InEXclusion* challenges the medical dominance and professional discourses of special education as a way into a more compelling conversation on educational inclusion in both national and international contexts.

Ideology and the Politics of Inclusion: The Conference

The chapters included here were among several papers presented at a research conference sponsored by the Spencer Foundation in the summer of 1999 at the University of Rochester. The conference, *Ideology and the Politics of Inclusion,* explored the rhetoric and ideology of inclusion in both the United States and abroad, to explicitly trouble the complexity of this international reform movement and to reveal the multiple ways in which ideology impacts educational opportunity for disabled students. The conference was motivated by a critical essay that appeared in the *Review of Educational Research,* "Using Ideology: Cases of Non-recognition of the Politics of Research and Practice in Special Education" by Ellen Brantlinger (1997). Her critique cited the historic reluctance among scholars in the field of special education to recognize and claim their use of ideology in research and practice. Brantlinger dissected the division in the field between the *traditionalists* and the *inclusionists* in a close reading of the research of many well-known special education scholars. Her essay exposed the enhanced legitimizing forces that *traditionalists* utilize to obfuscate the discontinuities inherent in special education's progress narrative, most pointedly the disavowal of nonpositivist research. Specific to inclusion, Brantlinger summarized the chief concerns of the *traditionalists* as: a deep suspicion of inclusion's aims and outcomes; the desire to retain traditional placements; disengagement from broader school restructuring needs; a preoccupation with rational technical solutions and incremental reform; and the long-held disavowal of moral grounding for professional practice (430). In sum, *traditionalists* challenge the research knowledge base that informs the inclusion movement because they claim it lacks rigor and scientific objectivity and fails to conform to the linear model of positivist research privileged in their own scholarship. Their conceptual approach to understanding assumes objectivity through measured observation, calibrated interventions, and pursuit of singular truth that rests on an appeal to facts.

Brantlinger contrasted this stance with that of the *inclusionists*, who rely on multiple inquiry methods derived from postpositivist research paradigms that fully recognize ideology is "at work in everything we experience" (Zizek, 1994). Their conceptual approach privileges subjective, multiple truths and complex rather than simple analyses that tend to ignite the *traditionalists* to criticize their research and scholarship as "too ideological." These divisions, according to Brantlinger, predate the current conversation on inclusion and have long served to underwrite the contrived dichotomy between ideology and empiricism manifest in the interventions, procedures, policy, and beliefs that underwrite practice. Brantlinger's essay provoked both outrage and accolades in a field that remains divided on the issue of inclusion, divided on research methods, divided on the merit of insider accounts of living with disability, and divided on the uses of ideology. Brantlinger urged new conversations among educators to revisit the moral and ethical dimensions of special education policy and practice and to acknowledge the multiple forms of ideology that influence special education frameworks and practices.

The conference "Call for Papers" invited participants to read the Brantlinger essay and to contribute "cases of recognition" across international contexts. Researchers and participants from Australia, England, New Zealand, Scotland, Canada, and the United States engaged in a cross-cultural dialogue on educational reform and inclusion that addressed three primary goals:

1. To explore how a very narrow framework for understanding disability has led to the inequitable educational policy and practice;
2. To examine the historic relationship between disability, special educational needs/schooling, and general education;

3. To encourage understanding of the moral consequences of espoused ideology versus lived ideology among academic researchers.

Drawing from prior research, ongoing research, and theoretical investigations, these chapters serve as cases of recognition/multiperspectival analyses of ideology and the politics of inclusion within historical, educational, cultural, and social contexts. *Ideology and the Politics of inEXclusion* allows for a view from more than one balcony. The contributors reveal a terrain of discontinuities and explore the subtle and overt ways that both ideology and politics shape special education and that which has come to be called *inclusion*. Their task was to disrupt the prevailing discourse on educational inclusion as that which occurs in a vacuum, separate from social inclusion; and instead to consider the narrow frameworks, historic influences, and research tensions that underwrite *Ideology and the Politics of inEXclusion*.

Overview of the Book

The book is divided into three parts. Part I, "Narrow Frameworks/Endorsed Inequities," opens with "Ideologies Discerned, Values Determined: Getting Past the Hierarchies of Special Education" by Ellen Brantlinger. This opening chapter provides a brief overview of various definitions of ideology in which Brantlinger contends that ideological critiques are not merely a scholarly "fiddling" but are necessary for understanding social life. She argues that because ideologies operate largely at an unconscious level, they go unnoticed, especially those that are most common. Failure to attend to ideology or denial of its existence, Brantlinger contends, ensures that educators are left with "partial knowledge" of everyday events in schools and communities, and perhaps more dangerous, an "incomplete understanding" of their own work. Her chapter teases out the ideological roots of inclusive practice and explores how ideology critique can be used as a tool for discerning detrimental and beneficial ideologies. In Chapter 2, "The Aesthetics of Disability as a Productive Ideology," Julie Allan provides further discussion of ideology and its uses to explore what *counts* as ideological critique. She suggests the work of disabled writers to underwrite her example of "productive ideology" derived from versions of kynicism (Sloterdijk, 1987) and are illustrated with the works of Czechoslovakian writers Kundera, Kafka, and Hasek. Allan seeks to portray disabled people as both inside and outside ideology in that which she describes as an aesthetics *of disability* that can powerfully subvert and disrupt disabling barriers in pursuit of praxis as social change. Chapter 3, "Meaning in the Service of Power," by Roger Slee, follows on the concerns raised by both Brantlinger and Allan as he explores the production and reproduction of meaning relative to disability in the context of education. Slee brings together scenarios from his childhood, his experience in teacher preparation, and his years as a teacher, professor, and dean to support his claims that regardless of the context or era, inclusive education is about little else than the politics of recognition. Thus, the view of inclusion espoused by the special needs industry of rational technical outcomes merits critical reexamination. Slee further maintains that *traditional* special education is a dangerous liaison for those who seek to promote educational inclusion.

In Part II, "Historic Influences: Disability and 'Special' Schooling," the chapters explore the uses of ideology that have played out over time to impact disability and schooling. Collectively, the goal for this section is transparency—to reveal how ideology really "works" in social, economic, and educational systems otherwise held to be natural, inevitable, and good. In Chapter 4, "The Politics of Special Education: A Necessary or Irrelevant Approach?," Len Barton suggests that the question of school governance, educational funding, and the purpose of education have been redefined by the globalizing tendency of economic rationality. Barton holds that in this more politicized context schools are held hostage to increased control over the work context and the dehumanizing culture of teaching that follows. These new demands, in turn, prompt major changes to the purpose, content, and outcome of teacher training—all with negative implications for inclusion. The arguments made by Barton inform Chapter 5, "Race and Special Education," by Sally Tomlinson, who opens with a brief history of the stigmatization of minority and migrant students in the United Kingdom. She seeks to contextualize the question: Why, at the end of the 20th century, are children who are perceived as racially different persistently regarded as prime candidates for removal from mainstream education? Her case study examines the well-entrenched mechanisms in schools that ensure the overrepresentation of minority students in special education and that simultaneously reinscribe the eugenic impulse in everyday practice. Tomlinson contends that this historically disproportional data will be exacerbated by increased competition in the present moment through the marketization of schooling.

Chapter 6, "Ideology and the Origins of Exclusion," by Keith Ballard, considers the influence of New Right Ideology in New Zealand as it underwrites the social construction of "unworthy others" in a system of governance that promotes individualism, restricted government, and free market forces to authorize a "culture of contentment" (Galbraith, 1992). Citing current policy documents, Ballard, like Tomlinson, implicates enduring eugenic assumptions that continue to influence economic, education, employment, and welfare policy in New Zealand. Ballard maintains that in fact, "only ideology matters" to support Brantlinger's (1997) claim that discussions of ideology demand *continuous* examination in pursuit of the twin goals of democracy and inclusion. He reminds us that the task is one that can never be assumed complete or finished.

Chapter 7, "Accounting for Ideology and Politics in the Development of Inclusive Practice in Norway," by Marit Stromstad, opens with a useful discussion of definitions of ideology and the implication of each in consideration of the history that shaped the ideology of normalization and integration in Norway. Bolstered by the arguments of Ballard and Barton, Stromstad contends that while Norway was once synonymous with an *ideology of solidarity,* increasingly these communal values lack "currency" in the global market where solidarity amounts to little more than the exclusive domain of the elites. Her history includes ancient Norwegian legends and lore to show the pernicious influence of ideologies past in the configuration of ideologies present.

In Chapter 8, "Quality versus Equality? Inclusion Politics in Norway at Century's End," Kari Nes follows on the background provided by Stromstad. This chapter carefully unravels important distinctions at the micro level of practice in a case study that probes the reality rather than the mythology of Norway's ideology of solidarity. Nes peers into the workings of the "unitary school" in an age of increasing diversity resulting from immigration and troubles the limitations of retrofitting educational policy for language minority pupils that was originally designed for disabled students. The previously celebrated goal of "normalization" is, according to Nes, counterintuitive to inclusive ideology for disabled students, and far off the mark for language minority students.

Although the previous sections include both theoretical and empirical cases, the final section, Part III, "Research Tensions: Espoused versus Lived Ideology," considers cases of recognition in which personal struggle marks the contributors' openly ideological research and teaching. By the very design of their research, these contributors welcome multiple and diverse participant opinions and because they recognize the moral consequences of their scholarship, they acknowledge their own biases and viewpoints from the outset. Chapter 9, "Special Education Knowledges: The Inevitable Struggle with the Self," by Lous Heshusius, is an epistemology story that considers various aspects of participatory consciousness. Drawing on the work of Jean Vanier, the founder of an international network of communities for people with intellectual disabilities, Heshusius explores the meaning of an inclusionary mode of consciousness as the foundation for an *epistemological civil rights movement*. Heshusius' appeal to revise the traditional behaviorist approach to research in special education through confrontations in self-other constructions plays well against Chapter 10, "Tensions and Conflicts: Experiences in Parent and Professional Worlds," by Jude MacArthur. MacArthur explores the ideology of expertism to reveal the threat it poses to the creation of inclusive schools. Her chapter also raises questions about ethical concerns when researchers collaborate with parents to author research "about" disability and not as someone "with" a disability. Chapter 11, "The Politics of Ideology: A Pedagogy of Critical Hope," by Linda Ware, describes how students and teachers in one high school ventured to risk an ideological stand in support of inclusion. For the students, the risk invited the opportunity to transgress inherited identities as Julie Allan discussed in Chapter 2. However, the teachers were more cautious and initially less willing to challenge the limits of the system's pathological response to disability as fundamentally biological rather than cultural. The case reveals how resistant to change school systems can be at the same time teachers' discourse, alliances, and tactics can confront ideologies that undermine inclusion.

The book ends not with answers or tidy solutions promising that readers might reconcile the myriad of complexities that educational and social inclusion invite. Rather, our aim is to explore the silences that too often limit the debate on inclusion as mere procedural compliance. Our aim is to expose the silence and to inspire continuous conversations within a more broadly conceived discursive community. In the words of the poet Stephen Dunn (1989), "I'm just speaking out loud to cancel my silence."

References

Armstrong, F. (2002). The historical development of special education: Humanitarian rationality or "wild profusion of entangled events." *History of Education, 31*(5), 437–456.

Barton, L. and Tomlinson, S. (eds.) 1981. *Special Education: Policies, Practices, and Social Issues*. London: Harper & Row.

Brantlinger, E. A. (1997). Using Ideology: Cases of nonrecognition of the politics of research and practice in special education, *Review of Educational Research, 67*(4), 425–459.

Brantlinger, E. A. (2003, April). *The big glossies: How textbooks structure (special) education*. Paper presented at the annual meeting of the American Educational Research Association, Chicago, IL.

Dunn, S. (1989). "To a Terrorist." *Between Angels*. New York and London: W. W. Norton.

Eco, Umberto (2002, October 15). "The art of translation: A discussion of Baudolino." www.theconnection.org/shows. Boston: WBUR.

Gailbrath, J. K. (1992). *The culture of contentment*. Harmondsworth, United Kingdom: Penguin Books.

Heshusius, L. (1989). The Newtonian mechanistic paradigm, special education, and contours of alternatives: An overview. *Journal of Learning Disabilities, 22,* 403–415.

Richardson, John G. (1999). *Common, delinquent, and special: The institutional shape of special education*. New York and London: Falmer Press.

Safford, P. L. and Safford, E. J. (1996). *A history of childhood and disability*. New York: Teachers College Press.

Sloterdijk, P. (1987). *Critique of cynical reason*. Minneapolis: University of Minnesota Press.

Stiker, H. J. (1999). *A history of disability*. Ann Arbor: University of Michigan Press.

Trent. J. B. (1994). *The invention of the feeble mind: A history of mental retardation in the United States*. Berkeley: University of California Press.

Ware, L. (in press). Public Schools and the Development of the Medico-Pedagogic Approach. In D. Mitchell, S. Snyder & D. Braddock (eds.), *Eugenics in America, 1890– 1935: A disability studies sourcebook*. Ann Arbor: University of Michigan Press.

Winzer, M. and K. Mazurek (eds.) (2000). *Special education in the 21st century*. Washington D.C.: Gallaudet University Press.

Zizek, S. (1994). *Mapping ideology*. London: Verso.

I

NARROW FRAMEWORKS/
ENDORSED INEQUITIES

Ellen Brantlinger

1

IDEOLOGIES DISCERNED, VALUES DETERMINED: GETTING PAST THE HIERARCHIES OF SPECIAL EDUCATION

Given the complicated and obscure language of theoretical discourses, it is little wonder that practitioners and recipients of services are just not interested in the theories of university scholars. So, when I proclaim the imperative of the highly abstract endeavor of doing ideology critique, it may seem like more left-wing web-spinning in the ivory tower. Nevertheless, I contend that it is dangerous to design or engage inclusive practice without an understanding of its ideological roots.

Many mainstream scholars act as if the special education practices that involve labeling, ranking, and exclusion from general education are neutral—that they are the natural response to flaws in affected children. These scholars view programs and services through a technical, supposedly value-free lens and ignore how ideologies related to people and schooling can cloud or distort vision. When others claim that special education labeling and pull-out are neither effective nor moral, the champions of the special education status quo reject such claims and reassert that there is insufficient empirical evidence to prove them unsuccessful (Kauffman, 1999). Such reasoning, when combined with the dearth of attention to the value underpinnings of practice, means that no matter how much reform and innovation take place, it is likely that practices will continue to replicate current exclusions and stratifications albeit in continuously evolving "new" forms and changing terminology. Before turning to a discussion about the nature of ideology and its relevance to the lives of people with disabilities, it seems important to review some of the barriers to inclusive schooling.

Institutional and Perceptual Barriers to Inclusion

A perusal of special education and other journals reveals that much educational research is of little significance to teachers and students and has few real connections to schools. Preoccupied with technical agendas, the similar "interventions" are constantly (re)invented—or renamed. Aware of a gap between their ideas and school practice, scholars accuse practitioners of ignoring research. They believe that their ideas are more valid than those of practitioners in the field. Part of this may be a gender issue rather than a status issue, of course—the two are confounded. As Crocco, Munro, & Weiler (1999) write:

> Historians have generally depicted [Jane] Addams as a social worker rather than sociologist, positioning her as low-status practitioner rather than high-status theoretician. Such discursive formulations channel and control the impact of Addams's work; indeed, they emanate from the same gendered processes of historical reconstruction critiqued by this book. Addam's legacy is framed very differently from that of Dewey, the product of forces emerging over the last century through which the social sciences and academic institutions elevated theory over practice and identified women's work with the latter. (p. 8)

Whether gender or status, or a combination of the two, Vare (1995) draws from Foucault's (1980) theory of knowledge as normalized truth, to critique scholars' tendency to see research as having sacred qualities that privilege it over less powerful sources of truth. "Communication" is always in one direction: top down. Willinsky (1999) has written a book about how to get knowledge from the university to the public sector. Vare objects to the asymmetry that results when scholars position themselves above teachers and ignore teachers' views. Teachers, in turn, position themselves above students and their families and ignore these groups' preferences for schooling. Implicit in relationship hierarchies is an assumption about the superiority of educated people, especially credentialed experts.

In addition to the power factor, there is also the relevance factor. Many scholars work outside of schools and agencies, so their perceptions of causes and cures may not match social reality. Such scholars should go to schools to learn not only how schools work, but also what research might be beneficial. Contact with school personnel might keep them apprised of the university-produced knowledge that might be worthwhile. This approach still might be unproductive, however, because scholars tend to assume that formal academic knowledge is superior to intuitive or firsthand knowledge gleaned by teachers in the field.

Another hurdle faced in implementing inclusion is that people in the United States have been conditioned by their own education to see subject matter traditions and core curriculum as the legitimate content of public schools. And they think subject matter is best taught through lock-step sequences and student performance is best judged by how they fare in tests that cover ranked sequences (McGill-Franzen & Allington, 1993). Academic content is to get banked in students' minds for future use (Freire, 1973) or to be tested to enable access to further education or employment. These traditions are deeply entrenched, although there is little evidence that they lead to improved conditions for a broad range of humans and the environment. According to Freire's perspective, mentally banked academic content's value is mostly as cultural capital that serves to perpetuate stratifying rituals and sustain social hierarchies. Freire's emancipatory pedagogy is geared to developing students' understanding of life circumstances. Literacy involves acquiring reading and mathematical skills simultaneously with firsthand knowledge of the political and social aspects of their surroundings.

One more barrier to inclusion is the wrong-headed belief in the neutrality of school practice and research held by certain scholars (Martin, 1994). Indeed, research billed as apolitical and technical does solidify existing knowledge and status quo social relations (Anderson & Irvine, 1993; Brantlinger, 1997; 2003). Quite satisfied with the meritocratic (some win, some fail) nature of school and society, the middle class appears to be benevolent in looking out for a range of interests from the state of the economy to conditions of the poor. Nevertheless, because they are generally well-served by the status quo, they resist real change that threatens their security and status (Mirel, 1994). Wildman (1996) details the many ways that invisible middle-class privilege undermines democratic life in America.

By virtue of education and employment, scholars and teachers are middle class and have a middle-class standpoint (Gouldner, 1979; Habermas, 1978, 1983; Tyack & Tobin, 1994). With no direct access to the elite's riches and power, the middle class—what E. O. Wright (1985, 1989, 1994) calls a contradictory class—gains through its monopoly control of cultural capital, social institutions, and credential production. Technical remedies or compensatory treatments are aimed at changing losers. Not only does this approach create jobs for professionals but it puts others, including those with disabilities, in positions of dependency. Local, state, and federal governments designate funds for people with disabilities and who are poor. Funds, however, filter through professionally controlled institutions and rarely go directly to those in need. Whether purposely or inadvertently, professional intervention inevitably results in work for professionals and what might be called a (re)colonization of the oppressed for dominant class gains (Brantlinger, 1999b; 2003). Troyna and Vincent (1996) express skepticism about the benefits of the proliferation of credentialed positions and expansion of the professional class.

In an era when cultural capital along with economic capital determines status and power, credentials help define the social order by giving an "educated" class the authority to name and control others (Bourdieu, 1996). Psychological [and other social science] professions "naturalize oppressive standards of social adjustment" and "perpetuate inequities" (Schnog, 1997, p. 3). Normalizing technologies make use of social differentiations that are essentially political in that the powerless are particularly likely to be scrutinized and controlled (Boler, 1999). Indeed, control paradigms that entitle one group to scrutinize and police another are especially likely to arise in inegalitarian political and economic conditions (Rosaldo, 1984). Ubiquitous studies of the flaws and foibles of the "other" betray the widespread belief that people at lower ends of social continua constitute a/the problem—a scholarly assumption long ago pointed out as faulty by DuBois (1965). Focus on "at risk," "disabled," "underclass," or "culturally deprived" has been characterized as subscribing to "deficit hypotheses" and "blaming the victim" (Keddie, 1973; Ryan, 1971). Nevertheless, tales of others' inadequacies continue to surface in multiple forms and guises in social science research and writing (Wright, 1993).

Because of the phenomenon of burgeoning care-providing bureaucracies, my read on progress (i.e., reducing disparities and increasing equity) is that the scholarly gaze must be turned inward to learn how educated classes benefit from stratified social arrangements and upward at powerful, elite classes who gain from the low wages and poverty of "others" and who influence the media, politics, and public and private institutions. Elites win in ethically dubious races among multinational corporations and then make laws that protect their money and privilege (Farazmand, 1999; Gibson-Graham, 1996; O'Brien, 1998); that is, those who master economic life also regulate politics through media control (McChesney, 1997, 1999; McLeod & Hertog, 1999; Viswanath & Demers, 1999) and campaign contributions (Scatamburlo, 1998). Smith (1995) writes: "Everywhere education systems have been organizationally restructured and turned to the purposes of international capitalism" (p. 1). Smith and Epp (1999) report that, addressing a decline in national market productivity, the Canadian government has defined "the university" as a national asset in a competitive global economy and has mandated commercialization as a primary mission of the university.

Where Ideology Fits In

Powerful classes narrate stories of themselves as deserving people—more deserving than others—and as liberals who serve others. These stories are infused with ideological operations that obscure the self-interest of their practices (Thompson, 1990). Thompson defines ideology as "meaning in the service of power." Thus, ideology mystifies class relations. Mostly unaware of their complicity in unequal power relations, members of the middle class are surprised and angry when others bring it to their attention or when their motives or actions are doubted (Brantlinger, 2003; Brantlinger, Majd-Jabbari, & Guskin, 1996; Wildman, 1996). Again, to get at psychic inconsistencies between what is believed and what is happening, an ideological critique is necessary.

The stories we tell about ourselves, others, and the way life should be are forms of ideology that have a great impact on daily life in schools and communities. Because of ideology's profound influence, there is a need to discern how it works in order not to be stymied by "undesireable" ideologies. There also is a need to imagine ideal [inclusive] communities (Anderson, 1983) and develop moral missions likely to capture the imaginations of others (Schudson, 1998) and persuade them to adhere to ideologies that are conducive to inclusion and that provide direction and inspiration for actions. In this chapter, I delineate the values, beliefs, and stories embedded in common ideologies and show how some work against the realization of inclusive community. Then, I set forth ideas about a particular cluster of ideologies that provide the groundwork for inclusive, democratic schools and societies. These preferred ideologies are fairly general, so they apply to the many divisions and exclusions that arise along gender, race, ethnicity, language usage, sexual orientation, and supposed ability or competency lines. First, however, I will briefly describe some distorted uses of the concept of "ideology" among special education scholars and some of the limitations of Marxist definitions of ideology to creating a discourse of possibility for inclusive settings.

Denigrating and Denying Ideology

Pierre Bourdieu (Bourdieu & Eagleton, 1994) notes that the term "ideology" is often used disparagingly to dismiss an opponent's work as too political or impractical. Kauffman and Hallahan (1995), Fuchs and Fuchs (1994), and others use the term "ideology" as a negative epithet to denigrate the inclusionist position. Denying the existence of ideology in their own work and alert to the evils of subjectivity and ideology lurking in others, such prominent scholars condemn inclusion advocates for being idealists, dreamers, wishful thinkers, and leftists (see Brantlinger, 1997). Yet, like it or not and know it or not, the reality is that ideologies and values infuse all dimensions of social life (Zizek, 1994). However, because ideologies operate largely at an unconscious level, they go unnoticed, especially the ideologies that are the most common and widespread. The assumptions grounded in ideologies are taken for granted as children go to school, people live in communities, and professionals establish careers. Nevertheless, failure to attend to ideology or denial of its existence and impact leaves scholars and educators with only partial knowledge of life in schools and communities, and an incomplete understanding of their work. Such ignorance puts them in the position of deciding among a deluge of supposedly moral-free technical choices, most of which reinforce the status quo (Mirel, 1994). Technical details are produced as ends in themselves.

Mainstream special education researchers claim that values are irrelevant to the design of public agencies and imply that they hinder the collection and utilization of scientific data. They scoff at those who stress the need to base practice on clarified values (see especially the chapters in this volume by Allan, Ballard, Nes, Slee, and Ware). Given the prevalence of positivist sentiments in higher education, portrayals of objectivity/subjectivity as dichotomous and the severing of emotion from rationality, body from mind, and private from public are expected. Cynicism about values and attacks on idealism, however, are puzzling. Perhaps it is the nature of ideals linked with inclusion that conflict with these scholars' competitive ethos and personal ambitions. Or the assertion that classroom structure and practice should be based on ideals rather than on instrumental details may cause them to worry that their role as producers and conveyors of technical knowledge is threatened (Barton, 1997). Another plausible explanation is that they are so engrossed in and distracted by career pursuits that they have little time to "smell the roses" or "see the big picture"; that is, to ponder the purposes of their labors. Idealism draws its strength from having hope and purpose as well as visions of better circumstances. Perhaps those who proclaim the need for segregated services have lost hope and optimism about the human condition. They certainly have lost touch with the people they think they serve.

Some special education practices are so commonplace that they are taken for granted by professionals and the general public. Yet the views of insiders—those who receive services—reveal the pain and suffering caused by practices that make use of stigmatizing labels, differential treatment, and exclusions (Brantlinger, 1987, 1993; Clare, 1999; Cohen, 1996; Linton, 1998; Mairs, 1996 ; Oliver, 1990; Ware, 2000). Because it is typically the powerless in society—the poor, disabled, and racial minorities—who are subject to humiliating treatments and exclusions (Artiles & Trent, 1994; Harry, 1994; Oswald, Coutinho, Best, & Singh, 1999; Patton, 1998; Selden, 1999; Slee, 1996; Smith, 1997; Tomlinson, 1999; Wright, 1993), these aspects of practice go unnoticed or their negative impact is minimized by those in control (as discussed by Ware later in this book).

Determinism in Theories of Class Reproduction

Ideology critique is associated with Marx and his followers. Marxist analyses of the relations between the economic base and the ideological superstructure remain valid, yet a concern about Marxist theory is its somewhat outdated reference to oppositional social classes. Classes in postindustrial societies are complex partly because class identity and affiliation are confounded by a history of social mobility for certain waves of immigrants. Although class mobility obscures class distinctions, mobility only is pertinent to stratified societies. It is precisely stratification that must be diminished or overcome. Of concern regarding hope for societal transformation is Marx's prediction that hierarchical class relations would persist without a proletariat revolution (see Ortner, 1996). Similarly, social class correspondence theories have sound explanatory value for the persistence of inequalities, but they are deterministic and negative. Postmodern theories, many of which incorporate Marxist concepts of class and power, are more nuanced and dynamic. Foucault's writing resonates with Marxist ideas about uneven power relations (Ramazanoglu, 1993), but Foucault (1980) avoids the dualism of rigid dominant/oppressed class divisions and construes power not as present or absent but as circulating, partial, and unstable.

Another problem with Marx's binary class divisions is that there is a great deal of diversity within homogeneous groups. All members do not understand group interests in the same way—or, as implied by the idea of hegemony, in the "right" way (hooks, 1989; Robinson, 1994). Theories of hegemony proclaim that the worldview of the colonized mirror that of their colonizers; that subaltern voices echo the voices of masters because dominant ideologies have been taught to oppressed people in a myriad of subtle but influential ways (Spivak, 1988, 1994). Social reproduction theories support predictions of the inevitability of uneven class relations. Yet, the ideas about ideology and knowledge that are most attractive to me are the dynamic, responsive conceptions that allow for the possibility of human insight and agency (Holland, Lachicotte, Skinner, & Cain, 1998). No one would deny the fact that ideologies are stable over time — conservatives stay conservative, radicals stay radical. Nevertheless, both interpersonal relations and mental processes are multilayered and internally conflicted. Knowledge is received but not static or certain. Individuals inherit their cultures but are agents who constantly tamper with it (Bakhtin, 1981). Migration causes an influx of ideas from one culture to another which creates dissonance and fluctuations within recipient cultures. Diaspora results both in an intersectionality and dispersion of positions and perspectives across and within group borders (Deyhle & Swisher, 1997; Fuss, 1994; Hauser, 1997).

To move past forecasts of the inevitability of social class reproduction, the importance of agency and activism must be understood. While retaining ideas that help us understand differential power relations and conflict, we must turn to theories that recognize that intentional subjects can work toward the emancipatory, humanistic goals many of which were laid out during the Enlightenment. Latour (1993) observes that not only are we not postmodern, we have yet to be modern. Neither the human goals set forth during the Enlightenment nor the reasoning projected for modernity have been realized on any large scale. Composed of new texts and discourses, Enlightenment ideologies were interpellated by pre-Enlightenment received knowledge (see Althusser, 1971). Hierarchical and patriarchal domination by church and crown was reinscribed in scientific, technical, and material progress ideologies (Blunt & Rose, 1994; Haraway, 1988). Ideals for equity and full civic participation were sidetracked by "modern" gods and fetishes including the "difference" fetishism of racism, colonialism, and paternalism; "material" or commodity fetishism of capitalism and consumerism; and "status" fetishism of class distinction and credentialed expertise. These fixations are modern in that they now prevail, but in irrational devotion to social hierarchies, they prevent the realization of the humanistic goals of social equality and justice.

Rethinking Disability

For 20 years I taught in a program that prepares preservice teachers to work with students with mild disabilities. Because of that professional commitment, my focus mainly has been on mild disabilities that tend to surface in the context of school. Many claim that "school-defined" disabilities result from the structure of school rather than from impairments in children (Kutchins & Kirk, 1997; McDermott & Varenne, 1995 ; McGill-Franzen & Allington, 1993; Mercer, 1973). Thus, it is fitting to call mild disability a social construct that results from schools' inability (or lack of motivation) to accommodate students in general education, regardless of their diverse achievement levels or behavioral patterns. It has long been documented that children of powerless (poor and minority) families are overrepresented in special education (Artilles & Trent, 1994; Brantlinger, 1987, 1997; Patton, 1998; Tomlinson, 1982). As a long-term advocate of inclusion, I have always felt that my role was to prepare general and special education teachers to be more skillful in effectively educating a broad range of learners in integrated settings. My aim was to prevent the humiliating labeling and segregation that expanded during my 35 years as a special education professional—a proliferation that has not slowed down in spite of state and federal laws mandating mainstreaming and the rhetoric among professionals and scholars about the importance of inclusion.

The line of reasoning in which disability is viewed as a social construct is also relevant for some children and adults with more severe impairments and more substantial needs. Even in this population, what some call a disability others call a difference. An example of this perspective is the feeling that deafness is not necessarily a problem among members of the deaf community. Certainly, negative attitudes toward people with disabilities and practices that limit their lives aggravate rather than alleviate the impact of an impairment (Clare, 1999; Mairs, 1996; Oliver, 1990; Selden, 1999; Tomlinson, 1996). Still, there are individuals and families who choose to call themselves and/or family members "disabled" and feel they suffer not only from the impairment but from difficulties and frustrations they experience due to the lack of resources necessary for them to be full participants in inclusive communities (Clare, 1999; Cohen, 1996; Linton, 1998; Thoma & Wehmeyer, 1999). The term "suffer" may be patronizing, even maudlin; still, unique needs must be acknowledged[1] if extra resources are to be made available to people with disabilities by we the people/we the government.

Situating and Explaining the Incentives for My Work

Because I was troubled by the stratified and inequitable arrangements I observed in schools, I conducted a series of studies about the impact of social class on schooling (Brantlinger, 1985a, 1985b, 1985c, 1991, 1993). In turn, my analyses of interviews with parents, students, and school personnel led to my interest in the ideological overtones of stratified structures and practices (Brantlinger, 1996, 1997; 1999a, 1999b; 2003; Brantlinger, Majd-Jabbari, & Guskin, 1996; Brantlinger & Majd-Jabbari, 1998) and, concurrently, to the characteristics of moral classrooms, schools, and societies (Brantlinger, Morton, & Washburn, 1999). I became convinced that for a more equitable society to be realized, scholars would have to quit looking downward at those not making it and stop reinventing technical procedures that reinforced existing social hierarchies.

In response to special education segregationists' accusation that the grounding for inclusion comes from a values orientation rather than an empirical orientation, I admit that on the first count I stand guilty as accused. My support for inclusion most definitely comes from a set of values and ideologies. Yet, I also insist that my choices are empirically[2] driven. The direct observations gleaned during many years teaching special and general education and two decades observing field experiences in all types of classes and agencies (for 5,000 + hours) under both ideal and less-than-ideal conditions have informed and shaped my preferences. As I claim empiricism, I add the caveat that neutral empiricism is impossible. Perceptions are screened through personalized (biased) lenses and processed by subjective minds (Britzman, 1991); that is, subjectivity and affect are complicit in observation. So, any line drawn between objectivity and subjectivity is based on false premise and illusion. Instead of denying the subjective, value-ladden aspects of our humanity and our research, these should be honored and cherished. Yet we also must continuously scrutinize our work to be aware of its detrimental ideological underpinnings. Openness about values and efforts to align practice with specified values are tasks essential to valid research. It is likely that such clarification of values will lead to more widespread support for inclusion of students identified as disabled in general education classrooms. It will also address the social hierarchies that surround race, gender, sexual orientation, and class relations. Part of my agenda involves ecological projects that subvert practices that destroy the physical environment and allow people to live in balance with nature (Harvey, 1997; Irigaray, 1994).

Defining Ideology

As we begin this colloquium on inclusive education with its emphasis on how ideologies influence schooling and other aspects of social life, it is important to think about the implications of various definitions of ideologies. In my article "Using Ideology" (1997), I defined ideology in the classic Marxist way, as "meaning in the service of power" (Thompson, 1990), a definition that is based on social class positionality and conflict. In analyzing professional practice, I invoked Gramsci's essential question "Who benefits?" and concluded that dominant classes gain salary and status from "delivering services," while recipients receive stigmatizing labels and segregated low-status programs—that subordinates continue to be oppressed. As a tool of powerful classes, ideology is tied to notions of hegemony and the circulation of self-serving ideas by dominant groups (Gramsci, 1929–1935/1971). Credentialed experts control cultural capital through institutions that generate class distinctions and contain struggles of subjugated classes (Gouldner, 1979; Wright, 1989). Thompson's (1990) definition of ideology was useful for explicating the ways in which power intertwines with professional special education practice. At this point, to move beyond the indulgence and ease of critique, I engage in constructing a discourse of possibility about inclusive practice. I remain interested in the workings of ideology, but will assign both more neutral and enabling roles to ideological functions.

Although it is a useful concept for understanding social life, "ideology" is one of those grand terms with a number of loose and bewildering connotations. Moreover, it is used in distinct ways by various theorists. Zisek (1994) notes the ubiquitous presence of ideology in language, thought, and practice. Ideologies are systems of representations (images, myths, ideas, beliefs) that, in profoundly unconscious ways, mediate understanding of the world (Althusser, 1971, 1974/1976). Inscribed at the sociocultural level of mental life, there is an automaticity of ideological triggerings: people act with little realization of an action's ideological grounding.

Although some believe that mention of human universals digresses into essentialism, Brown's (1991) meta-analysis of anthropological studies identifying 108 "human universals" seems pertinent to my discussion of ideology and social hierarchies. The bad news is that all societies are structured by differentiated roles and usually a stratified division of labor; that is, people sort and rank each other. Ranked relations are based on the assumption that two groups are *fundamentally different* with an irreversible dissymmetry between them. As a Jewish refuge from Nazi Germany, Apfelbaum (1999) contends that the right to "mark" (brand, label, stigmatize) is concentrated on the side of the dominant group, or, as Eagleton (1990) concludes, the oppressor's privilege is to decide what the oppressed shall be. Furthermore, marking implies that a collectivity of individuals can be spotted and assigned the same identifying name on the basis of one distinctive feature. At the same time a mythical standard creates the impression that there is a homogeneous social body that meets the standard and another that does not; that is, "us" can be distinguished from "them." Bellamy (1998) recalls that Homi Bhabha, Frantz Fanon, and Jacque Lacan "theorize that the identity of the colonizer [or dominant person] is based on a lack that can only be filled by the colonized other" (p. 342). People take on the identity of gentiles as they define the Jewish other; the "abled" require the "disabled" to establish their normality. Intelligence is constructed against another's stupidity. Ideology works to dissimulate hierarchical practices for those it dignifies as much as those it excludes (Bourdieu, 1996). Without deep and total ideological conversion among those with the power to shape schools, schooling will always be "at risk" for having unfair, inequitable, humiliating, and painful practices (as discussed here by Slee and Ware).

Distinguishing Ideologies

In contrast to the hierarchical thinking that is so ubiquitous in human societies, Brown's (1991) good news is that the universal people also differentiate right from wrong and base many of their judgments on a morality in which human reciprocity and empathy are key elements. Although this depiction is oversimplified—and it makes use of problematic binaries—still, I suggest that there are two basic clusters of ideologies: (1) those related to establishing social hierarchies through interpersonal competition and stratifying practices, and (2) those based on the communal ideals that recognize human dignity, commonality, equality, and reciprocity. The former will henceforth be called "hierarchical" and the latter the "communal" ideology. Following my logic, it is easy to anticipate that I link what Brown (1991) identifies as reciprocal morality to communal ideology and sorting and ranking to hierarchical ideology.

On a theoretical level, communal and hierarchical ideologies are separable. However, as with most dichotomies, this model implies a continuum with a pure case at each end. Partly to avoid doing a "good guy/bad guy" take, I suggest that a tension between the two ideologies exists in most people and, except in rare instances, both interwine in mental life and surface differently regarding particular social issues. Certainly, some people are especially greedy, self-promoting, and ready to take advantage of weak people's vulnerability—acts firmly grounded in hierarchical ideology. Others are alert to social inequities and have a tenacious will to reform and a resilient optimism about improving the human condition. Such communally oriented people seem to suffer when they observe that all is not right in the world—apparently they have a large dose of empathy (Sober & Wilson, 1998). Perhaps some people find it easier to identify with the oppressed than do others. Some are willing to take unpopular stands on others' behalf regardless of personal risks and consequences. Individuals with high levels of communal ideology may become activists who courageously fight all forms of oppression (see Horton, 1998).

As evidenced by institutional practices that differentiate among humans, it is clear that hierarchical ideologies are prevalent in modern society and dominate social, political, and economic institutions and practices (see Table 1.1). Bourdieu (1998) argues that what he calls neo-liberalism, or the discourse of political submission to economic rationality, is hegemonic. This neo-liberalism postulates the withering away of the state and the undivided reign of the market and the consumer. Observing the recent flurry of dismantling social services in France, Bourdieu argues that neo-liberalism is an atavistic faith in the inevitability of productive forces that threatens democracy (and for that matter, as discussed by Ballard, Stromstad, and Nes later on in this book). Surely, similar phenomena have been witnessed on this side of the Atlantic.

In contrast to its hierarchical opposite, communal ideology articulates ways for people to relate across race, language usage, ethnicity, sexual orientation, gender, and other personal attributes and be equal. Communal ideology can encompass

TABLE 1.1. Structures/Practices Grounded in Hierarchical Ideology

Ability-based reading groups
Secondary school tracking or streaming
Special education pull-out
Class/race segregated schools
Property-tax-based school funding
Segregated living and working arrangements
Disparate public (and private) wages
Nonprogressive taxes
Public universities requiring tuition
Segregated organized religion
Within-district disparities in school funding and human resource distribution
Institutional barriers and exclusions

inanimate as well as living things. As informed by postmodern writers, it seems reasonable to assume that human thinking is fluid, dynamic, multilayered, and conflicted, and that humans have the potential to think and act in a number of ways (Holland, Lachicotte, Skinner, & Cain, 1998). The extensiveness of strong feelings about reciprocal morality among humans is heartening. Laws, regulations, and codes are often based on this ethical positioning. Nevertheless, their enforcement tends to be impeded due to the prevalence of hierarchical ideology. Another reason for optimism about communal ideology is the continuing popularity of Rawls's (1971, 1999) work on distributive justice, which prescribes that the most vulnerable and needy individuals receive the most resources. Christensen and Rizvi's *Disability and the Dilemmas of Education and Justice* (1996) centers around Rawls's work. Moral societies are to allocate a greater proportion of resources, for example, to the self-identified disabled who have special needs. Rawls's ideas of justice also pertain to people with school-defined disabilities (Mercer, 1973). Instead of being relegated to the fringes of school life these students are entitled to fair portions of resources and respect and have the right to have access to the general curriculum and be part of the comprehensive school community. Margalit (1996) contends that a decent society does not humiliate any constituency and takes all citizens as they are.

Consciousness and Practice

To go further out on a limb in this analysis, I would like to reflect on the much-disputed and now often maligned Marxist concept of false consciousness. One way that the idea of false consciousness is problematic is that it often has implied a duping of working classes by ruling classes, thus an intellectual inferiority in the one class. Dual consciousness, however, is also an attribute of dominant groups. Middle-class parents claim to value progressive forms of inclusive, equitable schooling, yet still push for advantaged and segregated school arrangements for their children (Brantlinger, 2003; Brantlinger, Madj-Jabbari, & Guskin, 1996). They claim the temporary need for privileged circumstances so that their children will not to be held back by the "other." They perceive their children and, generally, children of their class, as smarter than poor children. The duality of this progressive rhetoric/desire for advantage split certainly is a false consciousness. The faulty construction of their own superiority, however, is the mirror reversal of the internalized inferiority common to the false consciousness of working or impoverished classes. It is necessary for both forms of false consciousness to be eliminated for there to be equity and social justice.

My reason for resurrecting the idea of false consciousness is that it is a reasonable way of conceptualizing the falsity of the ideologies that undergird thinking and acting in hierarchical ways. That *true* consciousness is empathetic and communal is consistent with Freire's (1973) idea of conscientization as a process of the becoming aware of the oppressive reality of life circumstances; that is, of overcoming false consciousness. Given the strength of hegemony—the circulation of ideologies that support advantage for dominant groups—working for equity and inclusion is bound to be a struggle. Freire was skeptical that dominant people in social hierarchies would voluntarily give up privilege or power. He recommended that oppressed people take charge of their own liberation. Indeed, the most effective advocacy has always been done by people with disabilities or their families. Similarly, other civil rights movements by oppressed and segregated groups are effective when there is a broad base of insider leaders and participants.

In terms of enacting possibilities for inclusion, one role of "communal" scholars is to deliberately monitor practice in search of hierarchical thoughts, beliefs, attitudes, tastes, desires, and false consciousness—for the ideologies that justify exclusions and disparities. Scrutiny can assure that professional pursuits pass the test of adhering to communal morality. When the nature of ideologies is discerned, detrimental ideologies can be avoided and purged. Scholars can also work to convince and inspire the public to enact policy and practice consistent with reciprocal morality (see Feagin, 1999).

The assertion that ideological critiques are not scholarly fiddling but are necessary for understanding social life is consistent with the ideas of several major theorists. Foucault's (1980) idea that power is not an either/or phenomenon but that it circulates suggests that power can have good or bad aims and effects and that power must be worked for to be gained. Bakhtin (1981) claims that knowledge is received through language structures, yet people's thoughts are not totally predetermined. Knowledge can be altered by insight and circumstances changed by informed agency. In defining hegemony, Gramsci (1929–1935/1971) postulates it as mostly a tool of the ruling class. Nevertheless, ideologies consistent with the position of working classes could dominate in society. Bourdieu (1984) explicates how groups distinquish themselves hierarchically, but claims that people can learn to recognize pluralistic forms of cultural capital and engage with others in equitable ways. Fraser's (1997) "universalism of common dreams" (p. 5) smacks of communal ideology and "misrecognition of differences" (p. 173) seems equivalent to a false consciousness that falls within the realm of hierarchical ideology. Discussing the conflict between a materialist position (associated with the economic base of Marxism) and representation (associated with diverse cultural identities) of postmodernism, Fraser stresses the need for both.

Including Spirituality

To go onto the thin ice of applying religion or spirituality to secular spaces, I dredge up the idea of false gods and suggest that false consciousness and hierarchical ideology can be linked to false gods. Greed, materialism, and ego investment in personal distinction distract people from worshipping true gods. By equating God with "good" I suggest that people think and act within the constraints of communal morality. Whereas ideological critique is a tool for discerning detrimental and beneficial ideologies, spirituality provides the impetus to envision cherished goals and the inspiration to work toward them (see MacDonald, 1995; Paley, 1999).

Those who know me may be surprised at my interest in spirituality. When the moral majority coined the term "secular humanist," I knew they meant me. My father experienced a break with his received religious knowledge in the 1920s (he was raised a fundamentalist Lutheran). During my father's confirmation classes, his minister repeatedly alluded to free thinkers who tended to congregate in the dangerous city of Minneapolis as opposed to the North Dakota farm town where my father was raised. The minister warned of the evils of free thinking. Nevertheless, by the end of his confirmation lessons, my father was a confirmed free thinker, albeit a closeted one. In our secular ways, my family was drawn to a reciprocal morality in which there was strong identification with and empathy for others. Communal ideology, reciprocal morality, and inclusive spirituality continue to create the impetus for my work.

It is encouraging to acknowledge that communal ideology and reciprocal morality already exist in the ideals of religions. A recent television advertisement cites "do unto others" themes from a range of world religions. James Banks's inspirational speeches include numerous metaphoric variations of the golden rule, a forceful edict for reciprocity and empathy. Communal ideology could unite religions, yet particularistic rituals, dogmas, and doctrines divide them. Claims to distinction from other religions and nonbelievers distract some organized religions from communal ideologies which, by definition, ignore borders and ranks. Hierarchical ideology is all too evident in religions that claim a monopoly on the good as well as the only path to heaven. Furthermore, there is evidence that only a small minority of congregations do social service activities in a substantial way (Miller, 1999). A local minister refers to a "faith community," by which he means Christians and mainly members of his congregation. Used more generically, faith can be attached to inclusive spirituality and such missions as have been articulated by Susan B. Anthony and Elizabeth Cady Stanton, Mohandas Gandhi, Martin Luther King, Rosa Parks, Myles Horton, and others. An optimistic point about the spirituality of communal ideology is that it exists outside of as well as within organized religions. The diligent work of conscientious and inspired people can make it possible for communal ideology and reciprocal morality to be expanded and perhaps eventually to be incorporated into every aspect of daily life. To enable an emancipatory agenda for social justice and equality, scholarly work needs to connect to humanist[3] projects and the idealism of envisioning a good life. Just as false ideologies must be distinguished and extinguished, so values associated with inclusive, moral communities must be determined and articulated.

Using Rationality and Empiricism

Spirituality should be a celebrated part of humanity, but the critical, rational scholarship of ideology critique also is essential. So-called rationality has been debunked as patriarchal and Eurocentric; however, little scholarly work done by men or women has been truly rational. Many put on a facade of objectivity to establish scholarly careers. Few turn the gaze inward to inspect their own roles in sustaining social hierarchies. What is needed is an empiricism that looks at the reality of life conditions of self/other to discern social hierarchies and uneven power relations. The deep rationality of genuine curiosity (Nader, 1996), hard objectivity (Harding, 1987), and [merciless] introspection (Ellis, 1991) can dislodge the irrational roots and tangles of hierarchical ideology. Ideology critique comprehends subjectivity to inform agency so that incorrect, distructive ideologies—those not aligned with inclusive, democratic, moral communities—can be identified and eradicated. In subscribing to an emancipatory agenda that seeks social justice and equality, and in asserting the superiority of critical scholarship for progressing toward those ends, I stress that modernity must be dislodged from irrational roots and tangles and be (re)connected to humanist projects. Ideologies are linked to subjectivity and the unconscious; yet for people to be truly rational, ideologies must be understood and controlled.

In closing, I recommend that scholars do transformative work in which we: (1) are explicit about the values that undergird our research and practice; (2) identify the political and personal agendas our research is likely to serve; (3) direct our gaze inward at ourselves and upward at those in charge, in control, in dominance (i.e., those with power); (4) integrate private and professional lives (engage in praxis); (5) exercise agency when and where activism can have an impact; and (6) act to eliminate oppression.

Notes

1. By this I do not mean to imply that classification is necessary.
2. Empirical: derived from or depending upon experience alone; empiricism: empirical method or practice, the doctrine that all knowledge is derived from sense experience (*Webster's Desk Dictionary of the English Language,* 1983 [New York: Gramercy Books, p. 294]).
3. Humanism has many definitions and the definition of being connected to rationality and control have been the target of postmodernists' criticism. I define humanism as involving empathy, social reciprocity, and full, equitable participation for all members of a community.

References

Allen, J. (1999). *Actively seeking inclusion: Pupils with special needs in mainstream schools: Studies in inclusive education.* Philadelphia: Falmer Press.

Althusser, L. (1971). Ideology and the ideological state apparatus. In *Lenin and philosophy.* New York: Monthly Review.

Althusser, L. (1976). *Essays in self-criticism* (G. Lock, trans.). London: New Left Books (Original work published 1974).

Anderson, B. (1983). *Imagined communities*. London: Verso.

Anderson, G. L., & Irvine, P. (1993). Informing critical literacy with ethnography. In C. Lankshear & P. L. McLaren (Eds.), *Critical literacy: Politics, praxis, and the postmodern* (pp. 81–104). Albany: State University of New York Press.

Apfelbaum, E. (1999). Relations of domination and movements for liberation: An analysis of power between groups (Abridged Featured Reprint). *Feminism & Psychology, 9*(3), 267272.

Artilles, A. J., & Trent, S. (1994). Overrepresentation of minority students in special education: A continuing debate. *Journal of Special Education, 27,* 410–437.

Bakhtin, M. M. (1981). *The dialogical imagination* (C. Emerson & M. Holquist, trans.). Austin: University of Texas Press.

Banks, J. A. (1995). The historical reconstruction of knowledge about race: Implications for transformative teaching. *Educational Researcher, 24*(2), 15–25.

Barton, L. (1997). Inclusive education: romantic, subversive or realistic? *International Journal of Inclusive Education, 1*(3), 231–242.

Bellamy, E. J. (1998). "Intimate enemies": Psychoanalysis, Marxism, and postcolonial affect. In Robert Miklitsch (Special Issues Editor), *Psycho-Marxism: Marxism and psychoanalysis late in the twentieth century* (pp. 341–359). *South Atlantic Quarterly, 97*(2).

Blunt, A., & Rose, G. (Eds.) (1994). *Writing women and space: Colonial and postcolonial geographies*. New York: Guilford.

Boler, M. (1999). *Feeling power: Emotions and education*. New York & London: Routledge.

Bourdieu, P. (1984). *Distinction: A social critique of the judgment of taste*. Cambridge, MA: Harvard University Press.

Bourdieu, P. (1996, first published in France in 1989). *The state nobility: Elite schools in the field of power)* (with the collaboration of M. de Saint Martin) (L. C. Clough, trans.). Stanford, CA: Stanford University Press.

Bourdieu, P. (1998). *Acts of resistance against the tyranny of the market*. New York: New Press.

Bourdieu, P., & Eagleton, T. (1994). Doxa and common life: An interview. In S. Zizek (Ed.) *Mapping ideology* (pp. 265–277). New York: Verso.

Brantlinger, E. A. (1985a). Low-income parents' perceptions of favoritism in the schools. *Urban Education, 20,* 82–102.

Brantlinger, E. A. (1985b). Low-income parents' opinions about the social class composition of schools. *American Journal of Education, 93,* 389–408.

Brantlinger, E. A. (1985c). What low-income parents want from schools: A different view of aspirations. *Interchange, 16,* 14–28.

Brantlinger, E. A. (1987). Making decisions about special education placement: Do low-income parents have the information they need? *Journal of Learning Disabilities, 20,* 95–101.

Brantlinger, E. A. (1991). Social class distinctions in adolescents' reports of problems and punishment in school. *Journal of Behavioral Disorders, 17,* 36–46.

Brantlinger, E. A. (1993). *The politics of social class in secondary school: Views of affluent and impoverished youth*. New York: Teachers College Press.

Brantlinger, E. A. (1994). High-income and low-income adolescents' views of special education. *Journal of Adolescent Research, 9*(3), 384–407.

Brantlinger, E. A. (1996). The influences of preservice teachers' beliefs on attitudes toward inclusion. *Teacher Education and Special Education, 19*(1), 17–33.

Brantlinger, E. A. (1997). Using ideology: Cases of nonrecognition of the politics of research and practice in special education. *Review of Educational Research, 67*(4), 425–459.

Brantlinger, E. (1999a). Class moves in the movies: What *Good Will Hunting* teaches about social life. *Journal of Curriculum Theorizing, 15*(1), 105–119.

Brantlinger, E. (1999b). Inward gaze and activism: Moral next steps in local inquiry. *Anthropology and Education, 30*(4), 413–429.

Brantlinger, E. A. (2003). *Dividing classes—how the middle class negotiates and justifies school advantage.* London & New York: Routledge.

Brantlinger, E., & Majd-Jabbari, M. (1998). The conflicted perspectives of middle-class mothers. *Journal of Curriculum Studies, 30* (4), 431–460.

Brantlinger, E., Majd-Jabbari, M., & Guskin, S. L. (1996). Self-interest and liberal educational discourse: How ideology works for middle-class mothers. *American Educational Research Journal, 33*(3), 571–598.

Brantlinger, E., Morton, M. L., & Washburn, S. (1999). Teachers' moral authority in classrooms: (Re)structuring social interactions and gendered power. *Elementary School Journal, 99*(5), 491–504.

Britzman, D. P. (1991). *Practice makes practice: A critical study of learning to teach.* New York: State University of New York Press.

Brown, D. (1991). *Human universals.* Philadelpia: Temple University Press.

Christensen, C., & Rizvi, F. (Eds.) (1996). *Disability and the dilemmas of education and justice.* Buckingham, UK & Philadelphia: Open University Press.

Clare, E. (1999). *Exile and Pride: Disability, queerness, and liberation.* Cambridge, MA: South End Press.

Cohen, M. D. (1996). *Dirty details: The days and nights of a well spouse.* Philadelphia: Temple University Press.

Crocco, M. S., Munro, P., & Weiler, K. (1999). *Pedagogies of resistance: Women educator activists, 1880–1960.* New York: Teachers College Press.

Deyhle, D., & Swisher, K. (1997). Research in American Indian and Alaska Native education: From assimilation to self-determination. In M. W. Apple (Ed.), *Review of Research in Education, 22* (pp. 113–194). Washington, DC: American Educational Research Association.

DuBois, W.E.B. (1965). *The souls of Black folk.* New York: Avon Books.

Eagleton, T. (1990). *The ideology of the aesthetic.* Oxford, UK: Basil Blackwell.

Ellis, C. (1991). Sociological introspection and emotional experience. *Symbolic Interaction, 14*(1), 23–50.

Farazmand, A. (1999). The elite question: Toward a normative elite theory of organization. *Administration and Society, 31*(3), 321–360.

Feagin, J. R. (October 15, 1999). Soul-searching in sociology: Is the discipline in crisis? *The Chronicle of Higher Education.* B4–B6.

Foucault, M. (1980). Truth and power. In C. Gordon (Ed.), *Power/knowledge: Selected interviews and other writings, 1972–1977.* New York: Pantheon.

Fraser, N. (1997). *Justice interruptus: Critical reflections on the "postsocialist" condition.* New York & London: Routledge.

Freire, P. (1973). *Education for critical consciousness.* New York: Seabury.

Fuchs, D., & Fuchs, L. S. (1994). Inclusive schools movement and the radicalization of special education reform. *Exceptional Children, 60*(4), 294–309.

Fuss, D. (1994). Reading like a feminist. In N. Schor & E. Weed (Eds.), *The essential difference* (98115). Bloomington, IN: Indiana University Press.

Gibson-Graham, J. K. (1996). *The end of capitalism (as we knew it): A feminist critique of political economy.* Malden, MA: Blackwell.

Gouldner, A. (1979). *The future of intellectuals and the rise of the new class.* New York: Oxford University Press.

Gramsci, A. (1929–1935/1971). *Selections from the prison notebooks.* (Q. Hoare, & G. N. Smith, trans.), New York: International. (Original work published, 1929–1935).

Habermas, J. (1978). Knowledge and human interests (2nd ed., J. Shapiro, trans.). London: Heinemann. (Original work published 1971).

Habermas, J. (1983). Modernity—An incomplete project (S. Ben-Habib, trans.). In H. Foster (Ed.), *The anti-aesthetic: Essays on postmodern culture* (pp. 3–15). Seattle: Bay Press.

Haraway, D. (1988). Situated knowledges: The science question in feminism and the privilege of partial perspective. *Feminist Studies, 14,* 575–599.

Harding, S. (1987). Conclusion: Epistemological questions. In S. Harding (Ed.), *Feminism and methodology* (pp. 181–190). Bloomington, IN: Indiana University Press.

Harry, B. (1994). *The disproportionate representation of minority students in special education: Theories and recommendations.* Alexandria, VA: National Association of State Directors of Special Education.

Harvey, D. (1996). *Justice, nature and the geography of difference.* Cambridge, MA: Blackwell.

Hauser, M. E. (1997). How do we really work? A response to "locked in uneasy sisterhood": Reflections on feminist methodology and research relationships. *Anthropology and Education Quarterly, 28*(1), 123–126.

Holland, D., Lachicotte, W., Jr., Skinner, D., & Cain, C. (1998). *Identity and agency in cultural worlds.* Cambridge, MA: Harvard University Press.

hooks, b. (1989). *Talking back: Thinking feminist thinking Black.* Boston: South End Press.

Horton, M. (1998). *The long haul: An autobiography.* New York: Teachers College Press.

Irigaray, L. (1994). Equal to whom? (R. L. Mazzola, trans.). In N. Schor & E. Weed (Eds.), *The essential difference* (63–81). Bloomington, IN: Indiana University Press.

Kauffman, J. M. (1999). Commentary: Today's special education and its messages for tomorrow. *The Journal of Special Education, 32*(4), 244–254.

Kauffman, J. M., & Hallahan, D. P. (Eds). (1995). *The illusion of full inclusion: A comprehensive of the current special education bandwagon.* Austin, TX: Pro-Ed.

Keddie, N. (1973). *The myth of cultural deprivation.* London: Penguin.

Kutchins, H., & Kirk, S. A. (1997). *Making us crazy: DSM: The psychiatric bible and the creation of mental disorders.* New York: Free Press.

Latour, B. (1993). *We have never been modern* (C. Porter, trans.). Cambridge, MA: Harvard University Press.

Linton, S. (1998). *Claiming disability: Knowledge and identity.* New York: New York University Press.

MacDonald, B. J. (Ed.). (1995). *Theory as a prayerful act: The collected essays of James B. MacDonald.* New York: Peter Lang.

Mairs, N. (1996). *Waist-high in the world: A life among the nondisabled.* Boston: Beacon Press.

Margalit, A. (1996). *The decent society* (N. Goldblum, trans.). Cambridge, MA: Harvard University Press.

Martin, J. R. (Ed.). (1994). *Changing the educational landscape: Philosophy, women, and curriculum.* New York: Routledge.

McChesney, R. W. (1997). *Corporate media and the threat to democracy.* New York: Seven Stories Press.

McChesney, R. W. (1999). *Rich media, poor democracy: Communication politics in dubious times.* Champaign: University of Illinois Press.

McDermott, R., & Varenne, H. (1995). Culture as disability. *Anthropology & Education Quarterly, 26*(3), 324–348.

McGill-Franzen, S., & Allington, R. L. (1993). Flunk 'em or get them classified: The contamination of primary grade accountability data. *Educational Researcher, 22*(1), 1922.

McLeod, D. M., & Hertog, J. K. (1999). Social control, social change and the mass media's role in the regulation of protest groups. In D. Demers & K. Viswanath (Eds.), *Mass media, social control, and social change: A macrosocial perspective* (pp. 305–330). Ames, IA: Iowa State University Press.

Mercer, J. R. (1973). *Labeling the mentally retarded.* Berkeley, CA: University of California Press.

Miller, D. W. (1999, November 26). Measuring the role of "the faith factor" in social change. *Chronicle of Higher Education,* A21–A22.

Mirel, J. (1994). School reform unplugged: The Bensenville new American School Project, 19911993. *American Educational Research Journal, 31,* 481–518.

Nader, L. (1996). Anthropological inquiry into boundaries, power, and knowledges. In L. Nader (Ed.), *Naked science: Anthropological inquiry into boundaries, power, and knowledge* (pp. 125). New York: Routledge.

O'Brien, J. (1998). Introduction. In J. O'Brien & J. A. Howard (Eds.), *Everyday inequalities: Critical inquiries* (pp. 139). Malden, MA: Blackwell.

Oliver, M. (1990). *The politics of disablement.* New York: St. Martin's Press.

Ortner, S. B. (1996). *Making gender: The politics and erotics of culture.* Boston: Beacon Press.

Oswald, D. P., Coutinho, M. J., Best, A. M., & Singh, N. N. (1999). Ethnic representation in special education: The influence of school-related economic and demographic variables. *The Journal of Special Education, 32*(4), 194–206.

Paley, V. G. (1999, May/June). K is for kindness. *Teacher Magazine,* 51–57.

Patton, J. M. (1998). The disproportionate representation of African Americans in Special Education: Looking behind the curtain for understanding and solutions. *The Journal of Special Education, 32*(1), 25–31.

Ramazanoglu, C. (1993). Introduction. In C. Ramazanoglu (Ed.), *Up against Foucault: Explorations of some tensions between Foucault and feminism* (pp. 1–25). London & New York: Routledge.

Rawls, J. (1971). *A theory of justice.* Cambridge, MA: Harvard University Press.

Rawls, J. (1999). *The law of peoples: With the idea of public reason revisited.* Cambridge, MA: Harvard Press.

Robinson, J. (1994). White women researching/representing "others": From antiapartheid to postcolonialism. In A. Blunt & G. Rose (Eds.), *Writing women and space: Colonial and postcolonial geographies* (pp. 197–226). New York: Guilford.

Rorty, R. (1997). *Achieving our country: Leftist thought in twentieth-century America.* Cambridge, MA: Harvard University Press.

Rosaldo, M. (1984). Toward an anthropology of self and feeling. In R. A. Shweder & R. A. LeVine (Eds.), *Culture theory: Essays in mind, self, and emotion.* Cambridge, UK: Cambridge University Press.

Ryan, W. (1971). *Blaming the victim.* New York: Random House.

Scatamburlo, V. L. (1998). *Soldiers of misfortune: The New Right's culture war and the politics of political correctness.* New York: Peter Lang.

Schnog, N. (1997). On inventing the psychological. In J. Pfister & N. Schnog (Eds.), *Inventing the psychological: Toward a cultural history of emotional life in America* (pp. 3–16). New Haven, CT: Yale University Press.

Schudson, M. (1998). *The good citizen: A history of American civic life*. Cambridge, MA: Harvard University Press.

Selden, S. (1999). *Inheriting shame: The story of eugenics and racism in America*. New York: Teachers College Press.

Slee, R. (1996). Disability, class and poverty: School structures and policing identities. In C. Christensen & F. Rizvi (Eds.), *Disability and the dilemmas of education and justice* (pp. 96–118). Buckingham, UK & Philadelphia: Open University Press.

Smith, R. (1995). Prologue. In R. Smith & P. Wexler (Eds.), *After postmodernism: Education, politics and identity*. London & Washington, DC: Falmer Press.

Smith, T. J. (1997, March). *Storying moral dimensions of disordering: Teacher inquiry into the social construction of severe emotional disturbance*. Paper presented at AERA (American Educational Research Association) Annual Meeting, Chicago: IL.

Smith, D., & Epp, R. (1999). Curriculum in higher education. *Journal of Curriculum Theorizing, 15*(2), 107–109.

Sober, E., & Wilson, D. S. (1998). *Unto others: The evolution and psychology of unselfish behavior*. Cambridge, MA: Harvard University Press.

Spivak, G. C. (1988). Can the subaltern speak? In C. Nelson & L. Grossberg (Eds.), *Marxism and the interpretation of culture* (pp. 271–313). Urbana: University of Illinois Press.

Spivak, G. C. (1994). Bonding in difference. In A. Arteaga (Ed.), *An other tongue: Nation and ethnicity in the linguistic borderlands*. Durham, NC: Duke University Press.

Thoma, C., & Wehmeyer, M. (1999). Students talk about their roles in transition planning. *TASH Newsletter, 25*(5/6), 810.

Thompson, J. B. (1990). *Ideology and modern culture: Critical social theory in the era of mass communication*. Stanford, CA: Stanford University Press.

Tomlinson, S. (1996). Conflicts and dilemmas for professionals in special education. In C. Christensen & F. Rizvi (Eds.), *Disability and the dilemmas of education and justice* (pp. 175–186). Buckingham, UK & Philadelphia: Open University Press.

Tomlinson, S. (1999, June 15). *Race and special education*. Paper presented at the International Research Colloquium on Inclusive Education, University of Rochester, New York.

Troyna, B., & Vincent, C. (1996). "The ideology of expertism": The framing of special education and racial equality policies in the local state. In C. Christensen & F. Rizvi (Eds.), *Disability and the dilemmas of education and justice* (pp. 131–144). Buckingham, UK & Philadelphia: Open University Press.

Tyack, D., & Tobin, W. (1994). The "grammar" of schooling: Why has it been so hard to change? *American Educational Research Journal, 31*, 453–479.

Vare, J. W. (1995). Gendered ideology: Voices of parent and practice in teacher education. *Anthropology & Education Quarterly, 263*, 251–278.

Viswanath, K., & Demers, D. (1999). Mass Media from a macrosocial perspective. In D. Demers & K. Viswanath (Eds.), *Mass media, social control, and social change: A macrosocial perspective* (pp. 3-30). Ames, IA: Iowa State University Press.

Ware, L. (2000). Inclusive education. In D. A. Gabbard (Ed.), *Education in the global economy: Politics and the rhetoric of school reform*, 111–120. Mahwah, NJ: Lawrence Erlbaum.

Wildman, S. M. (1996). *Privilege revealed: How invisible preference undermines America*. New York: New York University Press.

Willinsky, J. (1999). *Technologies of knowing: A proposal for the human sciences*. Boston: Beacon Press.

Wright, E. O. (Ed.) (1985). *Classes*. London & New York: Verso.

Wright, E. O. (1989). A general framework for the analysis of class structure. In E. O. Wright (Ed.), *The debate on classes* (pp. 3–48). London & New York: Verso.

Wright, E. O. (1994). *Interrogating inequality: Essays on class analysis, socialism, and Marxism.* London: Verso.

Wright, S. E. (1993). Blaming the victim, blaming society or blaming the discipline: Fixing responsibility for poverty and homelessness. *The Sociological Quarterly, 34,* 116.

Zizek, S. (1994). Introduction: The spectre of ideology. In S. Zizek (Ed.), *Mapping ideology* (pp. 1–33). New York: Verso.

2
Julie Allan

THE AESTHETICS OF DISABILITY AS
A PRODUCTIVE IDEOLOGY

Like the poor . . . ideology is always with us.
EAGLETON *1994*

And precisely because the remnants of Marx no longer form any logical system of ideas, but only a series of suggestive images and slogans [a smiling worker with a hammer, black, white and yellow men fraternally holding hands, the dove of peace rising to the sky . . .], we can rightfully talk of a gradual, general, planetary transformation of ideology into imagology.
(KUNDERA, *1991, p. 127; emphasis in original*)

Ideology has both remained the same elusive beast and become something else. The vast range of critiques of ideology has taken us no closer to pinning it down, no nearer to exposing its falsity. At the same time it appears to have transformed into something that is even more unknowable and which tempts us still further into the "trap that makes us slide into ideology under the guise of stepping out of it" (Zizek, 1994, p. 17). We cannot abandon ideology, since it continues to shape what we think we know; but neither can we grasp it in its essence. As Brantlinger's (1997) "attack on the attackers" (426) of inclusion illustrates, ideology has become a weapon for the denouncement of one group by another. The astonishing paradox here is that the inversion is no less ideological: "[I]deology is always, by definition, *ideology of ideology* . . . there is no ideology that does not assert itself by means of delimiting itself from another *mere ideology* (emphasis in the original) (Zizek, 1994, p. 19). Brantlinger illustrates this paradox vividly and highlights the importance of "using ideology" (425) in debates on inclusion. This chapter responds to Brantlinger's challenge to "optimistically keep an eye on the prize in everyday actions" (p. 449), without holding to a utopian vision of inclusion, and to Ballard's (1999) call for a debate around the concepts and ideologies that guide policy and practice. It considers briefly the range of activities that count as ideological critique, including those undertaken by disabled writers, and traces the shift in focus onto discourse analysis and deconstruction. It explores the possibilities of *productive ideology,* derived from versions of kynicism (Sloterdijk, 1987; Zizek, 1994) and illustrated within the novels of eastern European writers such as Kundera, Kafka, and Hasek), to enable disabled people to stand both inside and outside ideology. The final part of the chapter explores the "aesthetics of disability," a type of kynicism formed by disabled people, in which the body is used as a weapon to subvert and undermine disabling barriers.

Ideology and the Impossibility of Knowing

Eagleton's (1994) most valuable contribution to the debate on ideology is to remind us of its elusiveness, which is increased through the essentialism at work upon it:

> Social classes do not manifest ideologies in the way individuals display a particular style of walking: ideology is, rather, a complex, conflictive field of meaning, in which some themes will be closely tied to the experience of particular classes, while others will be more 'free-floating, tugged now this way and now that in the struggle between free contending powers.' Ideology is a realm of contestation and negotiation, in which there is a constant busy traffic: meaning and values are stolen, transformed, appropriated across the frontiers of different classes and groups, surrendered, repossessed, reinflected. (187)

Gramsci's (1971) main criticism of ideology concerned the way in which it has become pejorative "with the effect that the theoretical analysis of the concept of ideology has been modified and denatured" (376). His objections are purist, arguing that ideology has been damaged by the negative light in which it has been portrayed. Habermas's dissatisfaction with ideology was more concerned with its inherent inadequacy as an omnipresent omnipotent device. The pejorative connotations of ideology have led Bourdieu (1994) to suggest that it should be abandoned. Yet his alternative notion of doxa, which seeks to account for the ways in which "we accept many things without knowing" (268) seems no more effective a concept. "Symbolic violence" (Bourdieu, 1972), on the other hand, is helpful in exploring some of the unspoken rules by which we live our lives:

the gentle invisible form of violence, which is never recognised as such, and is not so much undergone as chosen, the violence of credit, confidence, obligation, personal loyalty, hospitality, gifts, gratitude, piety. . . . (p. 192)

The analysis of exclusion as a form of symbolic violence, then, would involve a consideration of how individuals are denied access to cultural capital by teachers and others and excluded for not possessing it. As Eagleton (1994) observes, this represents another version of hegemony, but it offers more scope for studying "ideology as *everyday life*" (p. 224; emphasis in original) by analysing the microprocesses within schools and other institutions.

Gramsci's analysis of hegemony has been useful to disabled writers such as Oliver (1990; 1996), Shakespeare (1994), and Vernon (1998), particularly in analysing the effects of normalisation. Oliver (1996) identifies three separate strands within the hegemony of disability—ontology, epistemology, and experience—and, somewhat confusingly, distinguishes three relative means to understanding these. Grand theory, he suggests, addresses questions about the nature of disability; middle range theories illuminate the causes of disability; and finally, methodology, within Oliver's framework, explores the experience of disability. Each of the three dimensions interact to produce the hegemony of disability. While Oliver's analysis of this process is somewhat opaque, he nevertheless illustrates how assumptions about "being disabled" are part of the oppression experienced by individuals. Abberley (1995) has continued to find ideology a useful form of critique, making use of Thompson's (1984) model of examining "the way in which creative imaginary activities serve to sustain social relations which are assymetrical with regard to the organisation of power" (6). Abberley's analysis illustrates how the ideology of partnership and the "holistic" approach to occupational therapy work to sustain notions of disability as an individual problem. He also demonstrates how this enables blame for the failure of therapy to be placed upon the clients rather than the professionals. Imrie's (1998) analysis of the ideology of architecture suggests that the perpetuation of ablist and masculine values contributes to the oppression faced by disabled people. Neither Imrie nor Abberley seek to expose ideology in all its falsity, but rather demonstrate its activities and its disabling effects.

Much of the critique of ideology, from Marx onwards, embodies the metaphors of unmasking, seeking to expose false consciousness. This reductionist "hermeneutic of suspicion" (Ricouer, quoted in Eagleton, 1994, p. 194) appears not to be up to the task of accounting for ideological processes. Furthermore, Mannheim's (1936) attempt to negotiate the metaphysical problem of presence within the space of the ideological critique merely reinforced the impossibility of standing outside the process:

[A]ny criticism of another's views as ideological is always susceptible to a swift *tu quocque*. In pulling the rug out from beneath one's intellectual antagonist, one is always in danger of pulling it out from beneath oneself. (Eagleton, 1994, p. 193)

Ideology has been denounced as self-defeating, useless, and premised on mis-recognition of social reality (Zizek, 1994b). Its uselessness is particularly galling to Rorty (1994), who argues that "all that matters is what we can do to persuade peo-ple to act differently than in the past" (231). Yet as Zizek (1994b) observes, it is this *practicization* of ideology that has obscured our understanding of it as a concept; as will be suggested later in this chapter, a greater problem appears to be associated with its loss of satire, in an effort to become respectable as theory (Sloterdijk, 1987). Paradoxically, the act of unpicking some of the obscurities in ideology, and helping to recover its sense of humor, could possibly alert us to its more produc-tive possibilities and put it to work more effectively. Zizek (1994) helps to explore some of the obscurities of ideology by demonstrating how each of the strands of the Hegelian triad of ideology "In-itself; For-itself and In-and-For-itself" rein-forces the impossibility of the reversal of ideology into nonideology, since the very act of stepping outside ideology immediately plunges us back inside.

The first of these impossibilities, *ideology In-itself* specifies ideology as a doctrine or set of beliefs that conspire to convince us of its truth while masking the power interests its serves. Critique within this tradition seeks to "discern the unavowed bias within texts" (Zizek, 1994, p. 10). The trap, of course, lies in the notion of the existence of a truth against which ideology has been set.

Ideology-For-itself denotes a shift of focus onto how rituals performatively gen-erate their own ideological formation. Althusser (1994) illustrates how this oper-ates in prayer, whereby individuals who kneel down to pray will arrive at their be-liefs through the act of kneeling down, rather than intrinsically through their beliefs. In other words, religious rituals generate their own ideological substance. The problem here, suggests Zizek (1994), is that the logical conclusion of attend-ing to doctrine rather than ideology somehow bypasses the latter. Once again, however, we cannot attempt to step out of the ideological process without imme-diately regressing back into it. Fascism, for example, can only be understood in terms of a series of rituals and practices *and* unconditional acceptance of ideology.

The third version of ideology, as *In-and-For-itself*, goes for the disintegration and self-dispersal of ideology. It is viewed as localised and working in social institutions, rather than in society as a whole. Ideology is, thus, bypassed as a system that regu-lates individuals by constraining them to act according to their beliefs; instead it is the system itself that regulates individuals. And herein lies yet another trap:

> Here, however, things get blurred again, since the moment we take a closer look at these allegedly extra-ideological mechanisms that regulate social production, we find ourselves knee deep in the already mentioned obscure domain in which reality is in-distinguishable from ideology. (Zizek, 1994, pp. 1415)

So, once again we fail to grasp ideology, even where we think we may have ap-prehended its workings. This is perhaps the most insidious wrong-footing among the three strands, perhaps because we live in the society of the spectacle (Zizek, 1994). That is, our perceptions of reality are structured by a series of aestheticised images of it through the media and advertising. So far, Kundera (1991) seems to be nearest the mark in suggesting that ideology has been replaced by a more powerful and omnipresent "imagology," which funtions to "create truth, the most democratic truth that ever existed" (p. 128), but in image only. Thus, "the wheels of imagology turn without having any effect upon history" (Kundera, 1991, p. 129).

From Ideology to Discourse (and Back)

Do these impossibilities imply that ideology is a useless construct or that ideological critique is a waste of time? Some writers argue that it is simply too limited, a form of "stunted reflexivity" (Gouldner, 1976, p. 48), to be of value. Foucault asserts that ideology "cannot be used without circumspection" (1984, p. 60) because its suggestion of false consciousness, the privileging of reality over ideology and the possibility of "true" knowledge (Cooper, 1997) compromises its analytical possibilities. Foucault is among those replacing ideological critique with discourse analysis, a "process by which ideology becomes 'textualised as knowledge or truth'" (ibid, 152). Veyne (1997) suggests that a Foucauldian study of discourse helps to unmask ideology:

> We are beginning to see what ideology is: a noble and vague style, apt for idealizing practices while appearing to describing them. Ideology is an ample cloak that dissimulates the crooked and dissimilar contours of the real practices that succeed one another in history. (156)

This is to miss the point entirely. Discourse analysis offers no essence of the "real," but seeks to show how certain statements come to count as the truth. In other words, discourse analysis (merely) helps us to see how the truth is performed. Jameson (1994) suggests that discourse analysis is simply ideological critique practised in a postmodern age and is no more effective. Foucault's version of discourse analysis, however, seeks to bypass ideology, which appears to be neither possible nor desirable.

Derrida's criticisms of ideology were based on what he saw as its historical limitations. Nevertheless, he considered it to have potential, providing certain relationships are taken into account. The relation of the ideological to the scientific is crucial, according to Derrida, but has hitherto been ignored. The relation of the ideological to the philosophical is also important, yet much neglected, leading Derrida to question the logic of claims to a theory of ideology. Finally, Derrida argues that ideology needs to be connected with an examination of the problematics of language and the science of writing.

Derrida's spectral analysis (1998) helps us to navigate the impossibility of distinguishing the "real" from the ideological, by suggesting that reality never appears "itself," but always through spectral apparitions. These spectres cannot uncover the real because they fill up the hole left by it. Or, put another way, they make up part of what is real, and so by taking it away, what is assumed to be real would be incomplete. While this appears helpful, insofar as it enables us to search for the ghosts or spectres that materialise, rather than the "spirtual, substanceless big Other of ideology" (Zizek, 1994, p. 20), it does not offer, as Zizek suggests, a "pre-ideological kernel." Rather, it offers us a more tangible grasp of what we are unable to see: "The specter *appears* to present itself during its visitation. One represents it to oneself, but it is not present, itself, in flesh and blood" (Derrida, 1998 , p. 145; emphasis in original). Furthermore, the spectre "first of all sees us" (Derrida) rendering us anxious, but nevertheless attentive to a variety of reversals such as presence/absence; ghost/nonghost; real/unreal. Derrida argues that rather than demanding the "real" presence of a spectre or chasing it away, the scholar must learn from the ghost in the way that Shakespeare's Mercellus enjoined Horatio in Hamlet: "Thou art a scholar; speak to it Horatio . . . Question it" (cited in Derrida, p. 163). Derrida suggests that the scholar should learn

> how to talk with him, with her, how to let them speak or how to give them back speech, even if it is in oneself, in the other, in the other in oneself: they are always *there,* specters, even if they do not exist, even if they are no longer, even if they are not yet. (p. 163)

This may take us too close to the edge to be bearable, forcing us to endure a series of "metaphysical phantasies" (Pecheux, 1994, p. 150). And like the Baron Munchausen, we might find ourselves lifting ourselves into the air by pulling on our own hair (ibid). On the other hand, spectral analysis might force us to "rethink the *there* as soon as we open our mouths" (Derrida, 1998, p. 163).

Zizek (1994) argues that far from being a useless construct, ideology has taken on a greater importance. Rather than seek to pin down the essence of ideology and our relationship to it, we should seek to obfuscate and estrange ourselves from it:

> Herein lies one of the tasks of the "postmodern" critique of ideology: to designate the elements within an existing social order which—in the guise of "fiction," that is of "Utopian" narratives of possible but failed alternative histories—point towards the system's antagonistic character, and thus *estrange* us to the self-evidence of its established identity. (7; emphasis in original)

He suggests that what seems like an impasse can be viewed as a productive insider/outsider space, in which

> [i]deology is not all; it is possible to assume a place that enables us to maintain a distance from it, *but this place from which one can denounce ideology must remain empty, it cannot be occupied by any positively determined reality*—the moment we yield to this temptation, we are back in ideology. (17)

This space is one in which splitting takes place, offering a series of oppositions (e.g., between state and market, society and self) which allows both to see and not see ideology by observing how those very oppositions unravel themselves. Ideology goes limp in its very presence/absence.

Kynicism and Productive Ideology

Kynicism (Sloterdijk, 1987), an ancient Greek form of "pantomimic argument," also seeks to make ideology limp and, by so doing, puts it to work in a productive way. It is similar to the strategy of disidentifcation described by Pecheux (1994), in which individuals work antagonistically on or against the prevailing practices of ideological subjection, so that identifications are displaced. It succeeds not by triumphing over ideology in any confrontational sense, but in forcing ideology to do its own unravelling. It is entirely different from the cynicism employed in versions of ideological critique in which the cynic understands the distance between the ideological mask and the social reality, but still insists on the mask: "[T]hey know very well what they are doing, but still they are doing it" (Zizek, 1994, p. 312). The problem with cynicism as enlightened false consciousness, according to Sloterdijk (1987), is that it has become

> a hard-boiled shadowy cleverness that has split courage off from itself, holds any-
> thing positive to be fraud, and is intent on somehow getting through life. He who
> laughs last, laughs as if in pleural shock. (546)

Ideological critique, in order to become respectable as theory, has lost its identity as satire and as a consequence has closed down avenues for dialogue rather than opening them up. Sloterdijk suggests that this has also forced it to become entangled in dogma and radical solutions such as psychopathology: "False consciousness appears first of all as sick consciousness" (19).

Kynicism, in contrast, uses subversive tactics to confront the pathetic phrases of the ruling ideology. It mocks solemnity through banality and ridicule, but does so by pragmatic, rather than argumentative, means. Or rather, its argument is panto-mimic—lived rather than spoken—and inspired by cheekiness. Sloterdijk's account suggests it requires a level of outrageousness, "pissing against the idealist wind" to achieve its disruptive goals:

> Ancient kynicism begins the process of *naked arguments* from the opposition, carried
> by the power that comes from below. The kynic farts, shits, pisses, masturbates on the
> street, before the eyes of the Athenian market. He shows contempt for fame, ridi-
> cules the architecture, refuses respect, parodies the stories of gods and heroes. . . .
> (1987, p. 103)

Kynicism appears to succeed, where ideological critique does not, in breaking the "structure of cares" (Heidigger, cited in Sloterdijk, 1987, p. 124) and attacking the piety of seriousness through the "physiologically irresistible energy of laughter" (Sloterdijk, 1987, p. 110). This form of critique is particularly embodied, in that bodies are used as weapons, as the following example from Sloterdijk illustrates. In 1969 demonstrators, including some women who attracted his attention by baring their breasts, prevented Adorno from giving a lecture. Sloterdijk suggests that the women were using their bodies as weapons of critique, and achieving "praxis as social change" (109), and argues that this was more effective than other forms of challenge. Kynicism, thus, is promoted as a kind of "healthy narcissism" (127) and self-affirmation that sets out to "laugh in the face of the impudent demands of such morose societies" (Sloterdijk). This form of activity seems to form the basis of much of the writing by disabled people. Kynicism has been also given a voice by nondisabled eastern European writers in the space of the novel, and while an examination of this risks accusations of self-indulgence and pretentiousness (as indeed it is), it is worth attempting briefly to identify the features of kynicism *at work* in the novel.

According to Kundera (1986), the greatness of the novel as a form lies not in its potential to capture the essence of humanity, but to explore the possibilities of human experience. Kafka's exaggeration of the bureaucracy and the fate of individuals in it articulates the fantasy that creates our own belief in the "almightiness" (Zizek, 1994, p. 318) of bureaucratic realities. Zizek suggests that this is a particularly persuasive form of ideological analysis because, rather than get at the essence of the ideological form itself, Kafka lets us explore the efficiency of the fantasy in our social reality. The novels of the eastern Europeans adopt a form of kynicism that takes us to the "horror of the comic" (Kundera, 1986, p. 104), where we are inside the "guts of a joke" (ibid) rather than looking at it from the outside. It is from this place, however, that we come to understand Ionesco's observation that "there is a thin line between the horrible and the comic" (quoted in Kundera, 1986, p. 136).

Hasek (1973) takes us to the horror of the comic through the eyes of the *Good Soldier Svejk* and his long-suffering Lieutenant Lukas. In this example, the two were having yet another apparently senseless exchange:

> "Svejk, tell me, what happened to those books you told me about?"
>
> "Humbly report, sir, it's a very long story and you are always pleased to get angry when I go into a lot of detail. Like the time you wanted to hit me over the jaw when you had torn up the document about the war loan and I told you that I'd once read in a book that in the old days when there was a war on people had to pay for their windows, twenty hellers for every window, and the same amount for their geese . . ."
>
> "Like this we'll never be finished, Svejk," said Lieutenant Lukas continuing his cross-examination, during which he resolved that what was strictly confidential must of course be kept completely concealed to prevent that bastard Svejk making some kind of use of it again. "Do you know Ganghofer?"
>
> "What should he be?"
>
> "He's a German writer, you stupid bastard," answered Lieutenant Lukas.
>
> "Upon my honour, sir," said Svejk with the expression of a martyr, "I don't know any German writer personally. I only once knew a Czech writer personally . . ."
>
> "Are you feeling bad, sir?", asked Svejk with concern, when Lieutenant Lukas, who had turned pale, steadied himself by holding on to the footplate of the boiler of the abandoned locomotive.
>
> There was no sign of anger in his pale face. There was just hopelessness and desperation.

"Go on, go on, Svejk. It doesn't matter. It's quite all right . . ."

"Humbly report, sir, please forgive me, but why shall I never learn what I've done that's so frightful? I only venture to ask, sir, so that next time I can avoid such a thing . . ."

"You miserable bastard, you, I shan't explain anything to you . . ."

Svejk got solemnly into his van. He felt respect for himself. It did not happen everyday that he committed something so frightful that he must never be allowed to learn what it was. (471–476)

Hasek's characters experience a kind of misrecognition of the other, which is both once horrible and comical, since, as Gogol suggests, "the longer and more carefully we look at a funny story, the sadder it becomes" (cited in Kundera, 1986, p. 136). The brutal meaninglessness of war, and of human experience, is foregrounded in the characters' conversations, but this unravelling is so profoundly idiotic that we must also laugh, as a kind of empty consolation. Kundera suggests that the art of the novel came into being, following Rabelais, as the echo of God's laughter: "Because man thinks and the truth escapes him" (Kundera, 58). Rabelais feared what he termed agélastes, who could not laugh, who thought the truth is obvious and who were convinced of certainty. The novel has perhaps a great deal to tell us about ideology and about those who cannot laugh at their own uncertainty.

The Aesthetics of Disability as Productive Ideology

Disability politics within the United Kingdom has been characterised recently by a vigorous debate over the place of the body within a social model of disability that seeks to challenge the hegemony of disablism (Oliver, 1996). The aim of this social movement has been to fight the able-bodied oppressors and "win the battle for a social model understanding of society and our lives" (Shakespeare & Watson, 1997, p. 299). Considerations of individuals' illness or impairment have been regarded as a show of weakness, likely to be seized upon by able-bodied oppressors. In Kundera's (1986) terms, the removal of the body from the social model amounts to a "rape of privacy" (p. 111) in which disabled people are forced to live a "life without secrets" (1986, p. 110) and without their own bodies. Attempts to remove the body from the social model of disability and to privilege unity and consensus over difference have met with howls of protest from some quarters (Casling, 1993; Morris, 1991). The fragmentation of this social movement appears likely to compromise its effectiveness.

The emergence of an aesthetics of disability represents a dramatic new social movement with the potential to challenge forms of oppression. It is driven by pride, beauty, and the celebration of difference, giving disabled people a voice while also ensuring that their voice is not valorized at the margins (Ram, 1993; Singh, 1995). It is also guided by a basic desire by disabled people to live a full life and to reject the invisibility imposed upon them, as the following poem by Napolitano, placed at the front of the United Kingdom consultation document on arts and disability policy (McLean, 1998), illustrates:

My Place

I don't want to live in bungalow land
On the outer edges of the urban sprawl
In the places designed for people-like-us
Kept safely separate, away from it all.
I want to live in the pulse-hot-thick-of-it,
Where the nights jive, where the streets hum,
Amongst people and politics, struggles and upheaval,
I'm a dangerous woman and my time has come.

(Sue Napolitano, 1998)

The aesthetics of disability seeks to "strategically deploy *difference* in order to make a political difference" (Singh, 1995, p. 197), and involves individuals portraying themselves as aesthetic objects, through dance, photography, art, and other cultural forms. Disability arts, as it is also known, performs a dual function:

> Disability arts also provides a context in which disabled people can get together, enjoy themselves and think in some way about issues of common concern. But it goes deeper than that as a disability culture really does offer a key into the basic process of identifying as a disabled person, because culture and identity are closely linked concepts. (Vasey, 1992, p. 11)

While these activities could have an important role in the empowerment of disabled people (Morrison & Finkelstein, 1993), they may, however, be limited in their capacity to challenge disablist ideologies. Sloterdijk (1987) suggests, for example, that "whatever wants to live demands more than beautiful illusion" (109).

A more challenging group of disabled people appear to be pursuing a form of kynicism, through writing that deliberately subverts "the normality genre" (Darke, 1998, p. 184) and discomfits able-bodied people by forcing them to examine their own normalising and disablist attitudes. This writing features prominently in the growing literature on disability studies texts (e.g., Davis, 1997; Mitchell & Snyder, 1997; Snyder, Brueggemann, & Garland-Thomson, 2002) and on Internet sites such as *Cripzine,* a magazine devoted to promoting disability arts and culture. It unravels the "politically correct" language of disability, using words like "cripple" and "freak" in ways that are both affirming and excluding. Nancy Mairs (1993), for example, describes herself as a "cripple," precisely because "people—crippled or not—wince at the word." She wants people to see her as someone who can "face the brutal truth of her experience squarely: As a cripple I swagger" (9). Similar disruptive images play into the work of Cheryl Marie Wade (1997) in her poem, *I am not one of the.*

I am not one of the
I am not one of the physically challenged—

I'm a sock in the eye with a gnarled fist
I'm a French kiss with cleft tongue
I'm orthopedic shoes sewn on a last of your fears

I am not one of the differently abled—

I'm an epitaph for a million imperfect babies left untreated
I'm an ikon carved from bones in a mass grave in Tiergarten, Germany—
I'm withered legs hidden with a blanket

I am not one of the able disabled—

I'm a black panther with green eyes and scars like a picket fence
I'm pink lace panties teasing a stub of milk white thigh
I'm the Evil Eye

I'm the first cell divided
I'm mud that talks
I'm Eve I'm Kali
I'm The Mountain That Never Moves
I've been forever   I'll be here forever
I'm the Gimp
I'm the Cripple
I'm the Crazy Lady

I'm the Woman With Juice
                    (Cheryl Marie Wade, Quoted in Davis, 1997)

Wade reverses beauty and ugliness, portraying herself as both a sexual object—
with lace panties—and as deformed—with a stub, and demands a presence which
has been denied through notions of being "physically challenged" by asserting that
she will be "here forever." Among the various themes located in the writing of
Cheryl Marie Wade are sexual and gendered identities presented in playful ways
which challenge the desexing discourses of disability (Allan, 1999), a move called
for by several writers (e.g., Finger, 1992; Shakespeare et al., 1996). Wade provides
an unassailable argument by presenting both itself *and its opposition,* unity and difference, ugliness and beauty, leaving nothing to contest. This playful irony disturbs
in the way that Kundera (1986) suggests the truly great novel irritates: "not because
it mocks or attacks but because it denies us our certainties by unmasking the world
as an ambiguity" (134).

The work of Audre Lorde (Garland-Thomson, 1997) provides a further example of writing by "powerful women" (Garland-Thomson, 1997, p. 240) who have embraced their liminality as black disabled women and foregrounded their difference. Lorde pursues a form of byomythography, a revisionist narrative of self as *Zami,* in which a cluster of excluding and affirming attributes—namely, "fat, Black, nearly blind and ambidextrous" (1982, p. 240)—frees her up from normalising and assimilating conventions, so that her very distinctiveness becomes the site of power and politics:

> The marked women inspire awe at the profusion of difference their bodies flaunt, challenging the supposedly superior status of normalcy by rendering it banal. These literary representations accentuate the marked body's historical context, infusing the material body with social meaning rather than metaphorical significance. By connecting physical being with individual history and culture, the extraordinary women figures define the self in terms of its uniqueness rather than its conformity to the norm. (Garland-Thomson, 1997, p. 261)

The abnormal body thus becomes sanctioned as a means of disrupting the unity and order of its opposite, and exposing it in all its banality (Garland-Thomson, 1997, p. 261).

This form of kynicism by disabled people is hard to take, because it is so raunchy and "in your face." It is also difficult to make judgments about, both as an art form and as ideological critique. The "horror of the comic" (Kundera, 1986, p. 104) and the experience of impossibilities of characters portrayed by Kafka, Hasek, Kundera, and others provoke in the reader a mixture of surprise and relief, along with a "clear implication that laughter is life's exception" (Stronach & Allan, 1999). But where disabled people are concerned, this laughter immediately renders us self-conscious and places us back within the "call of care" (Heidigger, cited in Sloterdijk, 1987, p. 417), where we judge such a response as inappropriate and disrespectful. It is impossible to say how effective it might be as a form of ideological critique, but it does appear to invite the kind of questioning of normalising and disabling ideology, which is absolutely necessary. As an approach that aspires to make ideology limp without ever promising to expose it, but which also forces able-bodied people to confront their own banality, to laugh at their stupidity and to recognise how this disables, it is more spirited and possibly more productive:

> Only the greatest impudence still has words for reality. Only anarchic waywardness still finds an expression of contemporary normality. (Sloterdijk, 1987, p. 546)

References

Abberley, P. (1995). Disabling ideology in health and welfare—the case of occupational therapy, *Disability and Society, 10*(2), 221–236.

Allan, J. (1999). *Actively seeking inclusion*. London: Falmer Press.

Althusser, L. (1994). Ideology and ideological state apparatuses. In Zizek (Ed.), *Mapping ideology*. London: Verso.

Ballard, K. (1999). Concluding thoughts. In K. Ballard (Ed.), *Inclusive education: International voices on disability and justice*. London: Falmer Press.

Bourdieu, P. (1972). *Outline of a theory of practice*. Cambridge, UK: Cambridge University Press.

Bourdieu, P. (1994). Doxa and common life: An interview with Terry Eagleton. In S. Zizek (Ed.), *Mapping ideology*. London: Verso.

Brantlinger, E. (1997). Using ideology: Cases of nonrecognition of the politices of research and practice in special education, *Review of Educational Research, 67*(4), 425–459.

Casling, D. (1993). Cobblers and song-birds: The language and imagary of disability. *Disability, Handicap and Society 8*(2), 199–206.

Cooper, D. (1997). Strategies of power: Legislating worship and religious education. in M. Lloyd and A. Thacker (Eds.), *The impact of Michel Foucault on the social sciences and the humanitie*. Basingstoke, UK: Macmillan.

Cripzine: Disability Arts and Culture. Web site *http://www.stanford.edu/-jarron/crip.htm*.

Darke, P. (1998). Understanding cinematic representations of disability. In T. Shakespeare (Ed.), *The disability reader: Social science perspectives*.

Davis, L. J. (1997). *The Disability Studies Reader*. New York, NY: Routledge.

Derrida, J. (1998). Spectres of Marx. In J. Wolfreys (Ed.), *The Derrida reader*. Edinburgh, UK: Edinburgh University Press.

Eagleton, T. (1994) Ideology and its vicissitudes in Western Marxism. In S. Zizek (Ed.), *Mapping ideolog*. London: Verso.

Finger, A. (1992). Forbidden fruit. *New Internationalist 233*, 8–10.

Foucault, M. (1984). Truth and method. In P. Rabinow (Ed.), *The Foucault reader*. New York, NY: Pantheon Books.

Garland-Thomson, R. (1997). Disabled women as powerful women in Petry, Morrison, and Lorde: Revising Black Female Subjectivity. In D. Mitchell and S. Snyder (Eds.) *The body and physical difference: Discourses of disability*. Ann Arbor, Michigan: University of Michigan Press.

Gouldner, A. (1976). *The dialectic of ideology and technology*. New York: Seabury.

Gramsci, A. (1971). *Selections from prison notebooks,* Southampton, UK: Camelot Press Ltd.

Hasek, J. (1973). *The good soldier Sjveik*. Harmondsworth, UK: Penguin.

Imrie, R. (1998). Oppression in the built environment. In T. Shakespeare (Ed.), *The disability reader: Social science perspectives*. London: Cassell.

Jameson, F. (1994). Postmodernism and the market. In S. Zizek (Ed.), *Mapping ideology*. London: Verso.

Kundera, M. (1986). *The art of the novel*. London: Faber & Faber.

Kundera, M. (1991). *Immortality*. London: Faber & Faber.

Lorde, A. (1982). *Zami: A new spelling of my name*. Freedom, CA: Crossing Press.

McLean, D. (1998). *Beyond barriers: A consultation paper on arts and disability policy*. Web site: *http://ndaf.org.Pages/BEYONDBARRIERS*

Mairs, N. (1986). On being a cripple. *Plaintext: essays*. Tuscon: University of Arizona Press.

Mannheim, K. (1936). *Ideology and Utopia: An introduction to the sociology of knowledge*. London: Routledge.

Mitchell, D. & Snyder, S. (Eds) *The body and physical difference: Discourses of disability*. Ann Arbor, Michigan: University of Michigan Press.

Morris, J. (1991). *Pride against prejudice: Transforming attitudes to disability.* London: Women's Press.

Morrison, E., & Finkelstein, V. (1993). Broken arts and cultural repair: The role of culture in the empowerment of disabled people. In J. Swain, V. Finkelstein, S. French, & M. Oliver (Eds.), *Disabling barriers—enabling environments.* London: Sage/Open University.

Napolitano, S. (1998). In D. McLean, Beyond Barriers: A consultation paper on arts and disability policy. Available:http://ndaf.org.pages/beyondbarriers.

Oliver, M. (1990). *The politics of disablement.* Basingstoke, UK: Macmillan & St. Martin's Press.

Oliver, M. (1996). *Understanding disability: From theory to practice.* Basingstoke, UK: Macmillan.

Pêcheux, M. (1994). Ideological (mis)recognition. In S. Zizek (Ed.), *Mapping ideology.* London: Verso.

Ram, K. (1993). Too "traditional" once again: Some poststructuralists on the aspirations of the immigrant/third world female subject. *Australian Feminist Studies, 17,* 5–28.

Rorty, R. (1994). Feminism, ideology and deconstruction: A pragmatist view. In S. Zizek (Ed.), *Mapping ideology.* London: Verso.

Shakespeare, T. (1994). Cultural representation of disabled people: Dustbins for disavowal? *Disability and Society, 9*(3), 283–299.

Shakespeare, T., & Watson, N. (1997). Defending the social model. *Disability and Society* 12(2), 293–300.

Shakespeare, T., Gillespie-Sells, K., & Davies, D. (1996). *The politics of disability: Untold desires.* London: Cassell.

Singh, P. (1995). Voicing the "Other," speaking for the "self," disrupting the metanarratives of educational theorizing with poststructural feminism. In K. Smith & P. Wexler (Eds.), *After postmodernism,* London: Falmer Press.

Sloterdijk, P. (1987). *Critique of cynical reason.* Minneapolis: University of Minnesota Press.

Stronach, I., & Allan, J. (1999). Joking with disability: What's the difference between the comic and tragic in disability discourses? *Body and society.* v5 (4), 31–46.

Snyder, S., Brueggemann, B., & Garland-Thomson, R. (2002). *Disability studies: Enabling the humanities.* New York: Modern Languages Association.

Thompson, J. (1984). *Studies in the theory of ideology,* Cambridge, United Kingdom: Polity Press.

Vasey, S. (1992). Disability arts and culture: An introduction to key issues and questions. In S. Lees (Ed.), *Disability arts and culture papers.* London: Shape Publications.

Vernon, A. (1998). Multiple oppression and the disabled people's movement. In T. Shakespeare (Ed.), *The disability reader: Social science perspectives.* London: Cassell.

Veyne, P. (1997). Foucault and his interlocutors. In A. Davidson (Ed.), *Foucault and his interlocutors.* Chicago: University of Chicago Press.

Wade, C. (1997). I am not one of the. In L. Davis (Ed.), *The disability studies reader.* New York, NY: Routledge.

Zizek, S. (1994). *Mapping ideology.* London: Verso.

3   *Roger Slee*

MEANING IN THE SERVICE OF POWER[1]

Expositions in the Baggage-Hall of Knowledge

This is a chapter about the production and reproduction of meaning as it adheres
to the intersection of disability [disablement] and education. Making meaning
through what Foucault terms "discursive practices" "forms the objects of which
they speak—they do not identify objects, they constitute them and in the practice
of doing so conceal their own invention."[2] The formation of disability, and
thereby its ideological representations, suggests and simultaneously restricts a
range of possibilities for inclusive education. It is with the creation and denial of
possibility that I am concerned. My purpose is opportunistic. I wish to use this
forum to rehearse a problem that confronts me as a dean of Faculty of Education
responsible for teacher education; namely, What goes into a teacher education curriculum pursuant to enabling the neophyte teacher to work in and lead inclusive
schools? From the outset I realize that the question is inscribed with assumptions
and suggestions that require unpacking. "What inclusive schools?," some may ask.
Others may question the nature of the inclusive educational project: "Is it tinker-
ing we have in mind, or are we talking of a radical educational reconstruction?"
Still others may be interested to inquire, "Who is doing the teaching and to
whom?" Such explication in the first instance assists the conversation, its fluency
and, more importantly, its candor.

Since I have been stopped and have placed my bags on the counter for inspec-
tion, I know that this case (sorry) will be referred to the Inspector of Epistemol-

ogy. You see, the problem is that I paused, gave away my nervousness, and have been detected. Stumbling over the taken-for-granted language of "special education needs" and more recently "inclusive education" is conspicuous in the company I keep. So many others appear quite relaxed in their language, immediately engaging in conversation about inclusiveness irrespective of the epistemological baggage they carry. For my part I still feel the need to consult the Lonely Planet guide to global education lexicons to check off meanings as the words are deployed (deliberate choice) by travelers from different culture, disciplinary, and political contexts. After all, words are more or less powerful instruments in the politics of disablement. They are charged with differential power and meaning according to whom is speaking, and according to who is entitled to speak. I am reminded of the British poet Roger McGough, who mused on the theme of language in his "Poem for a Dead Poet":

> He had a way
> With language . . .
> Words?
> Why he could almost make 'em talk.[3]

You might think this an indulgence, but collections of papers from previous meetings of this gathering reinforce my nervousness about meanings and purposes. Let me return to my problem of inclusive education for teacher education students. It is a problem for me because people in our program say there is no problem. I am told that, in order to have our graduates "fit" for the task, they are required to merely "complete" studies in special education. That is, the preparation of teachers for inclusive education is viewed as consonant with the banking model of education, traditional special education skill sets are presented and practice follows—or so it is assumed. This is troubling, as it seems to be the antithesis to the requirement for inclusive education. The inherent technicism of special education rooted in deficit bound psycho-medical paradigms of individual pathological defects,[4] impedes "vast opportunities for developments in [educational] practice."[5] In this discussion I will suggest that the discursive field of special education itself prevents our aspiring teachers from *thinking otherwise*[6] about the deep structure of disablement. The constitution of disability knowledge represents an arena for theoretical struggle within and between groups of disabled and non-disabled people alike.[7] To be sure, the struggle is ideological, though some are more likely to "fess up" to their epistemic affiliations than others. From where I sit, the way that inclusive education has been managed as a policy objective across a number of contexts suggests a choice between segregation and assimilation.[8] Here I side with Pierre Bourdieu, "between two evils, I refuse to choose the lesser."[9] Drawing from Barton and Clough, the task of the intellectual and education activist alike is to "make and articulate with difficulties."[10]

Inclusive schooling is an ambitious project, given that we seem to be commencing with an oxymoron as our organizing concept. Schools were never really meant for everyone. The more they have been called upon to include the masses, the more they have developed the technologies of exclusion and containment. Immediately a caveat is inserted to acknowledge that such a generalization, while adhering to systems levels and many schools, is disrespectful of the work of some schools and their communities in guaranteeing educational provision for all. An historical artifact, schools were established for a minority of privileged children who were prepared for the academy and the professions. The relatively recent advent of mass compulsory schooling merely elaborated the processes of social stratification and exclusion through a range of dividing practices in the school.[11] Segregated special education, together with the unskilled labor market, colluded with schools to conceal the inevitability of failure for the majority of children. A rational, indeed scientific, explanation was produced which attached blame to the defects and pathological inability of those who were failed by the narrow academic curriculum.

Crisis in the unskilled labor market and the concomitant extension of schooling for increasing numbers of young people has witnessed a number of trends that reinforce the claim that schools are reluctant when it comes to inclusion. First is the expansion and net widening of special educational provision both within and outside of regular schools.[12] There has been a formalization of exclusion as a permanent feature of the educational landscape in coexistence with discourses of inclusion. OFSTED [Office for Standards in Education] inspectors are dedicated to the assurance of the quality of Pupil Referral Units that pick up the students schools that are serious about their League Tables performance.[13] Second, there is a struggle over the constitution of the curriculum for the millennium. Stephen Ball writes of the "culture restorationists'" ideological project of maintaining the curriculum as a museum in the United Kingdom where no signs of life are evident amid the exaggerated celebration of the past.[14] In Australia the struggle between the "academic" and "vocational" curriculum endures. This is both actual and illusory, as we continue to accept that while medicine is an academic program of study, automotive mechanics is firmly maintained as vocational training. Associated panics over "standards in education" translates into curricular conservatism. The Australian panic over standards in literacy and numeracy has facilitated a rearticulation of equity policy as back to the basics for the disadvantaged.[15] Third, the operation of the state (public) schools sector as an educational marketplace to the mantra of competition and choice has privileged "well-resourced choosers" who

> now have free reign to guarantee and reproduce, as best they can, their existing cultural, social and economic advantages in the new complex and blurred hierarchy of schools.[16]

"Class selection," they argue, "is revalorized by the market."[17] A pivotal instrument to assist parents in their choice is the publication of national league tables of schools' performance according to criteria that revolve around student examination results. The notion of choice is illusory. Assumed is the notion that parents are mobile and informed. Moreover, there is little attention paid to the fact that schools are discriminating in their choice and eviction of students. Active consideration is being given to students' special educational needs statements being counted in the League Table calculation as if this will militate against discrimination against disabled students.

The thrust of policy largely conspires against an assertion of the legitimacy of a politics of identity and difference. This chapter takes the position of "talking back to power,"[18] that rehearsing special education with our trainee-teachers will reinforce the status of "other" for all who fall into the special educational needs category. More devastating is the potential for teachers to feel more confident that their hunches that some kids don't belong in *our* schools is vindicated by the special educational theory with which they are conversant.

Disability—How Do We Know? What Do We Know?

In *Post-modernity and Its Discontents,* Zygmunt Bauman considers the phenomenon of social "othering."

> All societies produce strangers; but each kind of society produces its own kind of strangers, and produces them in its own inimitable way. If the strangers are the people who do not fit the cognitive, moral and aesthetic map of the world—one of these maps, two or all three; if they therefore, by their sheer presence, make obscure what ought to be transparent, confuse what ought to be a straightforward recipe for action, and/or prevent the satisfaction from being fully satisfying; if they pollute the joy with anxiety while making the forbidden fruit alluring; if, in other words, they befog and eclipse the boundary lines which ought to be clearly seen; if, having done all this, they gestate uncertainty, which in its turn breeds the discomfort of feelings lost—then each society produces such strangers. While drawing its borders and charting its cognitive, aesthetic and moral maps, it cannot but gestate people who conceal borderlines deemed crucial to its orderly and/or meaningful life and so are accused of causing the discomfort experience as the most painful and the least bearable.[19]

It is worth considering an extract from Joseph Shapiro's book on disability politics in the United States, *No Pity,* in the light of Bauman's postulations about social strangers:

> Non-disabled Americans do not understand disabled ones.
>
> That was clear at the memorial service for Timothy Cook, when long-time friends got up to pay him heartfelt tribute. "He never seemed disabled to me," said one. "He was the least disabled person I ever met," pronounced another. It was the highest praise these non-disabled friends could think to give a disabled attorney who, at thirty-eight years old, had won landmark disability rights cases, including one to force public transit systems to equip their buses with wheelchair lifts. But more than a few heads in the crowded chapel bowed with an uneasy embarrassment at the supposed compliment. It was as if someone had tried to compliment a black man by saying, "You're the least black person I ever met," as false as telling a Jew, "I never think of you as Jewish," as clumsy as seeking to flatter a woman with "you don't act like a woman."

Here in this memorial chapel was a small clash between the reality of disabled people and the understanding of their lives by others. It was the type of collision that disabled people experience daily. Yet any discordance went unnoticed even to the well-meaning friends of a disability rights fighter like Cook.[20]

Elsewhere I have written about similar collisions in the chambers of the Australian federal parliament during the readings of the Disability Discrimination Bills, about pile-ups in the corridors of education as teachers, administrators, and civil servants fumble their way towards "inclusive education."[21] A range of epistemologies, and their composites, is on offer when it comes to *knowing* disability. Some of these stories advance the rights of those upon whom the status of "stranger" has been conferred; others continue to impede rights and exclude them from active citizenship. How do we come to know disability? What do we know about disability?

For most of us, the answer to the first question is "from a distance and through the powerful discourses and ideological frameworks of others." Discursive practices establish the field of knowledge from which we piece together our understandings and thenceforth reactions to that knowledge. For Foucault, discursive practices are

> characterized by the demarcation of a field of objects, by the definition of a legitimate perspective for a subject of knowledge, by the setting of norms for elaborating concepts and theories. Hence each of them presupposes a play of prescriptions that govern exclusions and selections. . . . A discursive practice brings together various disciplines or sciences, or it passes through a number of them and gathers several of their areas into a sometimes inconspicuous cluster.[22]

Discursive practices have established the legitimate perspective for the constructed category, official knowledge and treatment of "the disabled" or special educational needs student. This discourse of special educational needs in turn became a very powerful knowledge[23] that draws together and is used to map, regulate, and govern[24] a fragmented and unruly population of "strangers" with less than "docile bodies."[25] In order to chart the manner in which ideologies carried within powerful discourses may intersect and reinforce each other in this field of knowledge I will share, albeit reluctantly, my own recollections of the formation of my knowledge of disability. Implicit is the revelation of process—in other words, how we come to know disability. This is, of course, quite specific, but I wonder whether it is less than extraordinary and indicative. The first point to make is that I feel great shame about these disclosures of my schooling in an amalgam of what Mike Oliver would call personal tragedy and medical stories about disablement.

My first memory of an encounter with disability emerges from the days before I started primary school. My mother used to clean the houses of the wealthy folk in the small rural town in which I grew up. She did this with a friend who had a daughter who, I was told, was so-called Mongoloid. I do remember that this term was quite common at the time and remained part of my vocabulary right through school. I later replaced this term with Down's Syndrome. It took me considerably more time to remember the girl's name, Pauline, outside of her label. My mother used to meet her friend and the four of us would set off for the day's work. One morning we arrived at Pauline's house to find the curtains drawn and her mother in her dressing gown. The two women embraced and sobbed. I didn't understand what was happening but sufficiently knew the portents of calamity to render myself invisible. On the way home I interrogated my mother to find that Pauline had been electrocuted in the bath the previous night. My mother's summation: "It's sad, but it's also a blessing." I learned that death was a blessed release from a disabled life. A fact was established. I now understand this as personal tragedy discourse.[26]

For my schoolmates and I, special kids were sent to special schools (i.e., segregated schools) because they weren't "normal." Normal became a very powerful concept established in childhood that took some time to jettison. The definition of normality for us was simple. They aren't like us.[27] Nature had been unkind and they couldn't mix with us, as they couldn't learn as much. Some of them might hurt us. What they did learn took a longer time, so they had specially trained teachers to look after them. These teachers did looking after, our teachers taught. Their education after all was an extension of pastoral care. We never saw them except at the shops with their parents, but they didn't frequent the shops as much as we did either.

Their school was called Mullalatarong. Many special schools were given Aboriginal names. However, I don't think we are talking about the semiotics of solidarity. We used to use the other side of the street on the way home or dare each other to run past the school on the unsafe side, for we believed in the contagion of intellectual disability. What an admixture of distorted myth, common knowledge, and old science we carried. My parents' comments were always on the side of tolerance and benevolence for "but for the grace of God, there go I." Our teachers supplemented this view by occasional reference to the heroic disabled, such as Helen Keller. Our sixth grade teacher, Mr. Seagrave, read *Reach for the Sky,* the story of Douglas Bader, as one of our serialized stories. At my school we had an opportunity grade. An introduction by Hauser,[28] opportunity grades were euphemistic deflection for the practice of the gathering together across grade levels all of those different and difficult kids that didn't find their way into segregated schools. Of course, placement meant the closing down of all opportunity in the educational meritocracy for these kids. We used to joke and tease each other about being assigned to Miss Harris's room, to the "oppo" grade.

High school seems less dramatic, more a process of civilizing and sophistication. We gathered more sophisticated medical explanations for disability and listened to debating teams wrestling over euthanasia. What is significant is that the opportunity grade didn't lead to high school and that there were no disabled kids at our school. There was a boy at the technical school (nonacademic stream) down the road, but his parents, I was told at home, hadn't accepted his disability. Another lesson—acceptance meant compliance with official knowledge and treatment. My intention is not to make villains of my parents or teachers. Theirs was a generally accepted common knowledge.

If I leap forward to my time as a teacher, I remember that our training was for "normal" kids, and others would be at segregated schools. There was a postgraduate certificate we might consider if we had a calling. This was the stuff of missionaries. My first teaching post was a shock. In the year 12 (final year of secondary school) I was to teach politics to a class that had a blind boy, Brendan, in it. Brendan had been a victim of a school prank that resulted in a very serious accident. I was anxious and I am sure that it was obvious as I raised my voice to address the startled boy. His classmates were not so inept. His classmates didn't know him as a stranger, knowing that the only difference was that Brendan couldn't see anymore and that he got mad and depressed about it. The kids saw to it that his learning didn't suffer while they taught me how to teach him politics and unlearning some of my established knowledge about disability.

The acquisition of knowledge becomes more complex when I opted to work at a behavior unit for so-called disruptive students. The possibility emerged that disability knowledge was a contested site. A number of counter positions existed among the teaching staff at the behavior unit. Some had special education training and seemed to carry great authority. They had an explanatory diagnostic lexicon to support their interventions. Others saw schools as being the problem for these difficult kids. I determined to complete a Graduate Diploma of Special Education in order to help me to better *know* and help these kids.

In hindsight, and with my current ideological reckoner in hand, a great deal of symmetry existed between some of the foundational knowledge that I have described and what I was taught in the Special Education course. Notions about normality and defectiveness were reinforced and could be explained with a far more persuasive professional vocabulary. The gaze remained fixed upon individual pathology and sought no interrogation of the broader context of the educational exchange. Schools were excused from the diagnosticians' gaze. Special needs were conceptualized as originating from "deficits in the neurological, psychological, physical or sensory make-up of the child, analogous to an illness or medical condition."[29] I was introduced to the range of diagnostic instruments employed to ascertain the "etiology" of the student's condition or "syndrome" with a view to identifying the correct form of intervention; chemical, therapeutic, or educational. The preferred research orientation was positivist. All of this was described as a "scientific" approach to disability.

We could also elect one unit in social-emotional disturbance taught by a sociologist/criminologist. He seemed to be a lonely member of that faculty—he was the Department of Special Education's resident stranger. The impact of his encouraging us to refer to a different set of call numbers in the library was profound. Discovering a sociology of deviance and stumbling upon such titles as: *Special Education—Policy, Practices and Social Interests*,[30] *A Sociology of Special Education*,[31] and *Special Education and Social Control—Invisible Disasters*,[32] presented a direct challenge to the epistemological foundations of the special education program. When these people wrote about inclusion they did not grasp at "clauses of conditionality,"[33] there were no caveats about least restrictive or most appropriate environments, no cascade models to protect us from encounters with the most disabled children. Theirs was a discourse of rights and the foundations of their reading of disability suggested that disability and impairment were socially constructed, that they were historically, materially, and culturally specific.[34] Disablement referred to oppressive social relations as they were played out in institutions such as schools.

My work in the behavior unit was disrupted by thinking otherwise about the relationship between the so-called disturbed children and mainstream schools. Most telling was my increasing discomfiture in working in a unit that allowed schools to off-load those kids whom they had failed. Barton's claim that special educational needs was a euphemism for the failure of schools had struck an echoing chord.[35] There seemed to be an increasing incidence of difficult and failing students being diagnosed within the category of "socially/emotionally disturbed." Elsewhere this would equate with EBD or maladjusted students. This incidence of learning difficulties[36] was on an obvious increase. More behavior units were called for to deal with this growing population of special needs children. No one in Australian education, it seemed, had read Her Majesty's Inspectorate's report on behavior units in the United Kingdom, where they were suggesting that they were a deflection from the problems in schools which resulted in the suspensions and referrals of vulnerable and disadvantaged children.[37] More compelling was the racialization of special needs manifest in such reports and in the work of Sally Tomlinson.[38] I moved from the behavioral unit to pursue research into school suspension and exclusion. I believed that more attention had to be paid to the institutional and educational pathologies that pushed some children while making strangers of others.

This biography is advanced to suggest that my learning about disability was pretty unremarkable and that the formative common knowledge was born out of separation. Special education training did not disrupt this knowledge—rather, it smoothed the rough edges; provided medical terms for a panoply of syndromes, disorders, and conditions; and heightened my sense of benevolence for needy others. The epistemic fissure surfaced only through an elective that introduced a critical, rather than functionalist, sociological account of difference and social control and suggested qualitative approaches to educational inquiry.

Ideology at Our Table?

I do not intend to rehearse theories of ideology here, as this has been so thoroughly explored for us by Ellen Brantlinger.[39] My professor of Chinese politics, Chwei Liang Chiou, argued that Chinese ideology comprised two components, pure ideology or "theory" (*lilun*) and practical ideology or "thought" (*szuhsiang*). "Maoism in action"[40] he argued, was more practical, akin to Mannheim's schemata of a functional as opposed to a substantive rationality wherein a set of ideas that may in fact be "a more or less conscious disguise of the real nature of a situation" is used as a rationalization for a set of actions.[41] In this respect the appropriation of inclusive education discourse by the special needs industry and educational management may be seen as a functional rationale that achieves a number of desirable outcomes. Unruly populations are subjected to greater levels of surveillance and made governable through various protocols of exclusion and inclusion. The special education professionals amass more clients and now have, as Stanley Cohen declared, "the fertile fields of the larger community" to operate within.[42] The ideological agenda, though not readily explicated, exists just as does that of the "inclusionists."

Earlier in this chapter I suggested my anxiety about possible misconceptions and misrepresentations of meaning. This is most acute for me in the attempts by Catherine Clark, Alan Dyson, and Alan Millward to present overviews of the field.[43] That they have sponsored debate and discussion is commendable and my comments ought to be seen as rejoinders for the extension of this discussion rather than attacks on the works cited. The consignment of theorists to groups committed to critique and deconstruction or to more engaged research in the schools and with education authorities is misleading. It suggests a detachment of the former from engagement with "practical" activity and the immediate relevance of the latter. More recent has been their call for a reconnection to special education.

I do not contest the importance of work with local communities but I am equally fearful of the scope this provides for the silencing of dissent, for the dismissal of difficult questions. Engaged as an evaluator of the Education Department of Western Australia's "Students at Educational Risk" strategy, I feel conscious of colluding with a policy fundamentally flawed in its return to 20% notions of students with special needs (the predetermined formula calculated for the subset of pupils with special educational needs). Critique threatens future contracts and incrementalism sustains the fundamental epistemology previously described. More, Beazley and Maelzer[44] remind us of Mike Oliver's view that most disability research is a waste of time in that it holds little prospect for promoting the agendas of disabled people.[45] The deeply ideological question of whose interests are being served by our research reemerges. Is a reconnection to special education a dangerous liaison?[46]

More persuasive is Tony Booth's dictum that inclusion is understood through the robust analysis of exclusion as it operates in the school sector.[47] The politics of the ideological struggle should be acknowledged. It is not simply a question of an academic exchange between different education paradigms. Inclusive education is about the politics of recognition. To bring people together in a liberal exchange in order to blend our ideas to effect harmonious détente is counterproductive. Peter MacLaren provides counsel for the kind of cultural work in which we must engage:

> Diversity that somehow constitutes itself as a harmonious ensemble of benign culture spheres is a conservative and liberal model of multiculturalism that, in my mind, deserves to be jettisoned because, when we try to make culture an undisturbed space of harmony and agreement where social relations exist within cultural forms of uninterrupted accords we subscribe to a form of social amnesia in which we forget that all knowledge is forged in histories that are played out in the field of social antagonisms.[48]

Put simply, our work is as ideological as the project of antiracist education or the exposing of the deleterious impact of patriarchal education. Disablism is disablism. The centrality of minority voices in the setting of the research agenda is a fundamental requirement for progress toward inclusive schooling. The absence of these voices simultaneously absents stories that need to be told. The Australian historian Henry Reynolds, whose work on the European invasion of Australia has been influential in our progress toward native title legislation, puts forth the question, "Why weren't we told?"[49] Why weren't we told in our European histories about the invasion and genocide? Why weren't we allowed access to an Aboriginal history? Being told, we now move, albeit reluctantly for some including the Federal Liberal (conservative) government, toward reconciliation and apology (national "sorry books") from institutions, sheltered workshops, and segregated schools? If apologies need to be made, sorry books and alternative stories told, then surely it is this field of disability research.

Perhaps Now We Can Consider My Teacher Education Studies?

I reassert an early proposition, having a Diploma of Education students study special education to help them in inclusive schools obstructs inclusion. Let me give some provocative prompts for our discussion.

What would a replacement curriculum look like? More to the point, what is the place for old hierarchies of knowledge, and how do we differentiate knowledge to represent a range of needs and abilities?

Whose advice should we seek? In the construction of curriculum, whom do we consult? Do the experts retain their unequal share of power and authority, or is expertise weighed against insider knowledge? Later in this book, both Jude MacArthur and Linda Ware introduce the perspectives of parents and youth who possess valuable insider knowledge that might radically alter the curriculum. However, in both cases the challenge to the system necessitated personal risk to the individuals who challenged the status quo.

How does our research contribute to the development of a curriculum that liberates future teachers from the yokes of exclusionary special educational practices? This last question asserts an ideology of inclusion as a counter discourse to the prevailing hegemony of traditional ideologies in special education. Disabled researchers should lead us in this discussion. Disabled students should author the content informed of their own experiences and the parents of disabled children can likewise be included in the process to disrupt the "backward facing" described by Kate, the mother presented by Jude Mac Arthur (see Chapter 10). An even more bold curriculum might be influenced by that which Julie Allan describes as a productive ideology informed of "kynicism by disabled people" (see Chapter 2). Her examples are informed by self-authored accounts of living with disability that invites the very kind of questioning of normalizing and disabling ideology that is long overdue.

This chapter has no conclusion as such. The task I set is not written in stone. Nor do I start with a notion that we become the architects of a blueprint to be raced down to the patents office. Inclusion speaks to a fragmented, unruly, and discontinuous world—a world receptive to remaking and rediscovery.

Notes

1. I have borrowed this phrase from John B. Thompson (1984:7) who is cited by Ellen Brantlinger (1997) in her incisive exploration, *Using Ideology: Cases of Non-recognition of the Politics of Research and Practice in Special Education.*
2. See Foucault, M. (1974) *The Archaeology of Knowledge,* London, Travistock, p. 49.
3. Roger McGough (1979) Poem for a Dead Poet, *Holiday on Death Row,* London, Jonathan Cape Publishers.
4. For discussions of the trade special education paradigm, see, Barton, L. (ed.) (1987) *The Politics of special Educational Needs,* Lewes, Falmer Press; Skidmore, D. (1996) Towards an integrated theoretical framework for research into special educational needs, *European Journal of Special Needs Education,* Vol. 11, No. 1, pp. 33–47; Tomlinson, S. (1982) *A Sociological Special Education,* London, Routledge; Skritic, T. (1991) *Behind Special Education: A Critical Analysis of Professional Culture and School Organization,* Denver, CO: Love Publishing.
5. Ainscow, M. (1999) *Understanding the Development of Inclusive Schools,* London, Falmer Press.
6. I have italicized 'thinking otherwise' as I borrow it from Stephan Ball's reflections on the inhibiting effects of school effectiveness research and educational management theories on education studies. See Ball, S.J. (1998) Educational Studies, Policy Entrepreneurship and Social Theory, in R. Slee, G. Weiner and S. Tomlinson (eds.) *School Effectiveness For Whom? Challenges to the School Effectiveness and School Improvement Movements,* London, Falmer Press.
7. See Barton, L. and Oliver, M. (eds.) (1997) *Disability Studies: Past, Present and Future,* Leeds, The Disability Press; Shakespeare, T. (ed.) *The Disability Reader: Social Science Perspectives,* London, Cassell.
8. Jan Branson and Don Miller, in their paper 'Beyond Integration Policy—The Deconstruction of Disability', draw our attention to what is essentially a policy sleight of hand.
9. Bourdieu, P. (1998) *Acts of Resistance. Against the New Myths of our Time* (Richard Nice translation), Cambridge, UK: Policy Press.
10. Clough, P. and Barton, L. (eds.) (1995) *Making Difficulties. Research and the Construction of SEN,* London, Paul Chapman.
11. Clough, P. and Barton, L. (eds.) *Articulating with Difficulty. Research Voices in Inclusive Education,* London, Paul Chapman.
12. See Foucault, M. (1979) *Discipline and Punish: The Birth of the Prison,* Harmondsworth, UK: Penguin Books, p. 183.
13. Sally Tomlinson has spoken to this group about special education as a tactic to be deployed in the regulation of difference.

14. For an elaboration of this point see Parsons, C. and Castle, F. (1998) The cost of school exclusion in England, *International Journal of Inclusive Education*, Vol. 2, No. 4, pp. 277–294.

15. See Ball, S.J. (1994) *Education Reform: A critical and post-structural approach*, Buckingham, Open University Press, chapter 3.

16. See Bob Lingard (1988) The Disadvantaged Schools Programme: caught between literacy and local management of schools, *International Journal of Inclusive Education*, Vol. 2, No. 1, pp. 1–14.

17. Gewirtz, S., Ball, S.J. and Bowe, R. (1995) *Markets, Choice and Equity in Education*, Buckingham, Open University Press, p. 23.

18. Ibid, p. 23.

19. See op. cit. Brantlinger, p. 426.

20. Bauman, Z. (1997) *Post-modernity and its Discontents*, Oxford, Basil Blackwell, p. 17.

21. Shapiro, J.P. (1993) *No Pity. People with Disabilities Forging a New Civil Rights Movement*, New York, Random House, pp. 3–4.

22. Slee, R. (1993) The Politics of Integration—new sites for old practices?, *Disability, Handicap & Society*, Vol. 8, No. 4, pp. 351–360.

23. Foucault, M. (1997) The Will to Knowledge, in P. Rabinow (ed.) *Ethics. The Essential Works 1*, London, Allen Lane, the Penguin Press, p. 11.

24. Usher, R. (1998) Seductive Texts: Competence, Power and Knowledge in Postmodernity, in R. Barnett and A. Griffin (eds.) *The End of Knowledge in Higher Education*, London, Cassell.

25. Rose, N. (1989) *Governing the Soul*, London, Routledge.

26. Foucault, M. (1977) *Discipline and Punish: The Birth of the Prison*, London, Allen Lane.

27. See Oliver, M. (1990) *The Politics of Disablement*, London, Macmillan.

28. For that matter Aboriginality along with a host of other minority identities weren't 'normal' either.

29. For a history of special education in Victoria see Lewis, J. (1993) Radical Social History or Old Wine? In R. Slee (ed.) *Is There a Desk With My Name On It? The Politics of Integration*, London, Falmer Press.

30. Op. cit. Skidmore, p. 34.

31. Barton, L. and Tomlinson, S. (eds.) (1981) *Special Education—Policy Practices and Social Issues, London*, Harper and Row.

32. Tomlinson, S. (1982) *A Sociology of Special Education*, London, Routledge and Kegan Paul.

33. Ford, J., Mongon, D. and Whelan, M. (1982) *Special Education and Social Control—Invisible Disasters*, London, Routledge and Kegan Paul.

34. Slee, R. (1996) Clauses of Conditionality: The 'reasonable' accommodation of language, in L. Barton (ed.) *Disability & Society: Emerging Issues and Insights*, Harlow, Addison Wesley Longman.

35. Abberley, P. (1987) The concept of oppression and the development of a social theory of disability, *Disability, Handicap & Society*, Vol. 2, No. 1, pp. 5–20.

36. Barton, L. (ed.) (1987) *The Politics of Special Educational Needs*, Lewes, UK: Falmer Press.

37. Sigmon, S.B. (1987) *Radical Analysis of Special Education*, Lewes, Falmer Press; Franklin, B.M. (1994) *From "Backwardness" to "At-risk": Childhood Learning Difficulties and the Contradictions of School Reform*, New York, SUNY Press.

38. Her Majesty's Inspectorate (1978) *Behavioural Units: A Survey of Special Units for Pupils with Behavioral Problems*, London, Department of Education and Science.

39. Tomlinson, S. (1981) *Educational Sub-normality: A Study in Decision-Making,* London, Routledge and Kegan Paul.
40. Op. cit. Brantlinger, 1997.
41. Chiou, C.L. (1974) *Maoism in Action,* Brisbane, AU: University of Queensland Press, p. 12.
42. Mannheim, K. (1949) *Ideology and Utopia,* New York, Harcourt, Brace and Co., pp. 55–70.
43. Cohen, S. (1985) *Visions of Social Control,* Cambridge, UK: Polity Press.
44. See Clark, C., Dyson, A. and Millward, A. (1995) *Towards Inclusive Schools?,* London, David Fulton Publishing, chapter 12; and also (1998) *Theorising Special Education,* London, Routledge, chapter 13.
45. Moore, M., Beazley, S. and Maelzer, J. (1998) *Researching Disability Issues,* Buckingham, Open University Press, p. 12.
46. Oliver, M. (1992) Changing the Social Relations of Research Production?, *Disability, Handicap & Society,* Vol. 7, No. 2, pp. 101–114.
47. The purpose of the connection may be at the heart of our answer. In this respect it is worth referring to Julie Allan's study of pupils in a special school in Scotland. See Allan, J. (1999) *Actively Seeking Inclusion,* London, Falmer Press.
48. Booth, T. (1995) Mapping Inclusion and Exclusion: Concepts for All?, in Clark et al., op. cit. Peter MacLaren is quoted from bell hooks (1994) *Teaching to Transgress. Education as the Practice of Freedom,* New York, Routledge, p. 31.
49. Reynolds, H. (1999), *Why Weren't We Told?* Ringwood, UK: Penguin Books.

References

Abberley, P. (1987). The concept of oppression and the development of a social theory of disability, *Disability, Handicap & Society,* 2(1), 520.

Ainscow, M. (1999). *Understanding the development of inclusive schools.* London: Falmer Press.

Allan, J. (1999). *Actively seeking inclusion.* London: Falmer Press.

Ball, S. J. (1994). *Education reform: A critical and post-structural approach.* Buckingham, UK: Open University Press.

Ball, S. J. (1998). Educational studies, policy entrepreneurship and social theory. In R. Slee, G. Weiner, & S. Tomlinson (Eds.), *School effectiveness for whom? Challenges to the school effectiveness and school improvement movements.* London: Falmer Press.

Barton, L., & Tomlinson, S. (Eds.). (1981). *Special education—policy, practices and social issues.* London: Harper & Row.

Barton, L. (Ed.) (1987). *The politics of special educational needs.* Lewes, England: Falmer Press.

Barton, L., & Oliver, M. (Eds.) (1997). *Disability studies: Past, present and future.* Leeds, England: The Disability Press.

Bauman, Z. (1997). *Postmodernity and its discontents.* Oxford, UK: Basil Blackwell.

Booth, T. (1995). Mapping inclusion and exclusion: Concepts for all? In C. Clark et al. (Eds.), *Towards inclusive schools?* London: David Fulton.

Bourdieu, P. (1998). *Acts of resistance: Against the new myths of our time.* Cambridge, England: Polity Press.

Branson, J., & Miller, D. (1989). Beyond integration policy—the deconstruction of disability. In L. Barton (ed.), *Integration—Myth or Reality?* Lewes, UK: Falmer Press.

Brantlinger, E. (1997). Using ideology: Cases of non-recognition of the politics of research and practice in special education. *Review of Educational Research, 67*(4), 425–459.

Chiou, C. L. (1974). *Maoism in action*. Brisbane, Australia: University of Queensland Press.

Clark, C., Dyson, A., & Millwood, A. (Eds.) (1995). *Towards inclusive schools?* London: David Fulton.

Clark, C., Dyson, A., & Millwood, A. (Eds.) (1998). *Theorizing special education*. London: Routledge.

Clough, P., & Barton, L. (Eds.) (1995). *Making difficulties. Research and the contruction of SEN*. London: Paul Chapman.

Clough, P., & Barton, L. (Eds.) (1998). *Articulating with difficulty. Research voices in inclusive education*. London: Paul Chapman.

Cohen, S. (1985). *Visions of social control*. Cambridge, England: Polity Press.

Ford, J., Mongon, D., & Whelan, M. (1982). *Special education and social control—invisible disasters*. London: Routledge & Kegan Paul.

Foucault, M. (1974). *The archaeology of knowledge*. London, Travistock.

Foucault, M. (1979). *Discipline and punish; the birth of the prison*. Hammondsworth, UK: Penguin Books.

Focault, M. (1997). The will to knowledge. In P. Rabinow (Ed.), *Ethic: The essential works 1*. London: Allen Lane.

Franklin, B. (1994). *From "backwardness" to "at-risk": Childhood learning difficulties and the contradictions of school reform*. Albany: SUNY Press.

Gerwirtz, S., Ball, S. J. , & Bowe, R. (1995). *Markets, choice and equity in education*. Buckingham, UK: Open University Press.

Her Majesty's Inspectorate (1978). *Behaviour units*. London: Department of Education and Science.

hooks, b. (1994). *Teaching to transgress: Education as the practice of freedom*. New York: Routledge.

Lewis, J. (1993). Radical social policy or old wine?, In R. Slee (Ed.), *Is there a desk with my name on it? The politics of integration*, London: Falmer Press.

Lingard, B. (1998). The disadvantaged schools programme: Caught between literacy and local management of schools. *International Journal of Inclusive Education, 2*(1), 114.

Mannheim, K. (1949). *Ideology and utopia*. New York: Harcourt, Brace & Co.

McGough, R. (1989). *Blazing fruit*. London: Penguin.

Moore, M., Beazley, S., & Maelzer, J. (1998). *Researching disability issues*. Buckingham, UK: Open University Press.

Oliver, M. (1990). *The politics of disablement*. London: Macmillan.

Oliver, M. (1992). Changing the social relations of research production?, *Disability, handicap & society, 7*(2), 101–114.

Parsons, C., & Castle, F. (1998). The cost of school exclusion in England. *International journal of inclusive education, 2*(4), 277–294.

Reynolds, H. (1999).*Why weren't we told?* Ringwood, Hampshire, UK: Penguin Books.

Rose, N. (1989). *Governing the soul*. London: Routledge.

Shapiro, J. P. (1993). *No pity. People with disabilities forging a new civil rights movement*. New York: Random House.

Sigmon, S. B. (1987). *Radical analysis of special education*. Lewes, UK: Falmer Press.

Skidmore, D. (1996). Towards an integrated theoretical framework for research into special educational needs. *European Journal of Special Needs Education, 11*(1), 33–47.

Skrtic, T. (1991). *Behind special education: A critical analysis of professional culture and school organization.* Denver, CO: Love Publishing.

Slee, R. (1993). The politics of integration—new sites for old practice? *Disability, Handicap & Society, 8*(4), 351–360.

Slee, R. (1966). Clauses of conditionality: The "reasonable" accommodation of language. In L. Barton (Ed.), *Disability and society: Emerging issues and insights.* London: Longman.

Thompson, J. B. (1984). *Studies in the theory of ideology.* Berkeley: University of California Press.

Tomlinson, S. (1981). *Educational Sub-normality—a study in decision-making,* London: Routledge & Kegan Paul.

Tomlinson, S. (1982). *A sociology of special education.* London: Routledge & Kegan Paul.

Usher, R. (1998). Seductive texts: Competence, power and knowledge in post-modernity. In R. Barnett & A. Griffin (Eds.), *The end of knowledge in higher education.* London: Cassell.

II

HISTORIC INFLUENCES: DISABILITY AND "SPECIAL" SCHOOLING

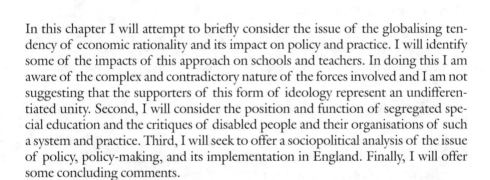

4   *Len Barton*

THE POLITICS OF SPECIAL EDUCATION: A NECESSARY OR IRRELEVANT APPROACH?

In this chapter I will attempt to briefly consider the issue of the globalising tendency of economic rationality and its impact on policy and practice. I will identify some of the impacts of this approach on schools and teachers. In doing this I am aware of the complex and contradictory nature of the forces involved and I am not suggesting that the supporters of this form of ideology represent an undifferentiated unity. Second, I will consider the position and function of segregated special education and the critiques of disabled people and their organisations of such a system and practice. Third, I will seek to offer a sociopolitical analysis of the issue of policy, policy-making, and its implementation in England. Finally, I will offer some concluding comments.

Globalisation and Commonality of Educational Policy and Practice

Within industrialised countries in particular, the centrality of economic rationality with regard to decision-making in education, at both a central and local level, has had an increasing influence on policy and practice. This has ushered in a series of significant changes in the values, priorities, and outcomes of education. Part of this pressure for change is due to the influence of globalisation and the interdependency of nations generating new economic conditions that challenge existing systems (Bauman, 1998).

In a paper examining the changing nature of educational policy across some industrialised countries Levin (1998) identifies several emerging commonality of themes:

> The need for change in education is largely cast in economic terms and particularly in relation to the preparation of a workforce and competition with other countries.
>
> Educational change is occurring in the context of large-scale criticism of schools.
>
> Large-scale change is not accompanied by substantially increased financial commitment to schools by governments.
>
> Changes in governance are typically among the key proposals for educational reform.
>
> In line with the economic rationale for educational reform, considerable attention has been given to making schooling more like a commercial or market commodity.
>
> An emphasis on standards, accountability and testing has been a feature of reforms in many countries. (pp. 131–133)

Reinforcing this perspective with regard to many Western societies in particular, there has been the increasing development of what Apple (1993) calls the conservative project, which has resulted in education becoming more deeply politicised. Thus, as Apple (1993) contends:

> The means and ends involved in educational policy and practice are the results of struggles by powerful groups and social movements to make their knowledge legitimate, to defend or increase their patterns of social mobility, and to increase their power in the larger social arena. (p. 10)

These struggles, as Apple argues, involve compromises and alliances at different levels, including ideological discourse, state policies, school knowledge; and interactions between teachers and pupils and at the level of understanding and making sense of such activities and experiences. Such relationships and struggles over, for example, defining what is a priority, a need, and how it is to be met, is not an encounter between or among equals. Nor is it a stable and uncontested activity. It is, at different times and within specific contexts, fragile, and entails the development of contradictory outcomes and spaces in which varying degrees of possible transformatory activities can take place.

Within this period of conservative restoration the impact of market ideologies has profoundly influenced how we think and talk about education. We view education through the lens of a form of economic rationality in which cost effectiveness, efficiency, and value for money has entailed the generation of a more competitive, selective, and socially divisive series of policies and practices. By encouraging notions of performativity and predefined outcomes, the whole question of the governance, funding, and purpose of education has been powerfully redefined. This includes a greater control over the work context and culture of teaching and major changes to the purpose, content, and outcome of teacher training.

In an analysis of these developments and their impact on teachers and teaching, Smyth and Shacklock (1998) perceptively illustrate the ways in which governments have strengthened their regulatory functions via directives, guidelines, and frameworks, legitimated by significant changes to legislation, while simultaneously seeking to appear fair and just through encouraging self-management, flexibility, and autonomy. All of this is undertaken through "maintaining external steering and setting directions at a distance" (p. 24). This, they continue, has had the following implications for schools:

> giving schools and teachers responsibility to implement local decisions—but within firmly prescribed guidelines;

> allowing schools discretion over expenditures—but in an overall context in which real resources are shrinking, and where centrally provided services are being wound down through the dismantling of educational bureaucracies;

> fostering the notion that it is fair (and indeed "good") for schools to compete against one another—that the efficient will survive, and that competition will cause the rest to lift their game or go out of business—regardless of whether they are all operating on a level playing field or not;

> devolving responsibility for achieving learning outcomes—but within a context of accountability, where resources are tied to demonstrating the achievement of guaranteed targets;

> redefining, at a policy level, who are the "consumers" of education so that there is much closer connection between education and industry. Industry is now the customer, and in the logic of the marketplace, the customer is always right, and we have to keep the customer happy. (pp. 24–25)

In presenting these claims in this way we run the risk of being criticised, as Hargreaves and Moore (2000) clearly illustrate, for providing examples of a totalising and uncritical application of state control to the specific phenomenon of educational outcomes. This, they maintain, also underplays, at least in some places, the progressive potential of an outcomes approach. Thus, the legitimacy, insightfulness, and applicability of such claims to specific cultural and social contexts needs to be carefully examined and demonstrated.

Within a climate of limited budgets, insufficient human resources, and increasing demands for higher standards and excellence, the work context and the culture of teaching is changing. Teachers are experiencing greater stress, loss of autonomy and control, intensification of work, and greater accountability. Within England and Wales during the past two decades teachers have become the scapegoats for factors over which they have little control. They have become the target of a sustained and systematic attack by the tabloid press, politicians, industrialists, and parents. The criticisms to which they have been subject include:

1. Failing to reach acceptable levels of numeracy and literacy with increasing numbers of pupils.
2. Being too politically motivated, supporting child-centred and progressive ideas within their teaching. Many teachers represent the loony left in education.
3. Failing to achieve and maintain acceptable levels of educational standards and thereby reducing the competitive performance of the country in the international marketplace.
4. Failing to attain and sustain acceptable levels of discipline within schools. This relates to both beliefs and behaviour.
5. Undertaking various forms of industrial action and thereby sacrificing pupil well-being for personal, selfish interests.
6. Failing to produce in pupils the sort of flexible, co-operative disposition that entrants into the modern work setting will require.

A significant feature of this period has been the number, speed, and cumulative impact of policies with which teachers and schools have had to deal. It is also important to recognise the ways in which "failure" has become a powerful conceptual tool within a more general discourse that applies to individuals and schools. Now, it is important to recognise that teachers are not homogeneous and schools are varied in ethos and quality. Thus, these changes and critiques have had a differential impact on teachers. The social/academic status of the school, the gendered nature of teaching, will have compounded or cushioned the degree of pressure that teachers and schools will have experienced. Nevertheless, some factors do seem to me to cut across the system as a whole: first, that there has been little participation of teachers in the development of these changing policies; and second, that teachers have increasingly become implementors of decisions made by external bodies. This includes decisions over the nature of the curriculum, assessment practices, and the funding of schools.

The Question of Hope

In a most lucid and powerful style Blackwell and Seabrook (1988) provide some very fundamental criticisms and insights concerning the decline of hope in British politics. One aspect of their analysis focuses on the topic of "helplessness." They persuasively argue that the

> [s]ense of aloneness is the cause of our helplessness. For so many are experiencing the same thing. It is a negative solidarity, a shared denial of the collective. In our isolation we are all the same. Up and down the country the same responses are heard, whatever evil confronts us. What can we do about it? If people are forced to seek a living rummaging through mounds of rubbish, if children are walking the streets of cities for the purpose of prostitution, if people are frightened to give up their jobs in sweat-shops redolent of Victorian England, if parts of London at night have the aspect of a vast funeral, with hundreds of people sleeping in rows of cardboard coffins,

few people will be found ready to declare that these things are evidence of a good or just society. (pp. 39–40)

They continue:

But what can we do about it? This is perhaps the most widely heard interrogative of despair in Britain today. (p. 40)

They maintain that this position of "impotence" in the light of such appalling and offensive conditions and relations comes from the depth and extent of our own unfreedoms, including, "the degree to which we are in thrall to the system, which lives through us, and in which we live" (p. 40).

While we may wish to raise important issues about their underestimation of market ideologies that have resulted in the very idea of "society" being rejected and which would encourage a view of individual failings with regard to their specific illustrations, nevertheless their analysis does have some serious implications. First, over a decade later we have even less experience within higher education of the vitality and empowerment of collective identity and solidarity. We work within and legitimate both in our positions and practices, institutional structures, and relations that reify and celebrate individual status and achievements. Second, we have been seduced by and actively perpetuate those deeply competitive values, rewards, and vested interests that are intensely socially divisive, exclusive in their outcomes, and mitigate against inclusive interests. Too often within our own institutions we are legitimators of and role models for a system we claim needs to be transformed. Third, the importance of anger, rage, and deeply felt commitment against the offensive, damaging aspects of an unjust system and our daily complicity have become sanitised, inhibited, and displaced into other less important and depoliticised endeavours. What is particularly upsetting, however, is that where some of these dispositions are even weakly evident, they are criticised (either directly or by inference and innuendo) by so called allies as a means of trivialising thinking and writing by encouraging polemic rather than analysis; as an indicator of dogmatism that restricts debate; as a reflection of complacency with regard to self-criticism, particularly over one's own values and ideas; finally, with the view that they will, if not controlled, lead to the ossification of ideas (Clark, Dyson, & Millward, 1998; Dyson, 1999). Finally, there is now an urgency about understanding the necessity of political analysis, which is inspired by a desire for emancipatory change and which reconstitutes hope at the centre of our struggles for inclusivity.

It is an informed historical view of hope that is needed, for as Apple (1996) contends, we "need to recapture our past to see what is possible" (p. 177). Hope is essential in the struggle for change in that:

1. It arises from within the contexts of inequalities and discriminatory social conditions and relations.
2. It is based on the strong conviction that current conditions are not natural, proper, or eternal, and that they can be changed.

3. It emphasises the importance of understanding the world in order to change it.
4. It acknowledges the significance of a vision as a means of motivation and inspiration.

However, we need to be aware of particular dangers. As Simon (1987) reminds us, we should not

> romanticise all dreams about the future. Not all fantasy is benign. The basis of what many people view as a "better tomorrow" sometimes includes the unjust and oppressive disparagement or control over others. Not all dreams are dreams of hope. (p. 382)

Disabling Barriers: The Case of Special Segregated Provision

A sociopolitical analysis of education raises questions about the complex and sensitive issue of the position and function of specific exclusionary factors. Special segregated provision is deeply entrenched within the system of schooling. This form of provision and practice has historically been justified by a series of ideological assumptions, including:

1. Such schooling is essential in order to provide the *type* of education and curriculum these children need.
2. Disabled children and young people need *protection* from the harsh and cruel realities of the world, including those to be found in mainstream schools — their size, the attitudes of staff and pupils, and verbal and physical abuse.
3. Normal pupils need to be protected *from the damaging influences* that disabled pupils will have on their development, especially their academic achievements.
4. Special schools are staffed by teachers *who have those special qualities* of patience, dedication, and love. Such schools provide good interpersonal relationships with staff and the small and necessary staff-pupil ratios.
5. Special schools are necessary on *administrative efficiency grounds*. Thus, specialist teachers, equipment, and support services are most effectively deployed.

With the increasing impact of industrialisation and the introduction of compulsory education, as well as the intensified emphasis on competition and selection, such schools began to serve a more ominous function — namely, that of enabling the smooth running of mainstream schooling. In other words, the difficult, objectionable, unwanted pupils were increasingly placed in segregated provision. Such developments have been depicted as being in the best interests of the child, peers, and society generally. Special education, from this perspective, entails a discourse and practice of exclusion. It is socially restrictive. Set within the wider context of institutional settings, social conditions, and relations, special education can be viewed as an important means of social control. The International Movement of Disabled People and the British Council of Disabled People are critical of special schools. Increasing numbers of disabled people, including those who are reflecting back on their experience of being pupils in such schools, are advocating the closure of such institutions in favour of an inclusive approach to education. Their criticisms of special schooling include:

1. Special schools are part of the disabling barriers within society and therefore need to be removed. This is a human rights issue (Oliver 1996).
2. Segregated provision tends to encourage negative labels, suspicion, stereotypes, fear, and ignorance of a reciprocal nature (Barnes, 1991; Rieser & Mason, 1990).
3. Pupils within such schools receive an education that is inferior to their nondisabled peers and the low expectations of teachers is a significant factor in this outcome. The rhetoric of "caring" and "supporting" often obscures this fact (Yates, 1994).
4. Such provision legitimates the notion of "professional" as "expert" and encourages passive dependency on the part of pupils (French, 1994).

While the rhetoric may be couched in facilitative and enabling forms, it is essential as Booth (1996) so shrewdly notes, that we recognise "compulsory segregation is never benign; it is always associated with devaluation" (p. 30). From a sociopolitical perspective, as long as there is a form of language that depicts some individuals as not "normal" and "special," separate segregated schooling will continue (Ballard, 1996; Booth, 1996). Thus, from this particular political analysis, "special educational needs" is to be understood fundamentally as a euphemism for *failure*.

In a comparative analysis of education policy and disability, Fulcher (1999) maintains "that disability is primarily a political construct rather than a medical phenomenon" (Fulcher, 25). Thus, what is of interest is the use to which the construct is put, by whom, in what context, for what purposes and with what consequences. For example, how far is it "used to exclude rather than include, and to oppress rather than enable" (Fulcher, p. 24). It is important from this perspective to distinguish impairment from disability, to recognise the position of categories in social relations, and to examine why particular categories are used in specific contexts. Fulcher, in contrast to the medical model, views disability as "a category which is central to how welfare states *regulate* an increasing proportion of their citizens" (p. 21).

What is significant from this perspective is that disability is not about something people cannot do, but instead is a *procedural category*. As Fulcher notes: "The social construction of disability is *relative* to particular social practices," and within education in particular, "independent of the presence of impairment" (Fulcher, 1999, p. 23). The position and power of professionals and the use of a range of nonnormative categories such as special educational needs are of fundamental importance in understanding "the practices which construct students' identities as disabled" (p. 35). Various discourses have been used to justify and maintain particular forms of policy initiatives and practice. Barton and Tomlinson (1981, 1984) have argued that in special education a discourse containing the themes of benevolence and humanitarianism have been used. This celebrates professionals as experts who know best and work in the interests of the child, and excludes the issue of rights and the perceptions of those labelled "disabled." The medical model depoliticizes, individualises, and professionalizes disability, viewing it as a technical issue, a personal trouble that requires professional judgment (Fulcher 1999). Disability is thus "an observable or intrinsic, objective *attribute* or characteristic of a person, rather than a social construct" (p. 26). In contrast, a perspective that emphasises the political nature of the category needs to, as Shapiro (1981) contends, examine "the ways that disability is constituted in utterances" (p. 87). This is a complex and demanding task in that, with regard to its use as a form of regulation, there are competing claims about it and its effects. Nor should we underestimate the formidable resistance that will be met by those who attempt to challenge medical dominance and professional discourses (Fulcher, 1999).

Politics, Policy, and Policy Making

Policy-making can be viewed as a struggle between different interest groups over meaning, participation, and practice. Individual biography, past experience, and learning will influence the ways in which policies are viewed and how they are engaged with. In the construction of policies the issue of choices is significant (Silver, 1990). Policies are never value-free or neutral and, more significantly, they are informed by wider concerns and questions than one might otherwise imagine. Policy must not be understood in a vacuum or compartmentalised manner: it entails a challenging process of understanding in terms of who is involved, who makes decisions, and whose values will be legitimated in both content and implementation.

To label something as a policy is to mark it out as having particular significance. A policy frames the way we think and act. It limits what we see (Colebatch, 1998). The importance of policy-making becomes apparent when it is viewed as a process of problem-solving and thus linked to issues of change. This includes engaging with the external and internal dynamics and the institutionalisation of change. Policy can be a means of excluding particular concerns from the arena of public debate as well as resisting specific claims made by particular interest groups. Thus, as Taylor et al. also maintain, policy is much more than a text or document; rather

> it is both process and product. In such a conceptualisation, policy involves the production of the text, the text itself, organising modifications to the text and the process of implementation into practice. (1997, p. 25)

Policies from this perspective need to be viewed as dynamic and interactive and always involve compromises between conflicting interests. To focus merely on the text is to fail to recognise the significance of factors within the context of policy creation that give the document meaning and influence (p. 15). These can include, the general economic climate, the position and status of teachers in public opinion and the nature of management.

In a detailed exploration of educational policy since 1945 in Scotland, McPherson and Raab have provided a wealth of insights into policy-making. They clearly demonstrate the contentious nature of educational ideas, policy, and practice. This includes the myth of ideological unity on the part of policy-makers; the disagreements over how a system *is* or *should* be governed, and the highly selective and evaluative nature of policies and their legitimation. Thus, for them, "policy-making is an aspect of power, and the control of awareness is a means of power" (1988, p. 5). They maintain that "power has as much to do with things that do not happen, as with things that do" (xiv). Thus, the nature and impact of particular policies can contribute to an ethos in which the development of alternative ideas and practice becomes much more difficult.

For some analysts policy is viewed as an authentic endorsement of specific objectives. This perspective, as Colebatch maintains:

> assumes that organisations exist to pursue goals, these goals are clear, and the best way to pursue them is a technical matter which can be left to experts. (1998, p. 83)

This supports a view of policy as that which governments decide to do. Now, while the significance of governments in terms of national policies cannot be denied, it is important to note, as Colebatch illustrates, that governments do not make policy in times and circumstances entirely of their own choosing, that official policy discourse is often experienced in a different way by participants in particular contexts and that contradictions are evident both within and across policies providing space for opposition and loss of control. In a top-down or hierarchical model of policy and policy-making, various groups and organizations are excluded or marginalised from the policy processes. It is important, therefore, that we recognise the contestable nature of policy and policy-making as Taylor et al. so forcefully remind us:

> Contestation is involved right from the moment of the appearance of an issue on the policy agenda. It is played out in regard to whose voices are heard, whose values are recognised in the policy, which groups ultimately benefit as a result of the policy. (1997, p. 28)

Policy-making always involves alliances, tactics, and negotiations. This is a complex, messy process raising concerns over the extent of agency that is involved, for example, in terms of the readers of policy and their ability to interpret the text in a variety of ways. This stands in contrast to those who emphasise the significance of power relations in shaping the possible ways in which texts can be read. Nor are these positions necessarily mutually exclusive (Taylor et al., 1997).

Fulcher (1999), an Australian academic interested in the issue of comparative policies and disability, questions the traditional top-down model of policy in which the role of government is given significant prominence. This scepticism included a critique of the distinction between policy and practice and theory and practice. By introducing the notion of arenas, Fulcher maintains that in these different forums struggles take place between contenders of competing objectives. Language is seen as crucial in this process. It is viewed by Fulcher as the instrument of power and thus how it is used tactically matters in the struggle for control of the power to define. Policy is seen as being produced in all these different arenas. The content may differ, the degree of conflict may vary, but the process of struggle over discourse, alliances, and tactics is the very substance of all these arenas. Thus, policy—in terms of the capacity to make decisions and act on them—is made at all levels. This perspective emphasizes the political nature of policy making and the struggle between groups over competing objectives. In seeking to advance analytical insights beyond mere claims to a gap between rhetoric and practice, Fulcher draws on the distinctions made by MacDonald (1981), who distinguishes between *written* policy (e.g., reports and laws), *stated* policy (what we say we do), and *enacted* policy (e.g., what we do in classrooms).

Policy-making is about establishing a set of claims about how the social world in terms of relations and interactions should or might be. We need to beware of an overly rational, linear model of policy-making. It is a messy process, and as Bowe et al. note, "it is important to acknowledge that policy intentions may contain ambiguities, contradictions and omissions (1992, p. 13). This messy, complex, and contradictory nature of policy-making can be seen in a recent Government Green Paper (Department for Education and Employment, 1997) entitled *Excellence for All Children: Meeting Special Educational Needs,* in which the newly appointed Labour government outlined their vision for these children. This consultation document has now resulted in the publication of a further document entitled *Meeting Special Educational Needs: A Programme For Action* (Department for Education and Employment, 1998). Two features of these documents are worth noting. First, in the Green Paper we have the unprecedented introduction within the foreword by the secretary of state for education and employment, of a commitment to a "comprehensive and enforceable civil rights for disabled people" (p. 4). This provides the context against which the document needs to be understood. Second, the documents are replete with references to inclusion in terms of both policy and practice.

However, several points of concern need to be raised in relation to these policy initiatives. First, the notion of "civil rights" is ambiguous and the tenor and overall thrust of the document does little to confirm the importance of disability as a human rights issue. Indeed, in the summary document that is circulated to all interested parties, the statement on civil rights in the secretary of state for education and employment's foreword has been removed. In the foreword to *Meeting Special Educational Needs: A Programme of Action,* there is no reference to civil rights, which is an influence of the Treasury. Second, the documents need to be read and understood in *relation* to other policy initiatives and documents that are *simultaneously* being promoted for purposes of policy coherence. Thus, for example, the White Paper (Department for Education and Employment, 1998) on Excellence in Schools celebrates those values and priorities that mitigate against the realisation of an inclusive system of provision and practice. Contradictions and tensions are thus evident both *within* particular policy statements and documents and *between* them. It is essential that we think about these policy developments *relationally*, which includes recognising which are more important than others and why. Finally, within these documents, the notion of "inclusion" involves a particular understanding of diversity and has been linked to other official concerns of standards and excellence. This provides ways in which open and covert selection can be legitimatised and extended. Thus, special schools can now be viewed as "centres of excellence" and justified within a discourse of inclusion. As the summary of the Programme for Action maintains: "We confirm that specialist provision—including special schools—will continue to play a vital role" (Department for Education and Employment, 1998 p. 6).

It is also crucial that we look beyond education to other developments that evidence the contradictory position of government with regard to disabled people. For example, recently Margaret Hodge, the minister responsible for disability concerns in the new Labour government, launched a new national campaign entitled "Hearts and Minds," which is intended to change public opinion. The slogan being used is "See the person *not* the disability." This represents one of the most *ominous* and *offensive* initiatives about which disabled people and their allies cannot afford to be complacent. It is about how disability is to be defined and whose voices are to be privileged and excluded. In the British Council of Disabled People's (BCDP) publication "Update," the editorial states the following with regard to this initiative:

> It is hard to believe that after nearly 30 years of campaigning on the Social Model, any Government, yet alone one that says, it is committed to our full rights and inclusion, could have launched a campaign which is so patronising to disabled people. (1999b, p. 1)

Or again in an earlier issue Bob Findlay, the acting chair of the organisation, charges, "[W]here have we heard this patronising, disablist bullshit before" (1999a, p. 1). This outrage prompted a national campaign in opposition to this disablist innovation.

Conclusion

I have attempted to briefly outline here some of the issues that continue to concern me, and while recognising the complex, messy, and contradictory nature of these factors, it is essential that we recognise and vehemently oppose all those deeply rooted, stubborn forms of discrimination, both subtle and overt, that are unacceptable barriers in the struggle for inclusivity. In this struggle, I do most passionately believe that a political analysis is now even more important and requires our most serious attention. Far from being irrelevant, it is an essential precondition for change.

References

Apple, M. (1993). *Official knowledge: Democratic education in a conservative age*. London: Routledge.

Apple, M. (1996). *Culture, politics and education*. Buckingham, UK: Open University Press.

Atkinson, R., & Savage, S. (1994). The Conservatives and public policy. In S. Savage, R. Atkinson, & L. Robins (Eds.), *Public policy in Britain*. Basingstoke, UK: Macmillan Press.

Ball, S. J. (1994). *Education reform: A critical and post-structural approach*. Buckingham, UK: Open University Press.

Ballard, K. (1996). "Inclusion, paradigms, power and participation." In E. Blyth & J. Milner (Eds.), *Exclusion from school: Inter-professional issues for policy and practice*. London: Routledge.

Barnes, C. (1991). *Disabled people in Britain and discrimination: A case for anti-discrimination legislations*. London: Hurst & Company.

Barton, L., & Tomlinson, S. (Eds.) (1981). *Special education: Policies, practices and social issues*. London: Harper & Row.

Barton, L., & Tomlinson, S. (Eds.) (1984). *Special education and social interests*. Beckenham, UK: Croom Helm.

Bauman, Z. (1998). *Globalization: The human consequences*. Oxford, UK: Polity Press.

Blackwell, T., & Seabrook, J. (1988). *The politics of hope: Britain at the end of the twentieth century*. London: Faber & Faber.

Booth, T. (1996). Stories of exclusion: Natural and unatural selection. In E. Blyth & J. Milner (Eds.), *Exclusion from school: Inter-professional issues for policy and practice*. London: Routledge.

Bowe, R., Ball, S., & Gold, A. (1992) *Reforming education and changing schools*. London: Routledge.

British Council of Disabled People (BCDP). (1999a, April). *Update*. Issue 33. Derby, UK: Author.

British Council of Disabled People (BCDP). (1999b, May). *Update*. Issue 34. Derby, UK: Author.

Clark, C., Dyson, A., & Millward, A. (1998) *Theorising special education* (Chapters 1 and 13). London: Routledge.

Colebatch, H. (1998) *Policy*. Buckingham, UK: Open University Press.

Department for Education and Employment (1997). *Excellence for all children: Meeting special educational needs*. London: DfEE.

Department for Education and Employment (1998). *Meeting special educational needs: A programme for action*. London: DfEE.

Department for Education and Employment (1998). *Excellence in schools*. London: DfEE.

Dyson, A. (1999). Inclusion and Inclusions: Theories and discourses in inclusive education. In H. Daniels & P. Garner (Eds.), *Inclusive education: World yearbook of education*. London: Kogan Page Ltd.

French, S. (1994). *Out of sight, out of mind: The experience and effects of a "special" residential school*. Unpublished paper.

Fulcher, G. (1999). *Disabling policies? A comparative approach to education policy*. Sheffield, UK: Philip Armstrong Publications.

Gamble, A. (1994). *The free economy and the strong state* (2nd ed.). Basingstoke, UK: Macmillan.

Gore, J. (1992). What we can do for you! What can "we" do for "you"? Struggling over empowerment in critical and feminist pedagogy. In C. Luke & J. Gore (Eds.), *Feminisms and critical pedagogy*. New York: Routledge.

Hall, S. (1980). Popular democratic versus authoritarian populism. In A. Hunt (Ed.), *Marxism and democracy*. London: Lawrence & Wishart.

Hargreaves, G., & Moore, S. (2000). Educational outcomes, modern and postmodern interpretations: Response to Smyth & Dow. *British Journal of Sociology of Education, 21* (1), 27–42.

Levin, B. (1998). An epidemic of education policy: (What) can we learn from each other? (Special Issue). *Comparative Education, 34*(2), 131–142.

MacDonald, I. (1981). Assessment: A social dimension. In L. Barton & S. Tomlinson (Eds.), *Special education: Policy, practices and social issues* (pp. 87–122). London: Harper & Row.

McClaren, P. (1995). *Critical pedagogy and predatory culture: Oppositional politics in a postmodern era*. London: Routledge.

McPherson, A., & Raab, C. (1988). *Governing education: A sociology of policy since 1945*. Edinburgh: Edinburgh University Press.

Morris, J. (1990). Progress with humanity: The experience of a disabled lecturer. In R. Rieser, & M. Mason (Eds.), *Disability equality in the classroom: A human rights issue*. London: ILEA.

Oliver, M. (1996). A sociology of disability or a disablist sociology. In L. Barton (Ed.), *Disability and society: Emerging issues and insights*. Harlow, UK: Addison Wesley Longman Ltd.

Rieser, R., & Mason, M. (Eds.) (1990). *Disability equality in the classrooms: A human rights issue*. London: ILEA.

Shapiro, M. J. (1981). Disability and the politics of constitutive rules. In G. L. Albrecht (Ed.), *Cross national rehabilitation policies*. Beverly Hills, CA: Sage Publications.

Silver, H. (1990). *Education, change and the policy process*. London: Falmer Press.

Simon, R. (1987). Empowerment as a pedagogy of possibility. *Language Arts, 64*(4), 370–383.

Smyth, J., & Shacklock, G. (1998). *Re-making teaching, ideology, policy and practice*. London: Routledge.

Taylor, I. (1990). Introduction: The concept of "social cost" in free market theory and the social effects of free market policies. In I. Taylor (Ed.), *The social effects of free market policies: An international text*. London: Harvester Wheatsheaf.

Taylor, S., Rizvi, F., Lingard, B., & Henny M. (1997). *Educational policy and the politics of change*. London: Routledge.

Yates, M. (1994). The Special School Survivor. *New Learning Together, 1*, 42–43.

5

Sally Tomlinson

RACE AND SPECIAL EDUCATION

In all countries that have developed special education subsystems to their mainstream education and also have racial, ethnic, or immigrant minorities,[1] these minorities have always been overrepresented in the special sector. On occasion, special education has been the only form of education offered to a substantial number of minority and migrant children. This has usually become a matter of great concern to minority parents and communities, often to the point of litigation. Those in charge of education have accepted or promulgated the situation as natural or inevitable, explained by unfortunate minority deficiencies or inabilities complicated by difficulties of assessment. Thus, in the United States Terman could suggest in 1916 that black, Spanish, Indian, and Mexican children exhibited "racial dullness" and inherited low intelligence (Terman 1916), which required special education. In 1923 Brigham produced, in his *Study of American Intelligence* (1923), a "race hypothesis" to explain his findings that Nordic immigrants to the United States had "genuine intellectual superiority" and in 1994 Hernstein and Murray could present elaborate evidence to demonstrate racial and ethnic difference in cognitive ability (1994). In the United Kingdom Eysenck suggested in 1971 that black Americans and Irish people are genetically intellectually inferior due to "crimes committed against their ancestors" (Eysenck 1971, p. 142), and in 1992 Lynn, himself a professor in Northern Ireland, offered a theory for the evolution of racial differences in intelligence (Lynn 1992). Lynn also theorised that as black Africans in Africa scored lower on Western IQ tests, black minority groups in other countries could not claim that racial disadvantage caused their educational problems.

Racial and ethnic minority and migrant groups in the United Kingdom, United States, and most European countries have always been concentrated at the lower-achieving end of mainstream education, and have been overrepresented in special education. A study of seven European countries carried out in 1987 noted that 6% of immigrant children were in special education, as opposed to 2.8% of "nationals" (Organisation for Economic Cooperation and Development [OECD] 1987), and a report for the European Community in 1992 concluded that:

> In all European Community member states, almost always ethnic minority groups do least well in education. They leave schools earlier, drop out altogether, obtain lower examination qualifications, and are overrepresented in special education. (Teunisson 1992)

In the United States the referral, testing, and overplacement of black, minority, and migrant children in special education provoked some bitter legislative battles (Sigmon 1990). In the United Kingdom children from colonial or former colonial countries had scarcely had time to settle in education before being labelled as potential low achievers and disproportionately relegated to special education (Coard 1970; Tomlinson 1981). In 1996 a review of the educational achievement of minority young people indicated yet again that black children have not shared in increasing rates of achievement (Gillborn & Gipps 1996) and that a disproportionate number of black students are excluded from school, relegated to pupil referral units, or placed in schools for the emotionally and behaviourally disturbed.

This chapter briefly reviews the situation in the United Kingdom beginning with the 1960s, during which period black children of African-Caribbean origin have been overplaced in stigmatised[2] forms of statutory and nonstatutory forms of special education such as schools for the "educationally subnormal" (ESN-M) and for the maladjusted. Until these categories were discontinued and relabelled in 1981 as "schools for the emotionally and behaviourally disturbed" (EDB), behavioural and pupil referral units (PRUs) and straight exclusion from school were and continue to be ways in which African-Caribbean children have been removed from mainstream education. The chapter raises the question as to why children perceived as racially different should continue to be regarded as candidates for removal from mainstream education. It suggests that one answer may lie in the 19th-century post-Darwinian racial thinking, which was structured around assumptions of biological inferiority and cultural deficiency of "other races," particularly those from slave ancestry or those who were living in colonised countries. By the end of the 19th century these assumptions were also applied to same-race (lower-class) white "degenerates" within the country. This thinking was bolstered by the development of mental testing in the early 20th century, creators and standardizers of mental tests such as Terman in the United States and Burt in the United Kingdom being particularly influential via their negative views of other races and lower classes (Burt 1937; Terman 1916). It is important to discuss the persistence of the assumptions and views behind the perpetuation of placements in the stigmatised forms of special education of racial and migrant minorities, since their situation, at the beginning of the 21st century, does not appear to be changing significantly.

The 1960s and 1970s: ESN and Maladjusted

The arrival of children from the Caribbean and the Asian subcontinent into the British school system in the 1950s and 1960s coincided with the expansion and consolidation of special education as an important postwar subsystem of education. In 1945 ten statutory categories of handicap were created. The largest group of children up to 1939 — educable defective — were to be merged with remedial and "dull" (slow-minded) children to become educationally subnormal. A new category of maladjusted was created for children who displayed behavioural and emotional problems with which mainstream teachers could not cope. ESN schooling (called "ESN-M" from 1970 onwards) expanded dramatically taking in children regarded as both learning and behavioural problems. The large number of immigrant — particularly black — children admitted to special schools was first noted by the Inner London Education Authority (ILEA) in the mid-1960s. In 1967 an ILEA survey of 22 ESN schools reported that "misplacement" was four times more likely in the case of immigrant children, and the schools noted that the children were largely admitted for behavioural reasons rather than low IQ. In 1970 Bernard Coard published a short book entitled *How the West Indian Child Is Made Educationally Sub-Normal in the British School System* (Coard 1970), and pointed out that the figures from ILEA in 1968 showed that while 17% of children in London schools were classed as immigrant, 34% of those in ESN schools were immigrants, of whom 75% were of West Indian origin. He suggested that teachers' cultural beliefs and low expectations of black children together with a white middle-class curriculum lay behind referrals. In the same year the North London West Indian Parents Association lodged a complaint against overplacement of black children in ESN schools in Haringey with the Race Relations Board, which resulted eventually in Department of Education guidance to Local Education Authorities (Department for Education and Science 1973). By 1972 children of West Indian origin constituted 1.1% of children in all maintained schools, but 4.9% of all children in ESN-M schools. An article by Dhondy in 1974 suggested that the ESN issue had become symbolic of the failure of the whole school system to incorporate and educate black children satisfactorily (Dhondy 1974).

But central and local government, schools, and teachers did not appear to regard the situation as particularly problematic, although the secretary of state for education — showing their findings to a House of Commons Select Committee in 1973, conceded that, "We probably have not yet got the right methods of assessing their abilities, bearing in mind the background from which they come" (Select Committee 1973, vol. 3, p. 647). Earlier, Thatcher had asserted that this background included badly structured family life. The Department for Education and Science, showing their findings to the same committee, noted that in London schools at that time, 20.5% of children in ESN schools were of West Indian origin and complained that there had been "no systematic appraisal of the reasons for this" but went on to blame language and dialect difficulties. A further report by a Select Committee in 1976 noted that black parents and teachers found the overplacement of black children in ESN schools to be "a very bitter area—the West Indian community is disturbed by the underachievement of its children at school and seriously disturbed by the high proportion in ESN schools" (Select Committee 1976, vol. 1).

During the mid-1970s I carried out a study following a group of children referred into ESN-M schooling. One aim of the study was to understand the views and beliefs of head teachers and other professionals as to why black children were overreferred to and placed in ESN schools. It was noticeable that black children were placed more speedily in special schools than were white children—11 months compared with 2 years at that time. The criteria used by head teachers to refer children corresponded closely to their perception of the "problems" of black children that they were likely to be educationally slow, behaviourally troublesome, and from disorganised families and disadvantaged socioeconomic backgrounds. Several head teachers felt the children had "natural" educational handicaps—"they are bound to be slower, it's their personalities . . . they are a representative bunch—slow, docile, low-functioning" while at the same time "they had the usual problems, hyperactivity and anti-authority" Tomlinson 1981, p. 160). One doctor interviewed in the study believed that "they have ebullient natures, they can go berserk in school." The professionals also took account of appearance in the 1970s. One child was described as "looking like a minstrel." Another as a "tragedy because she is ugly" and black families were generally regarded as deviating from the idealised family norm. I concluded that the characteristics of black children and their families were judged against white majority cultural norms, and the children and their families were judged to be deficient (Tomlinson 1981, p. 301). I also concluded "if race was taken into consideration, and the referral process took account of the position of the black child in a hostile, white society and the belief systems of the professionals, black children might start out equal in the assessment process" (p. 301).

A study into the process of referral and placement for maladjustment was also carried out in the 1970s by Ford, Mongon, and Whelan (1982). Although fewer children were referred into this category than for ESN-M, numbers of children attending schools for the maladjusted increased from zero in 1950 to 13,000 in 1978, with teachers in mainstream education commenting that "it was a relief to get the children out" (Ford, Mongon, & Whelan 1982, p. 54). This study also found that there were four times as many black children in these schools than would be expected (p. 135); boys and working-class pupils were heavily overrepresented; and the middle and upper classes did not seem to become maladjusted (p. 136). This study noted the "complex and delicate" questions raised by overrepresentation of black children and noted that features of ethnicity, culture clashes, school attitudes, and societal expectations might contribute, as might the medical model of maladjustment as "deviance and strangeness."

The 1960s and 1970s also witnessed the development of nonstatutory ways of excluding children from mainstream schooling. A variety of guidance centres, nurture groups, sanctuary units, support units, transitional classes, and intermediate treatment centres came into operations as a response to troublesome behaviour in schools. The Community Relations Commission noted in 1974 that in Birmingham, black pupils were overrepresented in these forms of education (Community Relations Commission [CRC] 1974), which had been developed primarily to prevent pupils from "disrupting the education of others" (Ford, Mongon, & Whelan, 1982, p. 89)—a common theme running through special education provision from the 1890s to the present day. A further formal investigation in Birmingham by the Commission for Racial Equality in 1984 found a disproportionate number of black children suspended from school, 10% of the school population being West Indian, but 43% of children in one special guidance unit alone were black. Black pupils tended to be referred for one offence, white children only after several offences (Commission for Racial Equality [CRE] 1985).

The introduction of the concept of special educational need, replacing the old categories of handicap, via the 1981 Education Act, did little to reassure black parents that their children would not continue to be overrepresented in special education. A Haringey Black Pressure Group on Education expressed their anxiety to the then shadow education secretary Neil Kinnock, who met the group to discuss the situation. (The London Times Educational Supplement, 1981)

The 1980s and 1990s: EBD and Exclusions

During the 1980s and 1990s information on the placement of minority children in special education could only be obtained by research studies or from individual Local Education Authorities (LEAs). Collection of information on the ethnic background of pupils was discontinued in 1972 and the 1989 requirement for schools to collect background information on pupils entering schools at ages 5 and 11 did not provide adequate data on the backgrounds of pupils moving into special education. There has been no requirement that the ethnic background of "statemented" children[3] be noted. Research in the 1980s indicated that as a group, black children continued to be regarded as potential low achievers and were overrepresented in the new forms of special education ESN-M schools, by then called MLD (mild learning difficulty) schools. However, the numbers of black children referred into these schools appeared to decline. What was happening was that black children were being referred instead into the new nonstatutory category of emotionally and behaviourally disturbed, which replaced the statutory maladjusted category. Studies began to take note of gender (Cooper et al. 1991). For black boys, the ESN issue was replaced by the EBD issue as they became the group most likely to be overreferred to and placed in EBD schools. Black pupils also continued to be overrepresented in behavioural units (new Pupil Referral Units [PRUs] were not developed until the 1990s) and suspended or excluded from school. Research studies continued to suggest that teachers still regarded black pupils, particularly boys, as potentially troublesome in mainstream (Bagley et al. 1982), Eggelston et al. 1986, Inner London Education Authority [ILEA] 1990). Bagley used National

Child Development Study data which showed that black pupils were six times more likely to be placed in special schools than whites and more likely to be described by their teachers as "delinquent, rebellious, aggressive and easily-led" (Bagley 1982, p. 127). Smith and Tomlinson noted in their study that teachers were more likely to regard black children as having emotional or behavioural problems (1989), and an ILEA survey in the late 1980s found black pupils twice as likely to be suspended or excluded as Asian or white pupils (ILEA 1990). The only large-scale study to date of EBD schools, carried out by Cooper and his colleagues in 1989, found that black boys were four times more likely to be overrepresented in these schools, and black girls were also more likely to be regarded as EBD than white girls (Cooper et al. 1991). While the researchers gave due weight to social class factors they suggested that teachers continued to stereotype black pupils, misunderstand cultural attributes, and perceive them as potentially deviant in ways that often led pupils to adopt deviant identities (p. 90).

In the 1990s research into the placement and experiences of ethnic minority students in special education continued to be minimal, and studies were mainly carried out by research students. Vernon (1998) produced the first study in the United Kingdom on the experience of black, disabled, ethnic minority women. Reviews of the position of minorities in mainstream education continue to report that African-Caribbean pupils, especially boys, have not shared in the general increase in educational achievements and "there is a growing gap between Afro-Caribbean pupils and their peers" (Gillborn & Gipps 1996, Gillborn & Mirza 2000, Office for Standards in Education [OFSTED] 1999). The 1996 Gillborn and Gipps review noted again that black pupils were between three and six times more likely to be excluded from school than white pupils, and Gillborn has noted elsewhere that "exclusions from school operate in a racist manner: they deny a disproportionate number of black students access to mainstream education" (Gillborn 1995). A study carried out for the Commission for Racial Equality in the mid-1990s introduced the notion of "replacement" education (Commission for Racial Equality [CRE] 1996). This was replacement in referral units or home tuition. Parsons and his colleagues at the CRE estimated that the cost of replacement education was twice as much as mainstream education but offered only 10% of the education offered in mainstream schools. This study referred to "a major crisis in the education of black males, in which exclusion plays a part" and "until racial inequality in exclusions is eliminated it will contribute to the development of an uneducated, unemployed and unemployable cohort of young adults" (p. 4).

The inequitable treatment of young black students continued to be researched and documented in the 21st century. Maud Blair, researching the teaching and learning of minority group students for the Department of Education, demonstrated yet again that teachers' ideological orientation towards the young people affected their effectiveness as teachers, but they were often unwilling to take responsibility and continued to blame the students for low achievements. Blair reported that:

Black students felt particularly angered by the stereotypes which they felt shaped teachers' negative judgements about them. . . . There was nothing biologically or culturally distinctive about black students that made them a particular problem for schools. The problem was that teachers perceived a collective difference and constructed it as a problem. This created an environment which effectively set black students up to fail, in both behavioural and academic terms, in ways which do not arise for white students." (Blair 2001, p. 136)

Markets and Education

By the 1990s, a competitive schools market had become established in the United Kingdom, adding a further dimension to the needs of schools to exclude pupils they regarded as troublesome and function unimpeded in the scramble to be regarded as good schools, high up in league tables of examination results. Competition between schools has been encouraged via the annual publication of raw scores of public examination results, and schools are rewarded by a funding formula for the number of pupils they attract. "Choice" allows schools to become more selective and to choose their pupils. In the schools marketplace, some students are regarded as "desirable customers," others as "troublesome customers," and unsurprisingly, social class, race and ethnicity, special educational needs, and behaviour problems have become filters through which the desirability or undesirability of particular pupils is understood. Pupils who are valued above others are those with a high measured ability, who are well-motivated and have supportive parents (Ball et al. 1996). There are various ways in which schools choose their desirable customers and discourage the undesirable, and exclude the latter if they demonstrate troublesome traits. Schools can overtly select pupils by testing for ability or aptitude, they can covertly select by interviewing parents, and they can discourage parents by suggesting their children will be better off in other schools. Once the pupils are in school, they can be excluded on the grounds that they have special educational needs or are behaviourally troublesome.

It is not accidental that as the marketisation of education has become more firmly established, rates of referral to EBD schools and the use of exclusion have risen. In market situations where desirable customers are wanted, quicker ways of removing the undesirables are needed. The irony of the situation is that the effects of the market lead to a concentration of children who had been rejected by some schools, in other schools that will accept them. Far from this situation being acknowledged and extra assistance offered to these schools, they are likely to be targeted as failing schools in need of "special measures" (Department for Education DfE), 1992). An extreme example of this was Hackney Downs School, closed on the advice of an Educational Association in 1995, at a time when its school population included 80% minority pupils, 70% of them second-language speakers, 50% from households with no employment, a high proportion of boys expelled from other schools, and almost two-thirds regarded as having some form of special educational need (O'Connor et al 1999). Evidence so far indicates that African-Caribbean students are faring particularly badly in the education market (Gillborn & Youdell 2000; Tomlinson 1997).

Nonpolicy

There has always been disinclination on the part of central and local policy-makers to link special education policy to any policies that took account of race and ethnicity, despite the constant presentation of evidence over the years of racial overrepresentation, and overexclusion in the various forms of special education. Troyna and Vincent (1996) have pointed to the persistence of "ideologies of expertism," benevolent humanitarianism and individualism in Special Educational Needs (SEN) policy-making, which contrasted with the assertive collective voice in the creation of antiracist policies, and noted that only recently had white parents begun to challenge the categorisation of their children. Daniels and his colleagues, studying special schools in two LEAs, also noted: "[T]he practices of SEN seem to have been insulated from the gaze and voice of equal opportunity initiatives" (Daniels et al. 1998). In their study schools, there was an overrepresentation of boys, in particular African-Caribbean boys. They suggested that causation models of individual deficiencies may preclude the kind of social explanations that drive equal opportunity policies. The Labour government appointed a National Advisory Group on SEN and produced two papers on policies and a programme for action in 1997 and 1998 (Department for Education and Employment DfEE 1997, 1998). The government was attempting to grapple with the contradictions of an education market that encouraged schools to exclude children who were difficult to teach, and with the resulting enormous cost of special education, especially as increasing numbers of parents were claiming resources for their statemented children (Tomlinson 2001). While the policies were more open and pragmatic than previous policies, race was once again a nonissue and the treatment of minority young people not a policy topic.

What Is Going On?

It is fair to ask what is going on? The use of a special subsystem, via either statutory or nonstatutory provision, to remove black children in disproportionate numbers from mainstream education must be questioned. Making sense of the situation requires a study of the historical and political context in which racial minorities have been incorporated into education systems originally designed for white majority pupils. It requires a study of the belief systems built up from the early 19th century in colonialist Europe, and postslavery in the United States, and it requires an examination of the way in which, via social Darwinism, the eugenics movement, and the use of IQ testing, the notion that some races are genetically inferior to others has been propagated. This historical understanding has become very necessary. It is a matter of concern that views expressed and accepted by Terman in the United States in the early part of the 20th century, concerning racial deficiencies in intelligence, the need for special school segregation, training for low-skill employment, and control of reproduction of particular racial groups (Terman 1916), should still be current, reflected for example in the work of Herrnstein and Murray (1994; see appendix). Their book is in the tradition of the pseudo-scientific research and literature that throughout the 20th century sought to demonstrate the supposed inferior intelligence of particular racial groups, and the social and economic danger these groups supposedly pose for the rest of society.

Education systems and their special subsystems are not neutral elements. The decisions that assign black children to special education or otherwise exclude them from mainstream, and nonpolicies that fail to recognise the links between race and special forms of education are a product of the residual historical beliefs that shape the values of policy-makers, professionals, and practitioners.

Conclusion

The purpose of this chapter has been to draw attention to the persistence of links between race and special education, using the overplacement of black children in stigmatised categories of special education in Britain as a case study. On a wider level the chapter also raises the question as to why, for over a century, children identified by racial, ethnic, or immigrant characteristics should be regarded as more likely to qualify for special education than their white or nonimmigrant peers. In developing a model or theory to explain this there is no doubt that residual historical beliefs structured around Social Darwinist assumptions of the biological inferiority, natural incapacity, and cultural deficiencies of racial groups defined on the basis of visible characteristics still influences many of those responsible for decision making in special education at the beginning of the 21st century. In addition, 19th-century eugenic beliefs in the genetic and cultural inferiority of the lower classes, which led to a "class racism" (Balibar 1991), is also still in evidence. Eugenic anxieties were concerned with promulgating racial and social purity. These beliefs can also be seen throughout the 20th century. The enemy within Britain in the early part of the 20th century was the poor feeble-minded woman who produced degenerate children and who "threatened the racial stock" (Royal Commission on the Care and Control of the Feeble-minded [RCCCFM] 1908, vol. 1), with the terms "race" and "nation" being conterminous at that time. Keith Joseph, a candidate for the leadership of the Conservative Party in England in 1974, was equally concerned with the nation moving inexorably towards degeneracy due to the high birth rate among "dull" lower-class women (Joseph 1974). Eysenk, a respected professor at London University, expressed the complexities of the interplay of race, class, and gender in deciding who was intellectually inferior in his book *Race, Intelligence and Education* (1971), coming to a startling conclusion for one who had escaped Nazi persecution in the 1930s:

Most of the lumpenproletariat are white, we are not dealing with a problem that is exclusively one of colour, but rather of social class. Colour comes into it but through the link between class and IQ on the one hand and race and IQ on the other. If this is so then there is . . . no solution exclusively concerned with coloured people. A solution is only possible in terms of the abolition of the lumpenproletariat as a whole, both black and white. (p. 150)

He goes on to note that such an "ambitious undertaking" is a matter for politicians rather than psychologists. Herrnstein and Murray also worried that an urban black underclass of low cognitive ability was increasing, but they did not go so far as Eysenck's suggestion of "abolition." Their solution was simply to abolish cash and services for low-income women and low-intelligence women (Herrnstein & Murray 1994, p. 548).

Beliefs in biological incapacity, expressed in terms of "low intelligence" and "subhuman qualities," and also of cultural deficiencies, have characterised theories about other races "outside" the society and a same-race underclass within the society for the whole of the 20th century. The black immigrant minorities who arrived in Britain in the 1950s and '60s from British colonial coutries were thus likely to encounter beliefs about the likely deficiencies of both lower-class and racial groups. It should not, perhaps, be surprising that beliefs in the lower abilities and problem behaviour of black children should lead to their overreferral and placement in the subsystem devised for removing from education those who are regarded as inferior and troublesome. Popular assertions of belief in "inclusive education" do not yet include the descendants of citizens of African-Caribbean origin in Britain, or of many black citizens in the United States.

Notes

1. This chapter refers to groups described as racial or ethnic on the basis of characteristics inputed to them by others (see Rex 1986, chapter 1).
2. Some forms of special education carry a stigma historically associated with low ability, low socioeconomic status, and poverty. Other recently developed categories are used by knowledgeable groups to gain extra resources without a stigma. (For example, specific learning difficulty, dyslexia.)
3. Following the 1981 Education Act, children in England and Wales assessed by Local Authority personnel receive a "statement" of their special educational needs.

Appendix

The following quotations, taken from Terman's 1916 writing, and Herrnstein and Murray's 1994 book *The Bell Curve: Intelligence and Class Struggle in American Life,* illustrate the enduring attempts to brand low socioeconomic and racial groups as being of lower intelligence, likely to be unproductive, and targets for eugenic policies:

"In the near future intelligence tests will bring tens of thousands of high-grade defectives under the surveillance and protection of society. This will result in the curtailing of the reproduction of feeble-mindedness, and in the elimination of an enormous amount of crime, pauperism and industrial inefficiency. . . . borderline deficiency is very common among Spanish-American and Mexican families and also Negroes. Their dullness seems to be racial . . . the whole question of racial differences in mental traits will have to be taken up anew . . . children of this group should be segregated in special classes, they cannot master abstractions but can often be made efficient workers . . . from a eugenic view they contribute a grave problem because of their unusually prolific breeding." (Terman, L. M.)

"There is such a thing as a factor of cognitive ability on which human beings differ, cognitive ability is substantially heritable . . . our thesis is that the twenty-first century will open on a world in which cognitive ability is the decisive dividing force. . . ." (Herrnstein and Murray, pp. 22–25)

"The dry tinder for the formation of an underclass community is a large number of births to single women of low intelligence in a concentrated spatial area." (ibid, p. 520)

"The most efficient way to raise the IQ of a society is for smarter women to have higher birth rates than duller women. Instead, America is going in the opposite direction." (ibid, p. 548)

References

Bagley, C., et al. (1982). "Achievement, Behavioural Disorder and Social Circumstance in West Indian Children" in (eds.) Verma, G. K. & Bagley, C. *Self-Concept and Multicultural Education*. New York. Macmillan.

Balibar, E. (1991). "Is there a Neo-Racism?" in (eds.) Balibar, E. & Wallerstein, I. *Race, Nation, Class: Ambiguous Identities* London. Verso.

Ball, S., Bowe, R., & Gewirtz, S. (1996). "School Choice, Social Class and the Realisation of Social Advantage in Education." *Journal of Education Policy* vol. 11 pp. 75–88.

Blair M. (2001). *Why Pick On Me? School Exclusion and Black Youth*. Stoke-on-Trent, UK. Trentham Books.

Brigham, C. C. (1923). *A Study of American Intelligence,* Princeton, NJ. Princeton University Press.

Burt, C. (1937). *The Backward Child London*. London. London University Press.

Coard, B. (1970). *How the West Indian Child Is Made ESN in the English School System*. London. New Beacon Books.

Community Relations Commission (CRC). (1974). *Education Guidance Centres in Birmingham*. London. Community Relations Commission.

Commission for Racial Equality (CRE). (1985). *Birmingham LEA and Schools: Referral and Suspension of Pupils*. London. Commission for Racial Equality.

Commission for Racial Equality (CRE). (1986). *Exclusion from School: The Public Cost*. London. Commission for Racial Equality.

Cooper, P., Upton, G., Smith, C. (1991). "Ethnic Minority and Gender Distribution among Staff and Pupils in Facilities for Pupils with Emotional and Behavioural Difficulties." *British Journal of Sociology of Education* vol. 12 no. 1 pp. 77–94.

Daniels, H., Hey, V., Leonard, D., & Smith, M. (1998). "Differences, Difficulties and Equity; a Study of Gender, Race and SEN" *Management in Education* vol. 12 no. 1.

Department for Education and Science. (1973). (November) Letter to Chief Education Officers.

Department for Education (DfE). (1997). *Schools Requiring Special Measures*. London, Department for Education.

Department for Education and Employment (DfEE). (1997). *Excellence for All Children: Meeting Special Educational Needs*. London. Department for Education and Employment.

Department for Education (1992). *Choice and Diversity: A New Framework for Schools*. London: Department for Education.

Department for Education and Employment (DfEE). (1998). *Meeting Special Educational Needs: A Programme for Action*. London. Department for Education and Employment.

Dhondy, F. (1974). (February) "The Black Explosion in Schools." *Race Today*.

Eggleston, J., Dunn, D., Anjel, M., & Wright, C. (1986). *Education for Some*. Stoke-on-Trent, UK. Trentham Books.

Eysenck, H. (1971). *Race Intelligence and Education*. London. Temple-Smith.

Ford, J., Mongon, D, & Whelan, H. (1982). *Special Education and Social Control*. London. Routledge.

Gillborn, D. (1995). *Racism and Anti-Racism in Real Schools*. Buckingham, UK. Open University Press.

Gillborn, D. & Gipps, C. (1996). *Recent Research in the Achievements of Ethnic Minority Pupils*. London. Office for Standards in Education.

Gillborn D. & Youdell, D. (2000). *Rationing Education: Policy Practice. Reform and Equity*. Buckingham, UK: Open University Press.

Gillborn D. & Mirza, H. (2000). *Mapping Educational Inequality: Race, Class and Gender*. London. Office for Standards in Education.

Herrnstein, R. & Murray, C. (1994). *The Bell Curve: Intelligence and Class Structure in American Life*. New York. Free Press.

Inner London Education Authority (ILEA). (1990). *Suspensions and Exclusions from School 1987–88* London. Inner London Education Authority.

Joseph, K. (1974). (October 17) Speech to Birmingham Conservative Association. Birmingham, UK. *Times Education Supplement*. June 3, 1981.

Lynn, R. (1992). "Intelligence, Ethnicity and Culture" in (eds.) Lynch, J., Modgil, C., & Modgil, S. *Cultural Diversity and the School*. Vol. 1. London. Falmer Press.

O'Connor, M., Hales, E., Davies, J., & Tomlinson, S. (1999). *Hackney Downs: The School that Dared to Fight*. London. Cassell.

Office for Standards in Education (OFSTED). (1999). *Raising the Attainment of Ethnic Minority Pupils*. London. Office for Standards in Education.

Organisation for Economic Co-operation and Development (OECD). (1987). *Immigrant Children at School*. Paris. Organisation for Economic Co-operation and Development.

Rex, J. (1986). *Race and Ethnicity*. Buckingham, UK. Open University Press.

Royal Commission on the Care and Control of the Feeble-minded (RCCCFM). (1908). Eight volumes. London. HMSO.

Select Committee of Race Relations and Immigration. (1973). *Education*. London. HMSO.

Select Committee on Race Relations and Immigration. (1976). *The West Indian Community*. London. HMSO.

Sigmon, S. (ed). (1990). *Critical Voices in Special Education*. New York. New York University Press.

Smith, D. & Tomlinson, S. (1989). *The School Effect: A Study of Multiracial Comprehensives*. London. Policy Studies Institute.

Terman, L. M. (1916). *The Measurement of Intelligence*. Boston. Houghton Mifflin.

Teunisson, F. (1992). "Equality of Opportunity for Children from Ethnic Minority Communities" in (eds.) Reid, E. & Reich, H., *Breaking the Boundaries: Migrant Workers Children in the EC*. Clevedon, UK. Multilingual Matters.

Tomlinson, S. (1981). *Educational Sub-Normality: A Study in Decision-Making*. London. Routledge.

Tomlinson, S. (1982). *A Sociology of Special Education*. London. Routledge.

Tomlinson, S. (1997). "Diversity, Choice and Ethnicity: The Effects of Educational Markets on Ethnic Minorities." *Oxford Review of Education*. vol. 23 no. 1 pp. 63–76.

Tomlinson, S. (2001). *Education in a Post-Welfare Society*. Buckingham, UK. Open University Press.

Troyna, B. & Vincent, C. (1996). "The Ideology of Expertism: The Framing of Special Education and Racial Equality Policies in the Local State" in (eds.) Christensen, C. & Rizvi, F., *Disability and the Dilemmas of Social Justice*. Buckingham, UK. Open University Press.

Vernon, A. (1998). "Understanding Simultaneous Oppression: The Experience of Disabled Black and Ethnic Minority Women." Ph.D. dissertation. Sheffield, UK. University of Sheffield.

6   *Keith Ballard*

IDEOLOGY AND THE ORIGINS OF EXCLUSION: A CASE STUDY

This chapter is based on a paper presented in June 1999 to the International Research Colloquium on Inclusive Education. To provide an initial focus for the colloquium, Linda Ware sent all participants a copy of Ellen Brantlinger's (1997) timely, challenging, and important article on "using ideology." In this paper, Brantlinger says that inclusionist ideology is "optimistic about school reform and individual transmutability" (449), focusing on "ideas for eliminating oppression from social structures" (448). Examining the politics of special education, Brantlinger shows how the theory and practice of inclusion, embedded in a values system emphasising democracy and social justice, represents a challenge to presently dominant views on education and on research into education. Brantlinger provides evidence of how that challenge is strongly resisted by those who assert the rightness of segregated provisions and the correctness of the positivist analysis that they use to support their beliefs.

In her careful presentation of this ideological struggle, Brantlinger has shown the importance of recognising the origins of the positions taken on both sides. These are the assumptions, models, theories and paradigms that we use to organise and make sense of our world and to direct our work in research, teaching, and writing. I found the essay valuable also in that it emphasised that what might appear to be a rather petty put-down, such as that of being "politically correct," in fact is part of a systematic and significant discourse aimed at controlling and eventually suppressing and excluding alternative views and actions.

I am familiar with the accusation that my work on inclusion means I am a "zealot," "emotional," "ideological," and "biased." But when I engage in what Patti Lather (1986) terms "openly ideological research," I believe that I take on a complex and ethically demanding task, and I strive to act from considered positions, avoiding reckless advocacy and unsubstantiated claims. At the 1998 meeting of the International Research Colloquium on Inclusive Education, I listened to some comments that described those who support inclusion as "self-righteous" and as "PC bullies" who "demonized" special schools and who did not recognise that "there are some kids who would not survive in the mainstream." I said a number of things to challenge and reject those assertions. One of them was that "only ideology matters." Hence this chapter.

I have previously written about the ideological context within which school reform has been undertaken in New Zealand (Ballard, 1996). This has been part of a worldwide phenomenon in which the New Right fundamentalist approach to economics and social organization has radically changed societies, from macrosystem to microsystem (Bronfenbrenner, 1979) levels. It has been evident for some time that societies grounded on the New Right belief that all people are fundamentally self-seeking and greedy are societies that do not wish to pay much attention to issues of minority rights, disability or otherwise. New Right Social Darwinism accepts the economic and social exclusion of people from mainstream society as part of a natural order, of how things inevitably are. Increasingly we see publicly funded schools operating in a commercial market environment in which catering for diversity is not in their interests because it threatens their ability to maintain or enhance their enrollments (Smyth, 1993; Walford, 1993). All of this has been written about and alternatives argued for, with often little success in promoting inclusionist policies and practices. Yet it seems to me increasingly urgent that we continue to examine and challenge this situation because New Right market ideology may be analysed as a threat to democracy and therefore to inclusion in education and in society.

As I write that, I can almost hear new labels being assigned to me—"conspiracy theorist" is a likely one, "socialist" another (although in New Zealand the media prefer the term "loony left"). Such stigmatising by slogan is an everyday occurrence in New Zealand where both major political parties, Labour (formerly a left-wing party) and National (traditionally conservative and right-wing), have embraced New Right economic and social policies. This is not the place to detail the history—it is well documented (Easton, 1997; Jesson, 1999; Kelsey, 1993, 1997)—that has led us to a situation in New Zealand where many politicians assert, in former English Prime Minister Margaret Thatcher's terms, "there is no alternative." What I will do in this chapter is to suggest why I believe the idea that "only ideology matters" is worthy of consideration. At least, perhaps, by naming a slogan of my own I can urge, as does Ellen Brantlinger, that we identify, analyse, and evaluate the ethical and social implications of the ideologies that guide our research and our actions in policy and practice.

The Social Construction of Humanness

To provide a focus to this account I will use Robert Bogdan and Steven Taylor's (1992) idea of humanness as a social construction. Bogdan and Taylor argue for a "sociology of acceptance" to operate alongside a "sociology of exclusion." The notion of "acceptance" needs to be problematized. It may imply a dominant normative position assimilating less valued "others." Nevertheless, Bogdan and Taylor stress that response to difference is not necessarily determined by the "social or cultural meanings" assigned to a person who shares certain identified features with others. Individuals, say Bogdan and Taylor, may elect to define another like themselves, an individual capable of thought, feeling, reciprocity, and of becoming a member of a family or other social group. Referring to people with severe disabilities, Bogdan and Taylor say that "we can show that they are human by proving that we are capable of showing humanity to them" (291). Then, once a person is "integrated into primary groups and have their humanness declared there, they have a vehicle to be included in the social web that defines community membership" (290).

The idea that labelling and stigmatising should not be seen as overly deterministic is an important one. Those individuals in a society who believe and act against cultural and other stereotypes may be the originators of ideas and of political advocacy that opposes racism, sexism, disablism, and other forms of subjugation. Yet I do not think we should ignore the power, for example, of the medical model in disability, or of the positivist paradigm in educational and social research. While we might, and I think should, celebrate those who resist what is hegemonic and harmful, we need, as Brantlinger shows, to attend to the power for naming and controlling things that the dominant ideology takes to itself. As Kincheloe and McLaren (1994) suggest, ideologies are not "simple descriptions" of thought; rather, they are part of our social and institutional arrangements that maintain a particular order, a hegemony in which "the virulence of oppression in its many guises (e.g., race, gender, class, sexual orientation), is accepted as consensus" (141).

In this chapter I suggest the role of ideology is to construct people as human ("like me"), and therefore to be cared about and included, and as not human ("not like me"), as not to be cared about, and as therefore eligible to be excluded. As an example, a discourse of humanness, of inclusion, may be seen in the statement of a teacher who said that:

> A person with a disability is a human being the same as everyone else, they have the same rights as everybody else, and the same as you have a responsibility for providing a learning environment for any child you have to provide a learning environment for a child with a disability. (Ballard & McDonald, 1998)

Experiences of a dehumanising, exclusionary ideology come from a parent who said:

I remember being told by a teacher three years ago at our daughter's previous school,
"No one wants your daughter in their classroom next year."
And why does it still hurt so much Colleen?
The teacher aide told us that the whole staffroom clapped when they learnt we were
leaving the school. (Brown, 1999:28)

The pervasive nature of ideology, its invisible, dominating presence, is important to grasp. Ideology involves unquestioned assumptions; it has the power to make arrangements that are based upon it seem natural and ordinary. That is why I suggest that it is central to the issue of inclusion. To take an historical example, part of the struggle for equity and justice by and for women involved challenging the justifications that had been made for excluding women from tertiary education. Petersen and Wilson (1978) have described how American women artists were denied access to many art schools in the late 19th century. If they were admitted, they were likely to be banned from human figure drawing classes because of the alleged harm such exposure would do to their minds and bodies. Petersen and Wilson record that in 1848 the Pennsylvania Academy of Fine Arts nude statue gallery was open to women only for one hour three days a week, and certain parts of the statues were covered at those times. They illustrate a "ladies" life drawing class at this institution in 1883—the photograph shows women "doing their best to learn the mysteries of anatomy" from a model, which is a live cow (85). This is an example of a male chauvinist ideology. It is also an example of special education involving a segregated location, inferior learning opportunities, and exclusion.

In many Westernised societies women are now included in most areas of education. It is not that women have themselves undergone cognitive or other change or that they have graduated from "special" teaching designed to remediate their "special needs" (Cook & Slee, 1995). The changes are the result of hard-fought struggles against an exclusionary ideology.

A Case Study: Locating Myself

This chapter presents a case study. The case is New Zealand and the study is of how a particular ideology—which I suggest involves powerful pressures for exclusion—has become overwhelmingly dominant since 1984.

New Zealand has a population of 3.3 million people and, until the mid-1980s, a post–World War 1 history of a society committed to state-funded education, health, and social welfare provisions. In 1984 a Labour government was elected with a manifesto that indicated that it would continue the social policies that were familiar to most New Zealanders. Instead, Labour introduced an unannounced New Right agenda that has seen a massive shift in the ideas that shape the lives of New Zealanders. Under Labour from 1984 to 1990 and then under National (conservative, right-wing) governments, changes have been made to almost all aspects of our public institutions, including education. As an indication of the moves undertaken in New Zealand since 1984, the government-owned telecommunications systems have been privatised, and the country's entire railway system has been sold to offshore interests. Removing tariffs on imports has meant that *all* car manufacturers in New Zealand have closed down, and dealers now import new and used (second-hand) cars (mostly from Japan). With the exception of one small regional bank, all banks are owned by offshore interests. New Zealand television, including the two state-owned channels, is entirely commercial. Only 24% of television programmes (including news) are made in New Zealand. Comparable figures elsewhere are Australia 55%, Canada 60%, United Kigdom 80%, United States 95% (Norris, Pauling, Lealand, Huijser & Hight, 1999). Despite the economic "reforms" and the sale of major assets, New Zealand's overseas debt in 1996 was 85.4% of its Gross Domestic Product (Kelsey, 1997:373), a significant deterioration since 1985 (Jesson, 1999:18).

The focus of this case study is New Right ideology and its role in exclusion in New Zealand. This is not to say that pressures for exclusion did not exist prior to 1984—they clearly did, for the indigenous Maori in particular (Kelsey, 1997). But we now see more widespread evidence of exclusion than has been the case since the economic depression era of the 1930s.

In this chapter I am concerned with the idea advanced in our international research group (Booth & Ainscow, 1998) that inclusion must mean inclusion beyond the classroom and school. I question whether we can have inclusive education in an exclusive society.

This is a case study also in the sense that it is clearly my study—this is my analysis of a complex social phenomenon, drawing on my interpretations and versions of events, referenced to data and policy documents and drawing on the analysis of others. With that goes an ethical responsibility to tell the tale as truthfully as I can. This is not a claim to an absolute truth, but an account that strives to avoid deliberate distortion, assembled in a persuasive but not fraudulent argument, which says that these things are as I experience and interpret them, and suggests that they have some relevance—perhaps importance—in understanding the meanings of inclusion and exclusion. This is a tentative, "narrative" truth (Ellis, 1997) open to alternative readings yet asserting its version as worthy of attention. Such work should, I think, involve "self-conscious criticism," researchers striving to be aware of their own ideological position, stating their assumptions in their writing, and being ready to question and change their metatheories and paradigms if they can be shown not to challenge inequality and injustice (Kincheloe & McLaren, 1994).

Without Carolyn Ellis's (1997) conceptual or authorial skills, I am "writing emotionally" as an act of self-disclosure that I do not find easy or comfortable. Nevertheless, to personalise writing is a deliberate strategy intended to challenge myself and the reader to interrogate what I claim in this chapter. In this work I reject an ideology that I suggest is directly responsible for discrimination, poverty, and injustice in my country and in others. Yet I am also aware that my beliefs, my ideological position, will equally focus, explain, distort, and ignore, as will other political, paradigmatic, and ideological lenses through which observation and analysis is undertaken. It becomes important, therefore, to be responsible for what is claimed. I do not take a relativistic position because I do not accept the idea that we cannot make value judgments about our constructions of the world. I believe that theory and research can and should be evaluated for ethical, moral, and practical implications (Goodman, 1992). I also suggest, with Donmoyer (1990), that it is the reader who generalises from a study, who determines how they could or should use research findings, and so who must share responsibility with the researcher for what effects a work may have on policy and practice.

A Political Ideology: Creating and Constructing the Poor as "Other"

In New Zealand the ideology promoted by government since 1984 has been that of the libertarian New Right. This emphasises "individualism, limited government, and free market forces" (Kelsey, 1993: 296). It is, says Kelsey (1993:16), a "rigid ideology that promotes the interests of the individual as paramount." At the same time, there have been strong themes of populist conservatism, emphasising so-called traditional values and identifying groups such as single parents and unemployed people as morally suspect, unworthy of state support, and the origins of crime, disorder, and other social problems. New Zealand law professor and writer Jane Kelsey (1993) says that such a position engenders an "ethnocentric and exclusivist conception of national identity . . . which feeds off a wide range of already established discourses, especially on race, gender and sexuality, to explain the ills of society" (296).

The discourse on unemployment provides a singular example. The Labour Party government of 1984–1987 privatized and corporatized government public services with an immediate loss of 15% of public service workers (11,000 staff). Kelsey (1993: 336) reports that between 1986 and 1991 jobs in the public sector almost halved. Overall unemployment went from 8.5% of the workforce in 1984 to 16.2% in 1990 (Kelsey, 1993: 335). The indigenous Maori people have been particularly affected as a result of job losses in manufacturing industries and in agriculture. Kelsey records that by 1991 Maori, who were 8% of the total labour workforce, represented 25.7% of all unemployed people.

American economist John Kenneth Galbraith (1992) identifies what he terms a "culture of contentment" within societies where an economically affluent group supports policies that impoverish a significant proportion of their fellow citizens. The poor, he argues, represent a dispossessed underclass that is so marginalised that they fail to vote. The wealthy, aware of disparities in their society, create a rationale for the privileged situation that they hold in such societies. Prominent in this is the need "to justify a reduced sense of public responsibility for the poor" so that they may "be seen as the architects of their own fate" (97). In Reagan's America, says Galbraith, justification was claimed to be found in the works of economist Adam Smith with his emphasis on freedom of trade "motivated by the universal force of self-interest" (99).

At the same time, writing that justified the pursuit of wealth and argued that the poor were responsible for their own situation became influential. Galbraith refers to Gilder's (1981) *Wealth and Poverty*, in which Gilder states that "in order to succeed the poor need most of all the spur of their poverty" (118, cited in Galbraith, 1992: 102). Galbraith is disparaging of Laffer's taxation theory—an "exercise of imagination" that no one of "sober mentality" took seriously (104)—which has been widely used to justify reducing taxation for those who have higher incomes. And Galbraith sees a third component underlying the culture of contentment in the work of Charles Murray, who argued that the poor are kept in poverty and dependency by welfare payments, and so welfare should be ended.

All of these ideas are strongly evident in New Zealand politics, policy, and the media, but no more so than the last. Economist Brian Easton (1997) argues that the New Zealand Treasury is dominated by "Chicago school extremists" (88) committed to a minimum of taxation and welfare provision. In this, the Treasury has significant support. A leading New Zealand political columnist wrote in 1998 with regard to the increase of people using food banks that "if you provide free food of course people will accept it in ever-growing numbers" (McLoughlin, 1998: 96). The claim here is that people are not really in need but will elect not to work if church agencies provide them with free food. Consistent with the view that the poor are in fact slothful and therefore become dependent on the state when welfare is available to them was a government policy introduced in 1998 that required people to undertake community or other work if they are to receive an unemployment benefit. This policy implied that unemployment is not the result of a lack of jobs, but of personal moral failing.

Opposing views, when they are heard, quickly attract the accusation of being "politically correct" and as reflecting "the politics of grievance, greed and envy" (McLoughlin, 1998: 96). New Zealand has an uncritical media that readily reports the endless slogans of the New Right that fit a short "sound bite" approach, devoid of analysis or depth of investigation. To express concern about poverty is said to reflect envy for the well off. Expressions of concern from church leaders have seen one National party minister of the crown accuse church leaders of "constant bleating about poverty" (Carter, 1995: 4). One response to church concerns was the publication of an article by English writer Paul Johnson (1996) under the title "Poor are poor because they are stupid" (C6). Johnson refers to research showing that the gap between rich and poor in New Zealand is growing faster than in any other industrialised nation. In a typical New Right discourse he describes the writers of such reports as "gloomy" and as "describing the same old phenomenon" (C6). Having trivialised the research and the data, Johnson says that the "most single" important reason that people are poor "is lack of intelligence." People, he says, "become poor because they are stupid and/or incompetent, and therefore the likelihood is that their children will do even worse." Johnson says that "any radical solution must involve eugenics" but that would not be acceptable and so ending welfare is an appropriate strategy.

While New Zealand has not ended its welfare system, significant cuts have been made to social services, with equally significant results. For example, cuts in health spending mean that the waiting list for surgery in New Zealand is five times the rate of Australia's, and three times the rate for Holland and Canada (Issues—Hikoi of Hope, New Zealand Health Review, 1998: 20). On the waiting lists, 42% wait longer than one year for treatment and 22% longer than two years (Issues—Hikoi of Hope, New Zealand Health Review, 1998: 20). Some patients needing heart surgery die while they are on waiting lists (Keene, 1998), while patients who can afford it receive prompt attention in the private health system.

Relatively high levels of unemployment and poverty are creations of the 1984–1990 Labour government and subsequent administrations in the interest, it would seem, of establishing a low-wage, manipulable workforce. Writing on child poverty in New Zealand, director of the Children's Issues Centre Anne Smith (1996, citing Stephens, Waldegrave, & Frater, 1995), noted that the percentage of households in poverty (annual salary less than $16,032, or U.S. $8,000) was 4.3% in 1984, and 10.8% in 1993 (annual salary less than $16,366). The number of single-parent homes in poverty went from 11.8% in 1984 to 46.2% in 1993. In a recent UNICEF report on infant mortality, a key indicator of a nation's well-being, New Zealand ranked 16th of 16 developed countries. In terms of the support that we provide for children and families, Anne Smith noted (9) that our child benefit package ranks us at 16 out of 18 OECD countries (for a recent detailed analysis, see Stephens, 1999).

This suggests that an increasing number of people in New Zealand—adults and children alike—are being excluded from participation in the workforce, in the wage economy, and therefore in experiences of independence, agency, and well-being. The ideological context has been effective not only in creating this changed society but also in labelling people who are unemployed and who are living in poverty as "dependants" (an illness model, requiring intervention and treatment) and as "stupid" (they lack skills, which is their fault through lack of effort). It is not the role of society to promote the inclusion of those now seen as deviant. Indeed, the opposite may be the case.

Sir Roger Douglas, minister of finance in the 1984–1990 Labour government, has been reported as saying that New Zealand "society is really breaking down" because of people on welfare benefits, and that "eventually there will be areas of the country where it is too dangerous to go. They will have to be fenced off, to protect" the rest of us (Clifton, 1996). As I have noted elsewhere (Ballard, 1999), this idea is to be found in an influential American book *The Bell Curve* by Hernstein and Murray (1994), two academics of the New Right. They propose that IQ, ethnic origin, and poverty are genetically linked; that a growing and intellectually inferior underclass is a threat to the well-being and order of society; and that an end to affirmative action and welfare payments would encourage the poor to work and discourage them from breeding. Hernstein and Murray envisage that the "cognitive elite" (91) will increasingly be segregated from those who are poor because "they are not very smart" (142).

Whatever your politics, these ideas, which I believe influence economic, welfare, and employment policy in New Zealand, are for an exclusive rather than inclusive society. In particular, it is difficult to see a valued place for people with intellectual or other disabilities in this ideology.

Ideology and Disability

There is evidence that disabled people confront particular difficulties in New Zealand's commercialised society. In 1994 The Assembly of People with Disabilities (DPA) noted that Northland Health proposed a list of criteria for restricting renal dialysis to patients with renal failure (McCarthy, 1994). The list included "blindness, intellectual handicap . . . and major antisocial behaviour" (5). DPA president Anne Hawker said that excluding people from treatment on the basis of disability "assumes that they are less valuable human beings." The International Disability and Human Rights Network (1999) recently noted that reports of such incidents are increasingly common worldwide, including evidence that babies with Down syndrome have been denied medical treatment available to other children.

Where might such thinking lead? Disability activists Jenny Morris (1992) in England and Anne Waldschmidt (1992) in Germany note that the idea of disabled lives as "unworthy of living" (Morris, 1992: 16) was the rationale for the 1939–1941 programme for the extermination of disabled people in Nazi Germany. Some present-day research on genetics and genetic screening, says Waldschmidt, sees the disabled as "waste products" or accidents in a genetically engineered reproductive process, in societies where people with disabilities are seen as an unproductive economic cost that should be eliminated by a programme of "friendly eugenics" (Rose, 1994: 193). Employers and insurers may increasingly insist that to get a job or to be accepted for health or other insurance, people must fit a preferred "genetic profile" (Rose, 1994: 193). In this "geneticization of human difference," an entire group of people—those whom their society labels as impaired—becomes "undesirable and unnecessary" (International League of Societies for Persons with Mental Handicap, 1994: 89).

Excluding Language

An ideology, like a culture, is carried through its language. New Right economic rationalism has its particular terminology that has become pervasive in New Zealand, nowhere more so than in education. This has come about because Treasury and both main political parties have supported the same ideological position. For example, Grace (1988) has persuasively shown that Treasury advice to an incoming Labour government, *Government Management*, Vol. 2 (Treasury, 1987), was not the impartial advice "expected of a non political state administration" (3), but a "distinct Treasury agenda which [had] the status of an ideological position" (4). This involved the idea of education as a commodity, which should, therefore, be traded in a market for such goods and services with consumers, rather than the state, having a major role in what is developed and purchased. Thus was introduced a new discourse on the nature of education, challenging and gradually replacing earlier notions of education as a public good which is publicly provided as a "fundamental right of all citizens" (Grace, 1988: 4).

From the 1930s until the mid-1980s, education in New Zealand was dominated by what Snook (1996) has referred to as the "powerful myth of equality of opportunity" (2). While researchers challenged the reality of this claimed equality in our schools, New Zealanders believed and acted on a belief that their state school system should and did provide a consistent quality of education across diverse communities. However, in their advice to the government, Treasury in 1987 argued that this system had failed, and so a new basis for educational thought was needed. This was to be derived from an "industrial production function" analysis of education, an accounting assessment of "inputs" and "outputs" (Grace, 1988: 67). Treasury set out to ensure that its market analysis became the new model of educational thought and practice. A key strategy was the constant use of the language of libertarian market ideology, with teachers and schools identified as providers, and which children, students, and parents crudely framed as consumers in an educational marketplace.

The cultural, social, emotional, moral, and interpersonal complexities of education were rendered into a dualistic model in which a commodity—like food, books, shoes, or any other—was exchanged. Treasury and its New Right supporters were successful in comodifying education in New Zealand because this market approach and its language were already dominating all economic, social, and political discussion.

Grace argued that education in New Zealand "is a public good because . . . it places high priority upon social justice, equity and the attempt to establish a fair society" (13). That was in 1988. In 1990 the New Zealand government established a National Qualifications Authority (NZQA) with the role of "approving, registering and monitoring all nationally recognised qualifications and their component parts" (Tuck & Peddie, 1995:10). One of the managers of this authority has explained that "qualifications act as a form of currency in society" (Barker, 1995:15), an indication that the educated person is essentially an economic being. The NZQA stresses that education is a product that must be driven by purchaser demands (Barker, 1995: 20). Barker goes on to note that the teacher-student relationship must be changed from a pedagogical one to a "contractual one" in which students are "consumers of services" who "demand to know what they are purchasing" and that they are getting "value for money" (20). Students will want to know in "precise terms" why they have been assigned particular marks not in terms "open to subjectivity" (21).

As Barker notes, the language with which we discuss education must be changed, and this change "will be intensely resisted" (1995: 20). There is a modicum of resistance. However, when all government and ministry documents are framed in market terminology, the world of education is being colonised by a narrowly focused, technicist and positivist ideology. Most importantly, the simplistic notion of teaching as a commercial relationship of providers and consumers dehumanises the complex nature of student-teacher relationships.

The Language of Commodity and the Language of Care

Student-teacher relationships should, in my view, include an ethic of care. Witherell and Noddings (1991) write that:

> The notion of caring is especially useful in education because it emphasises the relational nature of human interactions and all moral life . . . in a *caring relation* that requires contributions from both parties in the relation . . . [providing] a foundation of trust. (6)

Caring relations in New Zealand seem increasingly under threat. For example, in her important work on child poverty in this country, economist Susan St. John (1995) wrote of the difficulty of criticising New Right thought and policies. She wrote that presenting a case for welfare provisions means that "one feels the scorn before the ink is even dry" (2). Economists such as Susan St. John (1995) and Brian Easton (1997) express concern about the effects of the extremist, New Right ideologies pursued by Treasury and our main political parties. Ichiro Kawachi, from the School of Public Health, Harvard Medical School, has said that the significant increase in poverty in New Zealand caused by these policies is creating health problems "commonly seen in the third world," and a divided society that is "increasingly less able to work together for a common good" (Saunders, 1997: 6).

That a divided, exclusionary society is a deliberate outcome of a planned, ideologically driven agenda is well illustrated by a report from Infometrics Business Services (1991), a private organization used by government and business for policy advice and whose ideas are often referred to in the media (White, 1999). This report advises that there is "substantial scope" for New Zealanders to absorb cuts in real incomes and that the government should "cut welfare benefits further" in order to make "managers of home production units" (that is, people and their families) more "economically efficient" (2). People should make their own clothes, and if they used "more intensive labour techniques" for cleaning their home they could buy cheaper cleaning materials (4). "A car is out" (8), and "walking or public transport" should be used. Meals prepared by "more intensive home labour contribution" (I read this to mean that these lazy people must make more effort) could be provided for *a family of four* for $47.00 per week (U.S. $23), and a further $5.00 per week could be saved by "preserving fruit and vegetables" (4). With regard to this recommendation in the Infometrics report, it is relevant to note that each year the Department of Nutrition at the University of Otago works out "basic" weekly food costs such that spending less will not provide the nutrients necessary for health. For 1999 the basic weekly food cost for a family of four was between NZ$200 and NZ$215 (Else, 1999: 7). The Infometrics report goes on to suggest that the government's Guaranteed Retirement Income for the elderly should be reduced by $55.00 to $133.00 per week. This benefit might be "tailored to provide them with an incentive to participate in the home production sector"—that is, providing childcare and other services for the wealthy (13). The report says that community doctors may find that people cannot afford their services, so they will need to "adjust their own business" and accept bartering and "trade in kind" (11).

The goal of all this is quite explicit. It is "to move further away from welfare payments and use these savings to foster the generation of greater market wealth, through lessening the tax burden faced by business" (12).

The outcomes expected are also made explicit. These policies, says the report, "will likely accentuate the differences in material wealth" between those people "participating in the market economy" and those who "are more dependent upon home production" (15).

There is nothing unusual about any of this. This work is located in "rational" economic and social thought (Galbraith, 1992; Saul, 1997). As the Infometrics proposal states, "[W]hat is suggested is that a cultural change to more productive consumption [for example, they should grow their own food] will be forced [on people] as real incomes fall further" (9), and, as in "the corporate sector, adjustment will involve some pain" (10). Writer Rosie Scott (1995) has suggested that this report, along with our so-called reforms in New Zealand, involve a "process of returning to the social practice of 19th Century England" (18). Of particular significance for us in the Infometrics report is the proposal that "the government may well be spending too much on delivery of present education outputs" (14) and that "the relevance of a traditional education may diminish for many, if the market economy is unable to provide paid work for them" (11).

The message here seems clear enough. Why bother to educate "them" at all if "they" are unable to be employed, to be of economic use? Two kinds of people are identified: those who are seen as worthy of an education and those, "them," who are not worthy, who are constructed, therefore, as lesser humans or, perhaps, as less than human. Whatever one's politics, such ideas are, I suggest, about an exclusive, rather than inclusive, society.

In her paper on poverty in New Zealand, Susan St. John (1995) comments on the "power of ideas for evil and the danger of letting a certain style of discourse go unchallenged" (5). If we are to advance the idea and practice of inclusion in New Zealand and elsewhere, then I suggest that we must at the same time challenge ideas and practices that promote exclusion. Also, I think that, without losing our focus on disability issues, we will need to understand that inclusion must be about all those who are discriminated against, whether this be on the basis of gender, sexuality, poverty, or other minority or disadvantaged experience. Further, I think that we must attend to issues beyond the school. I cannot see that we can achieve inclusive schools in an exclusive society.

Resisting Ideological Colonisation

How do you challenge a system that you believe to be exclusionary and to be wrong? Whatever one decides in this regard, I anticipate that it requires effort at all levels of a society—political, social, and personal.

At the political level, we may challenge the Thatcherian notion that "there is no alternative." If we do not, then we will collude in the other belief proposed by Thatcher that there is "no such thing as society," and that only the individual and the family are real (Rose, 1994: 181). That means, I think, that notions of interdependence and of social responsibility are at risk. New Right theory reduces all social phenomena to individual, subjective choice. As John Codd (1998) explains, "[T]here is no such thing as the 'public good' because there is no such entity as society" (3). Individuals are primarily motivated by self-interest and, in the terms of public choice theory, are "rational utility maximisers" (Codd, 1998:3). As Codd notes, in such a world, "public duty" or even "social justice" are deemed irrelevant (3).

This is not simply an issue of an ideological theory operating at a broad, social level. The "back to basics" pressures from right-wing groups urge teachers to attend to the academic rather than the social and emotional needs of their students. In New Zealand the Education Review Office (ERO) is the government agency that "audits" the performance of each school. The accounting metaphor of "auditing" is a component of the commercial market orientation of this agency. ERO has described teaching and learning as the school's "core business and what a teacher is employed to do" (ERO, 1996:10, cited in Thrupp, 1998: 2), and is critical of the attention that teachers may give to students' personal and social concerns.

I believe we should seriously question the ideology of the marketplace, perhaps considering John Ralston Saul's (1997) contention that "Marxism, fascism and the market place strongly resemble each other. They are all corporatist, managerial and hooked on technology" (20). Saul states that a "standard reaction to ideology" is "passivity," a belief that individualisation and globalisation, for example, are inevitable. If, as I suggest in this chapter, New Right ideology is essentially exclusionary, and if we are to put into action a belief in inclusion, then we cannot afford to be passive about the societies in which we are living, and the ideologies used to direct their government. We cannot, in Saul's words, continue as an "unconscious civilization," unquestioning of the ideas that are clearly associated with the creation of poverty and social division. We should, I suggest, question, in John Kenneth Galbraith's terms, our "culture of contentment," our rationalisation of the inevitability of the suffering of others.

To do this, we need to recognise that exclusion *is* a feature of our society and that this does involve us as participants in that society. We may then "care" about what is happening and our part in it, linking the emotion of care with critical thought that may inform action. Canadian writer Anne Michaels (1998a) has written about the Second World War in Europe and about the holocaust. She suggests that we cannot comprehend such things through generalities, and that we should look at specific incidents to question what is moral or immoral. In an interview for *Listener* magazine, Michaels suggests that the "kernel of what morality is" involves linking thought and emotion (McLeod, 1998: 44). Along with some research colleagues, Lous Heshusius and I have suggested a similar position as a basis for undertaking research in education and the social sciences (Heshusius & Ballard, 1996). Anne Michaels illustrates the issue with her comment about her writing that:

> The way the language works and the way the images work is very deliberate. An image is very like music, in that it can enter you before you can respond. The right image takes the wind out of you; not only do you respond emotionally but, very soon after, you realise what the image means (Michaels interview in McLeod, 1998: 44).

Like Anne Michaels, English writer Louis de Bernieres (1998) has also written about war. De Bernieres suggests that in striving to understand the destruction of war we should not consider morality as necessarily the central issue. Rather, he suggests, we should consider the idea that people kill out of contempt—those they kill are constructed by the killer as less than human.

It is important not to diminish the significance of social and historical contexts, or to simplify the basis to complex human actions. For example, De Bernieres (1998) reports his father telling him how contempt as a motivation diminished for him when during World War II he found love letters in the pocket of a dead enemy soldier. From then, he said, he fought out of duty. Nevertheless, I suggest that dehumanising constructions have played a role in the killing of indigenous people in my country and in other places where colonisation has occurred. Distancing oneself from another's humanity would seem likely also to be implicated in the ethnic wars and killings today in Europe and in Asia. My concern is that dehumanising others will be part of the harm we now seem willing to impose on our immediate fellow citizens in the name of a "rational" economic theory that has clearly been shown wherever it has been put into effect (a "natural experiment" in Bronfenbrenner's 1979 terms) to benefit a privileged few and to deprive many. In this context we might also explore the dehumanising effects of television and other media which are saturated with violence. Why, in some cultures, is violence now a form of entertainment? In what ways does this link thought and emotion? What does this tell children about the human body, about their embodied selves, about their humanness and the humanness of others? Continuing exposure to violence in the media may mean that children distance themselves from a sense of pain and harm that they see inflicted on and being experienced by others. This distancing of the self would seem a "rational" response. It is "rational" economics that is currently creating impoverishment for millions around the world while a few recruit riches to themselves (De Brie, 1999; Saul, 1997). To distance the suffering of others would seem to be a useful mechanism in this context. The distancing strategies of positivist science also fit well into this context and have formed a useful position from which the New Right can reject evidence that does not meet the requirements of the dominant objectivist paradigm.

At the social level, we may engage with and challenge discriminatory institutions and practices. For example, in a research project (Ballard & Bray, 1997) we gave parents of disabled children control over our research grant money so that they may identify, critically evaluate, and act on policies, agencies, and people that are excluding them and their children. After the funding ended, the organization that the parents set up continues. One of the fathers said that he would emphasise that a most enduring outcome of the research was

> consciousness raising [for parents] that has left a group of committed and *informed* parents in the community, that reaches out into a range of endeavours. This would not be obvious at first glance, but the energy and commitment from the original project pops up, for example, in the [fathers'] video [a programme by fathers of disabled children]. (Ballard & Bray, 1997: 18)

Also at the social level, I think we should be aware of what researchers in America and New Zealand have recorded as the decline in sociability and social trust—a dire result, suggests Codd (1998), of the ideology of economic rationalism that defines people as individualistic and selfish, and has the material effect of declining economic social well-being for the majority of people. As one writer commenting on the legacy of Thatcher in England suggests, there has been "a thinning of the subtle, almost invisible threads of neighbourliness and common interest that ultimately tie a society together. Greed seemed to replace compassion as a core value" ("Comment," 1999).

At the personal level, it is not my place to suggest how others might respond, although I would urge that we resist and reject the language that carries the ideology of exclusion. An example of personal action that I like came from a radio report from a village in India where people objected to the idea of the ownership by private companies of knowledge about plants and their environment. The village set up a community biodiversity register, making this knowledge public, not private property. One of the villagers said that the idea of "free trade" (a key component of New Right economic ideology) meant the freedom of multinational companies over the rights of citizens (National Radio, 1997). These citizens resisted that ideology. In India there is a significant and growing movement to resist "recolonization" by multinational companies and by those agencies, such as the World Trade Organization and International Monetary Fund, that support them (Ainger, 1999).

For myself, I find the need to remind myself of another worldview—an ideology of engagement, of striving to recognise humanness. I find this in scholarship, for example in Joan Tronto's (1993) notion of an ethic of care that involves attentiveness (caring about), responsibility (taking care of), competence (care giving), and responsiveness (care receiving). Tronto reasons, "[C]are connotes some kind of engagement . . . [and] action" (102).

How do we "engage" with the effects of ideology? Again, I think this has something to do with our notion of being human, of "humanness." I think that we can examine the nature of research to see how that way of knowing might acknowledge and affirm the humanness of ourselves and those with whom we research (Heshusius, 1995; Israelite, 1996). That approach to research should include the ongoing interrogation of the assumptions, models, theories, paradigms, and ideologies we use, and how they shape what we claim to know.

But I will close by suggesting that it is in literature and the arts that we may also find both analysis and sustenance in a challenge to the mechanistic, technicist, and selfish ideology that has colonised our institutions and would colonise our minds. The arts embrace complexity and uncertainty, both of which challenge the certainty and inbuilt confidence of any ideology. And, as writer Anne Michaels (1998a) says, "[W]hat truth can fiction add?"

For example, in her novel *None to Accompany Me,* set in postapartheid South Africa, Nadine Gordimer's (1994) character Vera says, "Empowerment, Zeph. What is this new thing? What happened to what we used to call justice?" (285), evocatively contrasting an individualist with a community focus. Also Doris Lessing's (1997) Sarah, in *Love, Again,* listens to singing with words "half heard" that "were cries, or even laments, but from another time, the future perhaps, or another place, for if these sounds mourned, it was not for any small personal cause" (69). We are reminded then, that we can indeed imagine beyond ourselves. Canadian writer Anne Michaels (1997), in her painfully beautiful novel *Fugitive Pieces,* says that "the best teacher lodges an intent not in the mind but in the heart" (121), while Australian writer Sue Woolfe (1996), in *Leaning Towards Infinity,* speaking, I suggest, to my positivist colleagues as well as myself, asks, "[H]ow can we choose what to make up? So we can bear it?" (320).

Bogdan and Taylor (1992) say that we can show another is human "by proving that we are capable of showing humanity to them" (291). My case study suggests that an ideology, which is presently dominant in many Western and other industrialised countries, can create a culture of inhuman thought and action. As I wrote at the beginning of this chapter, ideologies are part of the social and institutional arrangements that maintain a particular order. Our children are most likely to learn that which is the preferred, dominant order. I suggest that in New Zealand, the dominant order has come to involve selfishness, a culture of contentment that dehumanises and marginalizes others. Within this ideological context lie the origins of exclusion. I think we will pay a high cost for this in material, moral, and spiritual terms. It seems to me that once we begin to consider ideology in this context, we may need to be not just overtly ideological but also overtly political in our analysis and actions. That is likely to be a contentious idea, but one, I suggest, worth thinking, and feeling, about.

References

Ainger, K. I. (1999, 21 February). The meek fight for their inheritance. *Guardian Weekly,* p. 23.

Ballard, K. (1996). Inclusive education in New Zealand: Culture, context and ideology. *Cambridge Journal of Education, 26*(1), 33–45.

Ballard, K. (1999). Concluding thoughts. In K. Ballard (Ed.), *Inclusive education: International voices on disability and justice* (pp. 167–179). London: Falmer Press.

Ballard, K. & Bray, A. (1997, 35 September). *Disability, families and action research: A four-year project and what happened after.* A paper presented to the International Conference on Doing Disability Research, Disability Research Unit, School of Sociology and Social Policy, University of Leeds, United Kingdom.

Ballard, K. & McDonald, T. (1998). New Zealand: Inclusive school, inclusive philosophy? In T. Booth & M. Ainscow (Eds.), *From them to us: An international study of inclusion in education* (pp. 68–94). London: Routledge.

Barker, A. (1995). Standards-based assessment: The vision and broader factors. In R. Peddie & B. Tuck (Eds.), *Setting the standards: The assessment of competence in national qualifications* (pp.1531). Palmerston North, New Zealand: The Dunmore Press.

Bogdan, R. & Taylor, S. J. (1992). The social construction of humanness: Relationships with severely disabled people. In P. M. Ferguson, D. L. Ferguson & S. J. Taylor (Eds.), *Interpreting disability: A Qualitative reader* (pp. 175–293). New York: Teachers College Press.

Booth, T. & Ainscow, M. (1998). From them to us: Setting up the study. In T. Booth & M. Ainscow (Eds.), *From them to us: An international study of inclusion in education* (pp. 1–20). London: Routledge.

Brantlinger, E. (1997). Using ideology: Cases of nonrecognition of the politics of research and practice in special education. *Review of Educational Research, 67,* 425–459.

Bronfenbrenner, U. (1979). *The ecology of human development: Experiments by nature and design.* Cambridge, MA: Harvard University Press.

Brown, C. (1999). Parent voices on advocacy, education, disability and justice. In K. Ballard (Ed.), *Inclusive education: International voices on disability and justice* (pp. 28–42). London: Falmer Press.

Carter, J. (1995, 1 February). Churchmen faulted. *Otago Daily Times,* p. 4.

Clifton, J. (1996, 3 March). The artful Roger. *Sunday Star Times,* p. C1.

Codd, J. A. (1998, 36 December). *Educational reform and the culture of distrust.* Paper presented to the Annual Conference of the New Zealand Association for Research in Education, University of Otago, New Zealand.

"Comment." (1999, 9 May). Thatcher's legacy. *Guardian Weekly,* p. 12.

Cook, S. & Slee, R. (1995, Summer). Schools, failure and disability. *Education Links, 49,* 11–13.

De Bernieres, L. (1998, 16 August). Panel discussion: "War Stories." New Zealand Post Writers and Readers Week. National Radio.

De Brie, C. (1999, May). Watch out for the MAI clone. *Le Monde Diplomatique,* p. 13.

Donmoyer, R. (1990). Generalizability and the single case study. In E. W. Eisner & A. Peshkin (Eds.), *Qualitative inquiry in education: The continuing debate* (pp. 175–200). New York: Teachers College Press.

Easton, B. (1997). *The commercialisation of New Zealand.* Auckland: Auckland University Press.

Ellis, C. (1997). Evocative autoethnography: Writing emotionally about our lives. In W. G. Tierney & Y. S. Lincoln (Eds.), *Representation and the text* (pp. 115–139). Albany: State University of New York Press.

Else, A. (1999). *Hidden hunger: Food and low income in New Zealand.* Wellington: New Zealand Network Against Food Poverty.

Galbraith, J. K. (1992). *The culture of contentment*. Harmondsworth, UK: Penguin Books.

Gilder, G. (1981). *Wealth and poverty*. New York: Basic Books.

Goodman, J. (1992). Theoretical and practical considerations for school-based research in a post-positivist era. *Qualitative Studies in Education, 5*(2), 117–133.

Gordimer, N. (1994). *None to accompany me*. London: Bloomsbury.

Grace, G. (1988). *Education: Commodity or public good?* Wellington, New Zealand: Victoria University Press.

Hernstein, R. J. & Murray, C. (1994). *The bell curve: Intelligence and class structure in American life*. New York: Free Press.

Heshusius, L. (1995). Listening to children. What could we possibly have in common? From concerns with self to participatory consciousness. *Theory into Practice, 34*(2), 117–123.

Heshusius, L. & Ballard, K. (Eds.) (1996). *From positivism to interpretivism and beyond: Tales of transformation in educational and social research (the mind-body connection)*. New York: Teachers College Press.

Infometrics Business Services Ltd. (1991). *Mitigating misery: A preliminary assessment of New Zealanders' capacity to absorb cuts in real incomes*. Wellington, New Zealand: Infometrics Business Services.

International Disability and Human Rights Network. (1999, April). Just die quickly dear. *Disability Awareness in Action, 71*, pp. 1–3.

International League of Societies for Persons with Mental Handicap (1994). *Just technology? From principles to practice in bio-ethical issues*. Toronto: Roeher Institute.

Israelite, N. K. (1996). On feeling right: A paradigmatic epiphany. In L. Heshusius & K. Ballard (Eds.), *From positivism to interpretivism and beyond: Tales of transformation in educational and social research (the mind-body connection)* (pp. 56–60). New York: Teachers College Press.

Issues—Hikoi of hope. (1998). *New Zealand Health Review, 1*(3), p. 20.

Jesson, B. (1999). *Only their purpose is mad: The money men take over New Zealand*. Palmerston North New Zealand: Dunmore Press.

Johnson, P. (1996, 28 January). Poor are poor because they are stupid. *Sunday Star Times,* p. C6.

Keene, L. (1998). Ration book surgery. *New Zealand Health Review, 1*(2), 10–12.

Kelsey, J. (1993). *Rolling back the state: Privatisation of power in Aotearoa/New Zealand*. Wellington, New Zealand: Bridget Williams Books.

Kelsey, J. (1997). *The New Zealand experiment: A world model for structural adjustment?* Auckland: Auckland University Press and Bridget Williams Books.

Kincheloe, J. L. & McLaren, P. L. (1994). Rethinking critical theory and qualitative research. In N. K. Denzin & Y. S. Lincoln (Eds.), *Handbook of qualitative research* (pp. 136–157). Thousand Oaks, CA: Sage.

Lather, P. (1986). Research as praxis. *Harvard Educational Review, 56*(3), 257–277.

Lessing, D. (1997). *Love, again*. London: Flamingo.

McCarthy, P. (1994). Plan to restrict dialysis on disability grounds. *NZ Disabled, 14,* 5.

McLeod, M. (1998, February 13). Daunted and haunted, an interview with Anne Michaels. *Listener,* pp. 44–45.

McLoughlin, D. (1998, November). Why the left is so damned happy. *North and South, 12,* 96–97.

Michaels, A. (1997). *Fugitive pieces*. London: Bloomsbury.

Michaels, A. (1998a, 16 August.). Panel discussion: "War Stories." New Zealand Post Writers and Readers Week. National Radio.

Morris, J. (1992, July). Tyrannies of perfection. *New Internationalist*, 16–17.

National Radio. Daily news. October 27, 1997.

Norris, P., Pauling, B., Lealand, G., Huijser, H., and Hight, C. (1999). *Local content and diversity: NZ On Air*. Wellington, New Zealand: NZ On Air.

Petersen, K. & Wilson, J. J. (1978). *Women artists: Recognition and reappraisal from the early middle ages to the twentieth century*. London: The Women's Press.

Rose, H. (1994). *Love, power and knowledge*. Bloomington: Indiana University Press.

St. John, S. (1995, 17 August). *The future of the poverty industry: Thinking about welfare in the 1990s: Liberal and conservative battle lines*. A paper prepared for the New Zealand Council of Christian Social Services.

Saul, J. R. (1997). *The unconscious civilization*. Ringwood, Victoria: Penguin Books.

Saunders, J. (1997, 17 February). Rapidly growing underclass in NZ. *Otago Daily Times*, p. 6.

Scott, R. (1995, February/March). The dark abyss of pish. *New Zealand Political Review*, 17–23.

Smith, A. B. (1996, 9 September). *Issues affecting the wellbeing of children and families in New Zealand*. The Patricia Coleman Lecture, University of Otago, New Zealand.

Smyth, J. (1993). Introduction. In J. Smyth (Ed.), *A socially critical view of the self-managing school* (pp. 1–9). London: Falmer Press.

Snook, I. (1996). The privatisation of education. *Input, 18*(1), pp. 1–12.

Stephens, R. (1999). Poverty, family finances and social security. In J. Boston, P. Dalziel & S. St John (Eds.), *Redesigning the welfare state in New Zealand: Problems, policies, prospects* (pp. 238–259). Auckland: Oxford University Press.

Stephens, R., Waldegrave, C., & Frater, P. (1995). *Measuring poverty in New Zealand*. Unpublished paper.

Thrupp, M. (1998, 12 December). *The caring role of schools: Teachers' and children's perspectives*. Paper presented to the Children's Issues National Seminar, Child Wellbeing at School, University of Otago, New Zealand.

Treasury, the. (1987). *Government management: Brief to the In-coming government, Vols 1 and 2*. Wellington, New Zealand: Government Printer.

Tronto, J. (1993). *Moral boundaries: A political argument for an ethic of care*. New York: Routledge.

Tuck, B. & Peddie, R. (1995). Introduction. In R. Peddie & B. Tuck (Eds.), *Setting the standards: The assessment of competence in national qualifications*. Palmerston North, NZ: Dunmore Press.

Waldschmidt, A. (1992). Against selection of human life—people with disabilities oppose genetic counselling. *Issues in Reproductive and Genetic Counselling, 5*, 155–167.

Walford, G. (1993). Self-managing schools, choice and equity. In J. Smyth (Ed.), *A socially critical view of the self-managing school* (pp. 229–244). London: Falmer Press.

White, M. (1999, April 3). Right angles. *Listener*, 28–29.

Witherell, C. & Noddings, N. (1991). Prologue: An invitation to our readers. In C. Witherell & N. Noddings (Eds.), *Stories lives tell: Narrative and dialogue in education*. New York: Teachers College Press.

Woolfe, S. (1996). *Leaning towards infinity: How my mother's apron unfolds into my life*. Sydney: Vintage Books.

Marit Stromstad

7

ACCOUNTING FOR IDEOLOGY AND POLITICS IN THE DEVELOPMENT OF INCLUSIVE PRACTICE IN NORWAY

Readers are advised that my chapter works in tandem with that of my colleague, Kari Nes, who in Chapter 8 provides a more thorough discussion about inclusive schooling practice in Norway. While each chapter stands alone in purpose, the two work well in dialogue with one another to provide the reader with greater insights into the Norwegian context for inclusive schooling.

In this chapter I examine the ideology and policies leading up to the idea of inclusive practice in schools and society in Norway. Neither school nor society is consistently inclusive in Norway, but regarding people with special needs, we have come along way. We have a legal system, which to some extent ensures inclusion in school and society. However, as is often the case with policy, coherence is lacking between the ideology of the official state authorities—the basis for legal changes and the ideology—and the attitudes of the public society in general. People simply do not conform to state ideologies they do not hold as their own—even when this ideology is reflected in laws and provisions. That is, in fact, the nature of ideologies. Since ideology is an ambiguous term, before I advance to Norwegian ideology and policy, I want to explain how the term "ideology" will be employed in this chapter.

Uses of Ideology in This Chapter

It seems that the term "ideology" is sometimes used in a very superficial way. When controversial utterances of an opponent are characterised as ideological it simply means that they are unrealistic or idealistic and not to be taken seriously. Others have a more elaborated understanding of ideology. As long as authors fail to explicitly clarify their use of ideology, I find it difficult to know exactly what is meant. In traditional Marxism, ideology is associated with "false consciousness." If one is described as ideological it implies not only stating a lack of consensus but also suggests that his or her ideas spring from a distorted view of the world. The problem is, however, as Mannheim points out, that ideology is a characteristic not only of the opponent's but also of one's own thought (Mannheim, 1936). Most people take their "reality" and "knowledge" for granted. Further, if you subscribe to the arguments of sociologists, who view reality as a social construction (Berger & Luckmann, 1967), it becomes very difficult to talk about reality as opposed to appearances (Skritc, 1995). Or as Mannheim suggests, "henceforward the problem implicit in the term "ideology"—what is really real?—never disappears from the horizon" (Mannheim, 1936: 64). The term "ideology" employed in this chapter is congruent with Mannheim's general ideology; that is, "when ideology is no longer *falsches Bewusstsein* (false consciousness), but a perspective on life among other perspectives where none of them has priority" (Skjervheim, 1973:63). Citing Mannheim (1936) then, "the general form of the total conception of ideology is being used by the analyst when he has the courage to subject not just the adversary's point of view but all points of view, including his own, to the ideological analysis" (69).

Thus, ideology in this chapter is employed somewhat differently from Ellen Brantlinger (1997) in her critical essay "Using Ideology: Cases of Non-recognition of the Politics of Research and Practice in Special Education." Referring to Althusser (1976), Brantlinger defines "ideology" as a "system of representations (images, myths, ideas) which, in profoundly unconscious ways, mediate one's understanding of the world" (438). When Althusser employs the term "ideology" it implies the false consciousness of Marxist traditions, "an imaginary distortion of the real relations" (Therborn, 1981). To Althusser the opposition is between ideology and science. I find this understanding futile and I break with it in this chapter. I will, however, consent to Althusser's understanding of ideology on two other important points. The first is that ideology is not necessarily a body of ideas or thoughts, but rather is more akin to a social process of addresses or "interpellations" inscribed in material social matrices (Therborn, 1980).

Second, the most important functioning of an ideology is its contribution to the constitution of a person's subjectivity—that is, to a person acting as a particular subject in a particular context. Inspired by Therborn, I will employ a broad definition that is not restricted to forms of illusion or misconception. Thus, the conception of ideology employed here deliberately includes both everyday notions and "experience" and it is one that elaborates intellectual doctrines, both the consciousness of social actors and the institutionalised thought-systems and discourses of a given society (Therborn, 1981:2).

Since ideology operates as a discourse and constitutes a person's subjectivity, any text or utterance can be conceived as ideology, provided the focus is on the way it operates in the formation and transformation of human subjectivity. The formation and transformation of humans by ideology involves both subjection and qualification through three fundamental modes of interpellation: What exists, what is good, and what is possible. Foucault's concept of discourse may express much of the same—what can and what cannot be said, what questions may be asked, who can participate in that discussion, and so forth (Haug & Tøssebro, 1998).

Divergent conceptions of the same world frequently produce ideologies that are continually competing, uniting, and changing. Mannheim (1936) points out that vertical mobility between strata is most important for ideology to change. When a society is internally unstable and its relationship to nature and other societies is disrupted, ideological change is to be expected because these changes constitute the material determination of the ideologies. Though we all think about the world, not all of us engage in theorizing and construction of worldviews (Berger & Luckmann, 1967; Mannheim, 1936). According to Mannheim, there exists in every society an "intelligentsia" whose task is to provide an interpretation of the world for that society (9). In the Norwegian context, this is close to what we call "state ideology," although clearly all interpretations are not to be believed, and not every ideology is generally accepted in totality. Much depends on how the ideology is affirmed by people's everyday experiences and nondiscursive practices. The last point is important to keep in mind when inclusive practice is on the agenda.

Though the ideology of inclusion is held out as a nonclass ideology, we cannot completely exclude the notion of class, because even nonclass ideologies are linked to class. Analysing the ideology and politics concerning inclusive practices in Norway, it is evident that even the nonclass ideology of inclusion has been and still is inscribed within an overall system of social power constituted by conflicting classes of varying degrees of power.

From Thrall to the Nineteenth Century

Today we consider ideologies to be important in the formation of society. My ancestors found it convenient to call upon a god when they needed a justification for the existence of nonprivileged classes and people described in much the same way as a person with special needs:

> Once walked, 'tis said the green ways along,
> mighty and ancient, a god most glorious;
> strong and vigorous, striding Rig.

This poem, "Rigstula," from a collection called *The Poetic Edda,* recounts how the god journeyed among men and visited three different families: one very poor, one well off, and one very rich. Nine months after each visit three boys were born: the slave, the freeman, and the nobleman. The poem thoroughly describes the houses, the food, and the members of each family, and in those details assumptions for values and human worth. According to this legend, Thrall (the slave) failed to receive the approval of his father even though he was the most industrious among the three boys. The poem continues:

> Great-grandmother bore a swarthy boy;
> with water they sprinkled him, called him Thrall.
> Forthwith he grew and well he throve,
> but tough were his hands with wrinkled skin,
> with knuckles knotty and fingers thick;
> his face was ugly, his back was humpy,
> his heels were long.
> Straightaway 'gan he to prove his strength,
> with bast a-binding loads a-making,
> he bore home faggots the livelong day.

The implication here is that Thrall was cognitively disabled, or mentally retarded, as the labels used in Norway would suggest. The reader is expected to know that "thick" and "ugly" serve to mark his limitations, and that even today, cutting firewood in Norway is a task that is often assigned to those with similar cognitive limitations and physical brawn.

The poem continues, and in stark contrast describes Earl, the youngest brother:

> Light were his locks, and fair his cheeks,
> flashing his eyes like a serpent's shone
> to swing the shield, to fit the string,
> to bend the bow, to shaft the arrow,
> to hurl the dart, to shake the spear,
> to ride the horses, to loose the hounds, to draw the sword,
> and to swim the stream.

According to the lore passed down through the generations, Earl was of the class that should not work. The blessings of work were not for him. Keep in mind that Thrall was characterized with physical disabilities and presented in the poem as capable of hard labor given his lack of skills. He is not expected to become emancipated from the poverty of his class. Even the names of Thrall's children are expressive: Brawler, Cowherd, Boor, Lewd, Lustful, Stout, Stumpy, Sluggard, Swarthy, Lout, and Leggy. Again, the implication is that they, too, will perpetuate their father's destiny.

The ancient literature is not explicit regarding the disabled, the chronically ill, and the mentally retarded, but we have reason to believe that those who managed to survive shared a fate similar to Thrall's. For example, a common legend that told of the parents who had their child switched by underground creatures is passed on throughout the generations. According to this tale, in the cradle the parents found their own pretty child replaced by an ugly, screaming creature. Much is made of the punishment and mistreatment suffered by the ugly, screaming creature and the belief that the real parents would come back for their changeling child and return the proper child to its parents. Although many centuries have passed since the Norwegians were forced by sword to give up their ancient gods and folklore and create other explanations for human variation, such origins of difference continue to shape the fate of people who veer from the norm.

With very few exceptions, people with special needs are not visible in Norwegian history until the 19th century. More is known about those who were poor and labeled by early Norwegian law as "inheritance," which meant that their responsibility was placed on the family (Seip, 1984). But as early as the year 1100 a certain societal responsibility is implied as Frostatingsloven (one of the regional laws from early Christian times in Norway) institutionalized the system of "coming on the parish," which meant that those who for various reasons could not provide for themselves lived for a fixed time at one farm before moving to another. Here, the suggestion is that such provision was allocated for reasons other than impoverished circumstances. The group of poor people was divided in two. Help was justified for the old and the weak (and presumably the people with special needs), while those who were able to work received no help. Gradually the same system developed in Norway as in the rest of Europe, although madness was never interned to the degree described by Foucault (1973), as we had our own houses of correction. Of course, the church also helped to various degrees, with all its attendant pressures for conformity to Christian values (see below).

The historian Anne-Lise Seip (1984) provides a thorough description of how social care developed in Norway, in which it is evident that people with special needs are hardly taken into account until the beginning of the 19th century. The problem for the authorities was to discriminate between those who were worthy of help from society and those who were not. Too little is made explicit about the nature of those judgments and the arguments put forth to determine human worth. The 1863 law concerning poor relief states that only the sick, the mentally insane, and orphans had a legal right to any help.

Liberal Ideology: Helping People to Help Themselves

Compulsory Schooling

Education was gradually established in Norway as a consequence of compulsory confirmation (from 1736) that required a certain ability to read. If young people had not learned what the church demanded, they were not confirmed. Valerie Neumann (1988) considers confirmation a "proof of normality to God and men" (83). Confirmation was considered a changeover from child to adult. People who were not confirmed could not get work, which was rather important even for people with special needs as long as there was no system of social security. Children with special needs were not excluded from school, but when considering the methods of teaching and the standard for school equipment, very few disabled children attended school. It is also the case that school was not popular among parents who relied upon their children for their labor; hence many refused to send their children to school. These circumstances were unsatisfactory to both the church and to the politicians, thus school was subsequently made compulsory.

From the Left and the Right

In 1884 both the Left and the Right were constituted as official political parties, with the Left being elected into government that same year. The liberal politicians of the Left believed strongly in societal change through education and enlightenment of the people. Education was to be a right for everyone, and their aim was a uniform school maintained at public expense and open to every child regardless of socioeconomic class or background. Through education people should be helped to help themselves—a view still consistent with liberal ideology (Dahl, 1978).

This ideology may explain why a law concerning the Education for Abnormal Children was passed in 1881. Residential schools for the deaf and blind had been in existence since early in the century. The intention behind the law of 1881 was to make education compulsory for abnormal children because they have every essential qualification to live as conscious, responsible and working men (Neumann, 1988: 34). Education was a means to ensure these individuals would be enabled to help themselves. The aim was to educate them for participation in society and for gainful employment. However, not all "abnormal" children could be helped to help themselves. The aim of the institutions for abnormal children was obviously to make them independent, which for some was not possible. Thus the uniform school was never open to children with mental retardation, though this was repeatedly debated in the Norwegian parliament. The noneducable were either sent home or to institutions for mentally retarded. In the example of the maladjusted children who represented another problem distinct from those labeled mentally retarded, it was philanthropists and charities that provided care for nearly a century.

The Norwegian unitary school was established by law in 1889. It established free, compulsory school open to every child while simultaneously outlining the demands for the exclusion of certain children. Slagstad (1998) claims that the Left project of educating people was a project of creating a uniform normality as well. When parents from different classes were expected to send their children to the same school it was the duty of society to prevent the detrimental influence of mixing the masses. It was argued that "normality must be protected." Strange as it seems, the urge for a more democratic educational system made it necessary to exclude those children whose behavior or ability to learn might hinder the larger social mission. Those children with a demonstrated lack of ability could better be served in the system that was already established to contend with the social "misfits."

When it came to the maladjusted children, two professions had common interests—the jurists and the teachers. Dahl (1978) is of the opinion that this union primarily was brought about by professional interests, and not out of consideration for the children in question. The jurists believed in the criminologist ideology of punishment and upbringing, while the teachers needed to have the maladjusted children out of the classrooms because of their supposed detrimental influence. The two groups did not agree as to what was the best way of handling the children. While the jurists believed in repressive punishment, the teachers' opinion was that the children needed education in terms of understanding and love. The jurists would gradually change their view, and when the Law of Trusteeship was launched in 1896 the pedagogues won. Though the maladjusted children were not admitted to the ordinary schools, special schools were established for this group.

Finally, in the mid- to late 20th century a shift toward professional care began to emerge with force. Dahl (1978) connects this development with the influence of criminology as a positivistic science. It was argued that the maladjusted child should no longer be left to the philanthropists who had "warm hearts but weak heads" (Currie, 1975, cited in Dahl, 1978). This development was in many ways the result of the importation of ideology from more industrialized parts of Europe. The changes paramount in industrial societies also changed the structures of families. Children were increasingly left to themselves, and the professional handling of children was meant to take over where families failed and children were maladjusted. Separate schools approved to educate the maladjusted had two aims—defending the society against the "lawless and dangerous" child and adjusting that child to society.

This brief overview recounts some of the history of the efforts to launch the special school system as a separate and parallel project in Norway, informed by both the Education for Abnormal Children Law of 1881 and the Law of Trusteeship of 1896. For more than 100 years, efforts were undertaken to educate those whose difference excluded them from the ordinary school. However, in 1993 this separate system of schooling ended when calls for the "unitary school" were taken up in response to changing attitudes about ability and disability.

In the example of how ideology came into play, and limited by looking back to an era that is poorly documented relative to people with special needs, I offer the following analysis. Ideologies concerning people with special needs might be presented as nonclass ideologies, but in fact, class structures always influence ideology, and certain class ideologies are predisposed for certain nonclass ideologies. The first of the three ideological interpellations cited above was: What currently exists? The lawmakers of the Left recognized a society marked by poverty, class distinction, and social differences. Their answer to the second interpellation was, This is not right! Their solution, in response to the circumstances, was democratization and increased social mobility through education. However, the prevailing view was that success of this mission depended on the exclusion of those who could not easily be helped to help themselves. Exclusive practice in schools was therefore regarded as good and subsequently well established. Likewise the conservative Right agreed to exclusive practice, although their perspective was shaped by another ideological point of view. They argued that a society that privileged exclusion served to reduce social mobility.

The Ideology of Solidarity: Everybody Has a Right to Necessary Help and Assistance

Writing in 1906, Johan Castberg urged that social justice and solidarity were the "two most powerful forces in our time" (cited in Slagstad, 1998:140). In his view, society must protect the weak and be responsible for the welfare of all its inhabitants. The ideology of laissez-faire was gradually replaced by the ideal of a strong official state the authorities of which were to reform society through legal means. To Castberg, state and society were one in the same. The state expressed the sense of the society on an elevated level, free from the splitting interests of different groups. Though Castberg was never a member of Labor, which was established as a political party in 1887, he was in many ways a precursory ideologist for the course Labor was to choose when they came into power in 1935. Social democracy, which developed under the rule of Labor, was built on the foundation of developing a strong and expansive state. Following World War II, the welfare society was slowly and methodically constructed on the political aims of Labor. In a word, the belief was that every inhabitant should feel safe regarding education, housing, health, and work. Slagstad (1998) suggests that Labor was driven by a normative-ethical motive of justice secured by law and regulations. Modernization through law has been a distinctive feature of the Norwegian system. The ideology of the state, during the years from World War II until well into the 1990s, was synonymous with the ideology of Labor and implemented through legal changes. The development of inclusive practice under the Labor Government can be reflected over three different epochs, which I call here positivistic ideology, normalization ideology, and inclusive ideology.

Positivistic Ideology

In 1948 Paul Lazarsfeld gave his great Oslo lecture "What is Sociology?" At that time, the aim of sociology was to "develop in the end an integrated social science, which can help us to understand and control social affairs" (Slagstad, 1998: 373). In a visit to Oslo, Lazarsfeld had considerable impact on the development of sociology in Norway. For the young social democracies of Scandinavia the positivistic ideas of controlling and planning turned into a wildly embraceable overall ideology. He argued that on the basis of science a new world should be created, one that would perhaps yield "new" human beings as well. The aim was a better and improved society for all through research, planning, and legal change. This view was consistent with the progress of science narrative that was underway in many Western societies.

During this time, the uniform school system was further developed and extended to nine years of compulsory school. School was an important tool for Labor in the realization of a society without class distinctions. It was necessary to employ scientific methods to find the most effective pedagogical ways of teaching (Slagstad, 1998). This point of view reflected the influence of positivist ideology that invaded pedagogy from the United States. In 1956 the labor minister of education urged school reform through the application of science in the fields of psychology, pedagogy, sociology, and economy. New pressures emerged to employ empirical science to test out school reforms and pedagogical methods on the belief that a modern society must reflect these modern knowledge forms (op. cit.; see especially 330–333). Norwegian policy-makers espoused the idea that the good society should be brought about by a "scientifically enlightened rationality" administered by a technocratic governing elite (op. cit., 332).

The social democratic school technocrats viewed improved and repeated testing as the solution to establish a new scientific base for education. Tests were generated to measure intelligence, school preparedness, talents for English, and so on. Testing was justified as a means for educators to choose the optimal methods for teaching the particular child and because the last years of compulsory school required student placement by ability.

Technocratic intervention informed by positivism had bearings on special education and special schools as well. There was a firm belief in the right diagnoses followed by the right treatment. This was evident in the White Paper (St meld nr 42, 1965–1966) concerning the expansion of special schools, which stated that the children with special needs represent a challenge to pedagogy that can best be answered in a pedagogically organized institution in continual cooperation with other professional groups who have insight in the children's problems. Describing and analyzing the function of special education, the document concentrates on three points: (1) the pedagogical diagnosis (2) the pedagogical treatment, and (3) the pedagogical research. In diagnostic work one attempted, through systematic description, to determine the nature of and the reason for the problem so as to obtain a sound basis for treatment. The concept of diagnosis was originally linked to medicine, but has successively served a much broader application in education, particularly for students with special needs. It followed naturally that "the development of an optimal special educational effort will create an increasing demand for an individual guiding diagnosis" (ibid: 36–37). The development of special education as a field of highly trained professionals operating in schools as technocratic pedagogues was but another piece of the progress of science narrative embraced by education.

Education Politicians

Despite the enthusiastic embrace of scientific innovation there remained class distinctions, poverty, and lack of justice in Norwegian society. Labor took over government and developed further the program of the Left politicians: promote education in order to create a more democratic society, reduce class distinctions, and increase national integration. The positivistic approach was also good because it offered the possibility of a correct diagnosis from which an adjusted treatment could be derived. Many good things could be done to benefit the masses! Those once viewed as less worthy members of society—children with special needs—could now, by means of scientific methods, be helped back into society. The conclusion of the White Paper (St meld nr 42, 1965–1966) was to hasten the construction of special schools for an anticipated increase of three times as many pupils. But things were to change rather quickly, and this plan was never realized.

The Ideology of Normalization and Integration

Had I really made a friend without any help from the Norwegian government?[1]

When the White Paper (St meld nr 42, 1965–1966) was discussed in Parliament, the politicians wanted a further discussion of several points. First they wanted a coordination or integration of the Elementary School Law and the Special School Law. They also wanted special education as much as possible connected to the ordinary school as the ideology of normalization spread throughout Norway and other Scandinavian countries concerning the care for functionally disabled. The White Paper urged that an important principle of normalization was to avoid unnecessary dividing lines between functionally disabled and others specific to medical and social treatment, upbringing, education, work, and welfare (Ibid: 8).

Though there were institutions and special schools in Norway it is notable that most people with mental retardation and most children with special needs were not institutionalized. From 1955 onward the municipalities were obliged to provide special education to children who did not profit from teaching in the ordinary school. In 1966, records indicate that some 28,600 students with special needs received special education at their home school while 2,800 attended state special boarding schools. There were also approximately 4,000 students who were educated at different social medical institutions, including institutions for students with mental retardation (St meld nr 88, 1966–1967, 2425). It was this population of individuals that the government now targeted for inclusion. In this way, the welfare state was to be extended to include even those who had previously been among the most segregated and the most excluded in Norway.

In the section that follows I point out several reasons why this change of ideology came about in the mid-1960s. This background will support my later arguments.

A sociological critique of the welfare state project. According to Slagstad (1998) this critique worked to mobilize the inherent ideals of the Norwegian society to dismantle the social realities. He explains that the sociological confrontation between "realities and ideals created a sensibility for those who were not included in the welfare capitalistic system, the marginal, the deviants" (387). It was a critique of the society oriented toward reforms: Those who were not included by the project of modernization should be incorporated through social reform. In sum, this sociology of reformation wanted "more of what was already well developed: The well fare state" (op. cit., 387).

The critique against positivist ideology. In a critique that actually emerged in the late 1950s, it was suggested that science as a secularized ideology expanded at the cost of religion as an integrative ideology. Among the foremost critiques were those of philosophers Arne Næss and Hans Skjervheim. The latter took special interest in education, where his goal was to reestablish pedagogic concerns linked to ethics rather than to psychometrics.

The idea of normalization. With its origins in Denmark (Bank-Mikkelsen), Sweden (Nirje), and the United States (Wolfensberger), Norway interpreted normalization primarily through the work of Nirje in the Swedish context. Services and opportunities for people with mental retardation were now to be a part of the ordinary service for all Norwegian inhabitants. Thus, each individual should have his or her own house or flat, participate in work and leisure activities like others, and have access to the ordinary health and social services insured to all.

Ending centralization. At the end of the '60s there was general reaction in Norway against centralization and great enthusiasm in the promotion of decentralization. It was held throughout Norway that problems should be solved locally. Decisions were to be taken as close as possible to the person or institution in question for local resolution.

Disregard for institutions. A growing number of parents and professionals expressed doubts as to the suitability of institutions to provide the necessary context for human growth and development. The then-nascent deinstitutionalization movement underway in other Western countries prompted the media in Norway to document inhumane treatment of residents by institutions.

Readiness. The Norwegian welfare state was well developed and ready to include groups that had so far been excluded. These events mixed with the opportunity to enact beliefs in promotion of a new state ideology.

A new state ideology. The new state ideology was first applied to individuals with mental retardation, outlined in a White Paper (St.meld, nr. 88, 1974–1975) that recommended more decentralized and integrated care with more emphasis given to local service provision. The fundamental elements of care included housing, education or occupation, and leisure activities, none of which were sufficient when institutions predominated the service system. The White Paper declared that all societies have discriminated against deviant minorities who failed to live up to the expectations one might have for "good members of society" (78). However, it was now of greater interest to a society that as many of its inhabitants as possible be integrated, as this was deemed a condition for its survival. Integration was viewed as a process of living together where the partners are individuals, groups, and society, and whereby considering one another as different as well as being different must be possible "without suppression, exploitation or submission being the consequence" (ibid).

Over time the terms integration and normalization have been used with widely different meanings in widely different documents. Normalization described the process of making ordinary service in local communities accessible to mentally retarded persons, while the aim of integration was belonging and participation in society and school. In the 1970s integration was defined in policy documents as: (1) being part of a social collectivity (2) participation in the benefits of a community, and (3) shared responsibility and obligations (KUD, 1979). The same document urged that school exerts a strong influence on the attitudes children develop and as such serves as the base for their general outlook on their fellow beings and social purposes. If ideals such as "helpfulness, solidarity, understanding and tolerance" are to be realized, they must be grounded and nourished in home and school (38). Therefore school is regarded to be an important factor when the "aim is to create a society which is kindly disposed towards people with handicap" (ibid). In this document it is evident that the question now is not only the best method for education; just as important are the possibilities for people with special needs to belong and feel accepted as valued members of society.

This brief overview describes how, in 1975, the Elementary School Law and the Special School Law merged to ensure that every Norwegian school was open to every student. These laws signaled the end of a "unilaterally knowledge-based school [replaced by] a social-pedagogical institution" (Haug and Tøssebro, 1998: 16). However, that is not to suggest that state special schools disappeared. They did not fully cease operations until 1991. From that point on the municipalities became fully responsible for those inhabitants with mental retardation who still resided there. Some of those people returned home even though some 40 years lapsed since their institutionalization. I do not want to give the impression that these changes were made in the absence of struggle. We had reached a point where Norwegians did not automatically comply with state ideology. In the section that follows I outline reasons for the considerable resistance that followed these changes.

The Climate for Change

Social democracy has so far improved the lives of ordinary people—Norway has better social welfare than any other industrialized state, better health service, more leisure time, and better options for housing. This culture of improved care options also translated into improved living conditions, which ensured that the elderly were placed in homes for the aged and the young were served in pedagogically progressive kindergarten programs. Throughout society, credentialed professionals were entrusted with the power to provide solutions to our problems. The state ideology remained a social democracy despite the creation of a new liberal party established in the early '70s.

Increasingly, the costs associated with reform became a more focused concern as local authorities assumed increased responsibility transferred from the state to the local community. But in the process, local authorities failed to receive the money needed to support reform. Innumerable calculations and public discussions about the costs accompanied reform proposals. As a consequence the focus privileged the fiscal arena rather than the social intentions associated with the reform.

Looking back at the campaign for reform concerning disabled people, most educators would agree that it was far from a success. In fact, it would be no stretch of the truth to suggest that perhaps the effects of this campaign were even contrary to its aim. For example, the Department of Social Affairs distributed information booklets intended to promote the inclusion and integration of disabled persons. The flyers depicted a person with mental retardation who peered happily out of the window of his small new house while an eight-story brick institution towered in ominous threat in the background. The intended message of this portrayal was confusing and contrary. Over and over again it was argued that people with mental retardation are just like other people, or so the flyer informed us. Now, here was our new neighbor and we were urged to welcome him into our community. I regret to admit that to a high degree, many Norwegian communities failed to take up this aspect of reform. They knew from experience that there were substantial differences between themselves and their new neighbors and that these differences were not brought into the open for discussion. The similarities were highlighted, which was right, of course, but the obvious differences were dismissed as if none existed. According to the state ideology there were no differences and that was that! But any ideology operates within a matrix of affirmations and sanctions: it should come as no surprise that communities withdrew support in uncertainty and fear of the unknown. In this case state ideology was partly rejected as not coherent with prior experience. Regardless of whether that experience was inherited through powerful discourses and ideological frameworks discussed by others in this book (see especially the chapters by Allan, Slee, and Heshusius), the power of these beliefs prevailed.

It bears mentioning that the misapplied logic of this campaign to promote inclusion has actually been replicated in public schools, suggesting similar sabotage of our stated purposes. Eight years after the reform was launched there is no general agreement as to the outcome. For some individuals the situation is better, for some worse. Most of the approximately 5,500 people who left the institutions, at a minimum, enjoy better living conditions in their own homes as compared to life in the institution. But for the most part, they experience increased loneliness and isolation with only paid friendships supported by the state. In 1995 research sponsored by the Social and Health Department examined current living conditions and habits of people with handicaps (Sosial-og helsedepartementet, 1998). Researchers reported a decrease in social engagement between the years 1991 to 1995. While 15% of people with handicaps reported to have no intimate friend in 1991, the number had grown to 23% in 1995. Currently 33% reported that they have no leisure activities and the number of disabled people attending sporting events, concerts, and other public exhibitions has also decreased. Despite the official claims that ours is an educated and open society, there is every reason to ask why the data does not support the state ideology.

As I mentioned in my introduction, my colleague, Kari Nes, provides a closer examination of the schools in her Chapter 8. I want to mention briefly that during the 1980s the state special schools began to show a decline in enrollment. In 1989 there were 1,500 students in special schools; of that number, 500 students were in state schools (Skårbrevik, cited in Stangvik, 1998). The National Curriculum (KUF 1987) required that all children be taught in the class where they naturally belonged, based on where they lived. Moreover, every child had the right to receive adapted education (i.e., teaching should meet the individual child's abilities and interests). In 1991 Norway moved to restructure special education, a move that prompted the dismantling of many special schools, while others were transformed to national or regional competence centers. Today the new National Curriculum of 1997 states that public school shall be inclusive and that children with special needs should be taught in the framework of the class to which they naturally belong.

Attempting to trace what conditions may have existed so that present-day politicians might endorse this ideology, one analysis suggests justice and entitlement to equality. Disabled people are now viewed as worthy of the same rights as everyone else. If for no other reason, our wealth enabled us to ensure those rights to provision. Rights for the disabled were won at the level of policy and law, but what remains to be seen is how their actual lives will be transformed as a consequence.

The Ideology of Diversity

One might contend that in Norway the ideology of inclusion or diversity has been well underway for years under the guise of various terminology (Nes & Strømstad, 1999). As noted above, the term "adapted education" has been used as the ideological base for school development since the Left fought for the free, unitary school in the last part of the 20th century. The unitary school system has been extended to successively cover more groups of children. But this has, to a certain degree, been the result of a state ideology. As long as the aim was general enlightenment and democratization there was a general willingness to accept this ideology. Of course there have always been exceptions, but generally speaking the uniform school was upheld as important to Norwegians.

Since 1999 we have no institutions for mentally disabled people and no state special school where children can receive separate education (except for the deaf, who endorse this practice). Children are generally expected to be educated in the local school for their catchment area that is determined locally. Nes follows in Chapter 8 with a closer look into school practice, where it becomes more apparent that the perception of acceptance and inclusion is far from standard practice. The group of children who receive extra resources for education according to individually based resolution has grown from the expected 1.5% to 6%. Moreover, 10 % of pupils receive special education, and the school allocates 25–30% of the total time resources for special education (Haug & Tøssebro, 1998).

Conclusion: Do We Really Want Diversity?

Solidarity was the ideology of the social democracy. Solidarity was the glue that held community together. The aim was not to redistribute, but to develop new institutional arrangements in order to secure the rights of every inhabitant. The assumption was never that everybody should have the same, but most would agree that everybody should feel safe. In many ways social democracy in Norway has solved the problems it aimed to accomplish. Though the rich have grown richer and the poor have grown poorer, by the end of the 1960s most people had reason to feel a certain degree of safety relative to education, health, housing, and work.

It is obvious that since that time, although these problems were purportedly solved, new problems evolved for which the social democratic governments had no ideology and no preparedness. The ideology of one school for all is very much based upon an investment in solidarity and a firm belief in the worthiness of fellowship and community-based solutions. And yet, these ideals are threatened in Norway today. People have more money and want even more. Liberal ideology is advancing and the Liberal Party is steadily growing. In many ways Norway has developed into a country where people believe in private solutions. We are fast becoming a people completely taken up with private consumption. For the first time in the history of the public school system, grants to private schools have grown proportionally more than grants to public schools on the state budget. We still have fewer than 200, but the number is increasing.

Clearly, the face of solidarity is changing. We try to explain the changes with words like "market" and "globalization," as we have joined the European Union (EU) and our economy is more and more based on market demands. But when such values prevail, what is the market value of people with special needs? I would argue that Norway has come so far because solidarity was once the overarching state ideology. Indeed, solidarity is essential in the struggle to embrace the ideology of inclusion, but solidarity is unfortunately in decline in a society driven by market forces. My interpretation of the present circumstances in Norway may sound grim, but I want to suggest that while Thrall had no rights and no legal support in his lifetime, he might enjoy both today. While much remains to be done, at the moment we have both to protect what has been gained and to continue the fight for a more inclusive society.

Note

1. Elling is one of two characters in a film that captures his life following his release from an institution in Norway. The director, Petter Naess (Elling, 2001) succeeds by making seemingly uncommon events that would otherwise prompt professional intervention as just another part of everyday life.

References

Alveberg, D. (Producer), & Naess, P. (Director). (2001). *Elling*. [Film]. International distribution. First Look Distributors, Los Angeles, CA.

Berger, P. L., & Luckmann, T. (1967). *The Social Construction of Reality*. New York: Doubleday Books.

Brantlinger, Ellen (1997). Using Ideology: Cases of Nonrecognition of the Politics of Research and Practice in Special Education. *Review of Educational Research, 67*(4), 425–459.

Clark, Catherine, Alan Dyson, & Alan Millward (1995). *Towards Inclusive Schools*, London: David Fulton Publishers.

Dahl, Tove Stang (1978). Barnevern og samfunnsvern. (Protection of Children and Society) Oslo: UniPax.

Foucault, Michel (1973). Galskapens historie, Folie et déraison (Discipline and Punish), Oslo: Gyldendal Norsk Forlag

Gunnar Stangvik, Ann Elise Rønbeck og Ole Simonsen (1998). Kvalitet i spesialpedagogisk arbeid, HiF-forskning; 1998:10. (Quality in Special Education, Norway: Finnmark College)

Haug, Peder, Jan Tøssebro (1998). *Theoretical Perspectives on Special Education*, Oslo: Hoyskoleforlaget.

KUD (1979). Innstilling om lovregler for spesialundervisning (Monitoring Special Education Laws). Oslo: Ministry of Education and Church Affairs.

KUF (1987). National Curriculum, Oslo: Ministry of Education, Research and Church Affairs. Oslo: Ministry of Education and Church Affairs.

KUF (1996). Core Curriculum for Primary, Secondary and Adult Education in Norway. Oslo: Ministry of Education and Church Affairs.

Mannheim, Karl (1936). *Idelology & Utopia*. London: Routledge & Kegan Paul, Ltd.

Mordal, Kari Nes & Marit Strømstad (1997). Adapted education for all. In T. Booth & M. Ainscow, *From Them to Us*. London: Routledge.

Nes, Kari & Marit Strømstad (1999). Tilpasset opplæring i Stange, Rapport nr. 20, Norway: Høgskolen i Hedmark. (Adapted Education in Stange. Report nr. 20, Hedmark College).

Neumann, Valerie (1988). Fattig, forsømt, tungnem, Oslo, Statens Spesiallærerhøgskole. (Poor, neglected and slow). Oslo: Ministry of Education and Church Affairs.

Nilsen, Sven (1993). *Undervisningstilpasning i grunnskolen*, University of Oslo, Norway. (Adapation of Education in Compulsory School).

Nordahl, Thomas (1998). Atferdsproblemer i skolen (Behavior Problems in Schools). Norway: Spesialpedagogikk, nr. 5.Oslo: Ministry of Education and Church Affairs.

Seip, Anne-Lise (1984) Sosialhjelpstaten blir til (The Origin of the Welfare State). Oslo: Gyldendal Norsk Forlag.

Skjervheim, Hans (1973). Ideologianalyse, didaktikk, sosiologi (Analysis of ideology, didactics and sosiology). Oslo: PaxTeori.

Skrtic, Thomas M. (1991). The Special Education Paradox: Equity as the Way to Exellence. *Harvard Educational Review, 61*(2). 148–206.

Skrtic, Thomas M. (1995). *Disability and Democracy*. New York: Teachers College Press.

Slagstad (1998): De nasjonale strateger, Oslo: Pax Forlag A/S. (The National Strategists).

Sosial-og helsedepartementet (1998). Om handlingsplan for funksjonshemma. Oslo: Ministry of Health and Social Affairs. (People with Disabilities, A Report on Care and Participation).

St meld nr 42 (1965–1966). Om utbygging av spesialskolene, Oslo: Ministry of Education, Research and Social Affairs. (The Development of Special Schools, Ministry of Education White Paper).

St meld nr 88 (1974–1975). Omsorgen for psykisk utviklingshemmede, Oslo: Department of Education, Research and Social Affairs. (Care for People with Mental Retardation, Ministry of Education White Paper).

St meld 88 (1966–1967, 24–25). Om utviklingen av omsorgen for funksjonshemmede i samfunnet, Oslo: Department of Education, Research and Church Affairs. (People with Disabilities in the Community, Ministry of Education White Paper).

Therborn, Göran (1981). *The Ideology of Power and the Power of Ideology*. London: New Left Books/Zenit.

8

Kari Nes

QUALITY VERSUS EQUALITY? INCLUSION POLITICS IN NORWAY AT CENTURY'S END

In this chapter I present central aspects of inclusion in the Norwegian school system, with a focus on special education and the education of language minority students. I discuss current issues in the development of the Scandinavian welfare state ideology in relation to "the inclusive school" and the issue of quality versus equality. Similar to others whose work appears in this book, I show the multiplicity of ideologies that come to bear on inclusion in the Norwegian school system.

I begin with a quote that compares the good state with a good "people's home":

> The good home knows no priviliged or neglected people, no favourites and no step-children. The strong do not suppress and plunder the weak. In the good home, there is equality, care, collaboration, support. (Gustavsson, 1999:92)

This well-known image of the welfare state in Scandinavia was first articulated in the 1920s by the leader of the Swedish Social-Democratic Party. It is suggested that the state, in much the same way as the "good home," should provide security for its members in equal measure, for the strong and the weak alike. Health care and education should be accessible for all (i.e., free), and if necessary, basic living costs should be covered by the state. Over time, this generally accepted belief has influenced the way Norwegians approach our work as educators, particularly in this era of inclusion and the development of the unitary school.

The Scandinavian Welfare State Ideology[1] and the Unitary School

In the "people's home" there are no privileged or neglected people and basic needs are assumed to be provided. This image of the good state is over 80 years old and the Scandinavian countries enjoy a reputation for a high degree of social equality and welfare for all. By Scandinavia I here refer to the five Nordic countries—Denmark, Sweden, Norway, Finland, and Iceland—not only to the Scandinavian peninsula. These countries share much of their history. With the exception of Finland, we speak languages that stem from Old Norse; we practice Lutheranism in a state church system; this is the dominant religion, with more than 90% of the population belonging to this Protestant sect. The five countries are small and politically stable, and with the exception of Denmark, there remain vast areas that are scarcely populated. The labour movement has been strong in Scandinavian countries, and social-democratic governments have dominated the postwar period. On the whole, homogeneity, both socially and culturally, remain the undisputed norm. Only in the most recent years has immigration from third world countries increased and thereby challenged our collective sense of a shared identity, threatening to divide otherwise homogeneous communities.

Educational policies in Scandinavia have been strategically used to ensure social justice. Education became comprehensive early on and the content was common and compulsory for all. Ours has been a centralist school system intended to secure equality and justice characterized by "the unitary school" distinguished by the idea that education, in principle, remain free at all levels. Universities demand no fees and students who take up residence receive state loans and grants for living expenses. Higher education has been free for a long time, and accessible for all, although politically the emphasis on a "unitary system" has focused on primary (grades 1 to 7) and lower secondary schools (grades 8 to 10). It also bears mentioning that grades 1 to 10 are compulsory in Norway, which is slightly stricter than the requirements in Sweden and Denmark, where grades 1 to 9 are compulsory (see Eide, in Lauglo, 1998). Still, hardly any parental choice of schools occurs, as students age 6 to 16 in principle should attend the local public (state) school and not other schools. Pedagogically progressivist ideas like project work have been integrated in the common curriculum for years, suggesting an approach that is more developmentally sequenced and thus inclusive by design. Telhaug (1994) outlines four dimensions of the unitary school:

1. *The resources dimension.* There must be existing financing to support equality and justice between the municipalities and the schools in order to ensure equality of quality.
2. *The social dimension.* All students should be educated together in heterogeneous groups.
3. *The cultural dimension.* Students are not supposed to just meet one another; they are also expected to share the experiences of a common culture and a common knowledge base.

4. *The inequality dimension*. The concept of equality that is used is one that respects diversity. This means that some students will have to have more support
than others in order to receive equitable and suitably adapted education.

The Norwegian School System Today

In Norway some 98% of the children and teenagers[2] of compulsory school age go
to public schools (state schools) in the catchment area where they reside. A school
cannot deny the enrollment of any child from their catchment area, nor can students be expelled for more than three days. During the mid-1990s all educational
levels have undergone quite extensive educational reforms. For example, in 1997
the school starting age was lowered from 7 to 6, thereby extending compulsory
schooling from 9 to 10 years. For the last couple of decades there has been no
streaming or permanent grouping of students according to ability (up to age 16).
In an everyday context, boys and girls are educated together in the same class and
they participate equally in sports. Education within these guidelines is to be
"equitable and suitably adapted to all" according to the national curriculum, "irrespective of ethnic background, sex, social class, ability/disability" (KUF, 1997a).
Given this background, how is student diversity addressed in school? Let us take a
look at two groups of students for whom diversity is a descriptor: those found to
have special educational needs (SEN), and those students from an ethnic minority background.

Exclusion by Institutional Decree

In this small country (the population is now 4.2 million) there has never been a
large proportion of students in special schools, not more than about 1%. In 1996
0.6% of the students of compulsory school age received segregated education in
special schools; in 1980 the figure was 0.8% (Haug, 1998). Beginning in 1975 education policy called for the integration of *all students* "if possible." No careful
record was made of how schools made such determinations; however, separate
placement by categorisation of students with SEN was omitted. Even so, a parallel
school system for various categories of disabled pupils continued to exist until the
beginning of the 1990s. Specialty services was emphasized, rather than exclusion.
During this same era special schools and the institutions for the mentally handicapped closed down. Only the deaf community advocated to keep their state special schools, and they still remain in operation. In the school reform of 1997 the
deaf community received status as a language minority group, rather than a disability group as far as schooling is concerned. This coincided with other groups
that are bound by a national identity and a distinct language. National curriculum
secures elementary education in the mother tongue for language minorities, be it
sign language or Urdu, and in Norwegian as a second language for those who are

considered to need it. An option in lower secondary is a second foreign language (all have English) or the native language for students with another first language (KUF, 1997a).

Provision for Learning Needs Students

For students seen to be in need of special education, the local authorities and local schools now assumed full responsibility, as was slowly becoming the case for the SEN students. Education was to be individually adapted according to each student's special needs and strengths, and separate special schools were turned into competence centers that were supposed to assist the local level. Relative to the availability of local competence, across the general population, some 16% of the teachers in local schools have further studies in special education. Each municipality has a special staff which supplies special educational and psychological services to the schools. Based on the assessment from local or distant experts, every student with special needs is to receive a plan for their individual special education programme (IEP) in their own school, and extra resources are to be allocated to carry out the programme. Slightly more than 6% of the students fall into this group (KUF, 1998a), far more than originally expected (Haug 1998). Two thirds of them are boys. About another 4% receive some sort of extra support without an individual assessment and financial resource (Haug, op. cit.). This means that roughly 10% receive special education, in the broadest sense of the term. However, the term "special education" is restricted in its use, and in fact refers only to the 6% with individual "statements."

The organisational arrangement for teaching "special education" students varies from a few support lessons in or out of class, individually or in groups, to an almost complete separate and parallell system within the school. There are even examples of small separate units for the "special" pupils in or outside the school area that have developed (or continued as previously established), all in a country where special schools do not "officially" exist. The extent of this kind of "internal segregation" is difficult to assess since it is decided and administered locally and since there is little agreement on what to count. But are we, in fact, as Booth (1998) asks, witnessing a relocation of a parallel system in Norway?

Provision for Minority Students

Another group of students who often require specially adapted learning programmes in order to fully develop their learning potential are students from ethnic minorities, defined as "language minority." To date, their number has been small in Norway (6% of all students in 1997–1998), but this population is rapidly increasing and is now comparable to the number of students with SEN statements.[3] Increasingly, many in education have wondered what educational "fate" these children will experience over the course of their school years. In some respects the organization of their schooling is similar to the organization of special education—included or excluded across various dimensons determined by local authority. Only recently has integration become the official aim for language minorities joining in a shared campaign established for disabled students since the 1970s. According to the official language (KUF, 1997), integration is the preferred goal rather than assimilation as integration signals that the minority culture will be preserved (as long as it is within Norwegian law). The principle of the catchment area applies and only special reasons and formal application to the local education authorities may qualify a language minority child to enroll at another school. It holds as well that similar to some students with disabilities, language minority students are assigned to schools other than their neighborhood schools in order to interact with other language minority learners and to participate in larger groups for native language lessons, et cetera. This tactic, although clearly motivated by bureaucratic convenience, is recast into the language of the recipients' best interests and thus giving the appearance of privileging student needs (Skrtic, 1991). The minority student, like the SEN student, often spends several hours each day out of class attending group lessons in Norwegian as a second language or lessons in their own language. They line up to leave and return like visitors to the classroom which is never fully perceived as their homeroom.

Further, students who identify as Sami have recently won educational rights as a consequence of a long history of cultural and language discrimination. The indigenous Sami (the indigenous population native to Norway) pupils now have particular rights clearly established by law, in addition to their own national curriculum. They stand to be far better served educationally in their own language, at least on the level of policy formulation. Their access to these rights has been hard won and worthy of celebration by all. However, the distinction between indigenous populations, immigrant populations, and students with disabilities relative to the right to educational provision is clearly too complex to fuse together. All becomes muddled when we revisit the notion of a "good home" discussed earlier in this chapter.

Recent Research with Reference to Inclusion

Special Education Research

In Norway, research on inclusion is not focused exclusively on special education research. However, some aspects of current Norwegian special educational research has implications for all aspects of educational inclusion. Here I draw upon the recently completed five-year national research programme entitled the Development of Knowledge and Initiatives in Special Education (Haug et al., 1999). Given the breadth of this report, I will restrict my discussion to compulsory school-age findings and do not pretend to represent the full width of the programme. The report was appropriately titled *The Janus-face of Special Education*, one of the two-faced aspects reported is when so-called integrated students are withdrawn from class for support lessons designed for their benefit. However, when their removal results in conditions for the remaining students and their teacher that makes life easier for *them,* one is left to question who really benefits from this model. In fact, even when the majority of SEN students are in mainstream schools, pull-out programs still prove to be common. The use of individual lessons was reported to be 26% in 1990, about the same as it was ten years earlier. What has changed during those years is the use of a "two-teacher-system" in classrooms, which increased from 26% in 1980 to 43% in 1990 (Dalen and Skårbrevik, 1999). The rest of the individually adapted programmess consist of small group lessons delivered in settings outside of class. In total, students with documented "needs" tend to stay in class more time than before, but even so, differentiation of the teaching programme in class is poor, according to the research findings. The standard is set for "all" to achieve equally despite the initial reliance upon developmentally appropriate practice in the early years.

Some students are out of class most of the time. A majority of mentally disabled students spend less than five hours per week in their regular education classroom (Tøssebro, 1999). There is evidence that this kind of segregation is more widespread in densely populated areas (Tøssebro, 1997), and further, according to Pijl (1999), segregation in general is fairly low in scarcely populated areas, and increases with population density. Research confirms the impression of great geographical variations due both to numbers of defined SEN students and to the ways in which their teaching programme is organized, although patterns are mixed and not easy to explain (Dalen and Skårbrevik, op. cit.). Research into the social interactions between disabled and nondisabled students suggests that while they are not harassed, they report feelings of loneliness and isolation (Dalen, 1999). Proximity does not necessarily lead to good relationships between people with and without disabilities (Söder, 1997).

Models of Inclusion

Researchers who visited schools in Norway to determine what kinds of educational programmes were available for particular students often heard: "She gets 9 hours. He gets 7 hours" (Fylling 1999). Rather than describe the content covered in the programme, it was distinguished by the number of extra hours allocated to the student. This practice is similar to that described in the final chapter by Linda Ware who describes the ratios attributed to educational intervention (see Chapter 11). Both instances suggest the calculus of $[E = C + AR]$ Slee (1995) used to characterize educational intervention for disabled students. That is,

> Integration is thus framed within a Cartesian logic that forges disability as a problem for calculus rather than as a lateral testing of power and unequal social relations in need of reconstruction. "Disabled children have special needs, therefore they require expert special educators and additional resources to provide special programes albeit

at a change of address." The actuarialists are called in to determine levels of disability, levels of need and levels of resourcing. Equity equals child plus additional resources [E = C + AR]. (67)

In our own ethnographic studies we have observed how children are taken out of class for their special education lesson, regardless of what is going on in class at the time: The student was granted the "x" hours weekly support, and for bureacratic convenience this is the only time the special teacher can give it (Mordal and Strømstad 1998). One is left to wonder, *Is the emphasis on rights to special education so strong that educational content and quality comes second?* Actually, acording to Gunnar Stangvik, "yes" this is the rule of "The Royal Norwegian Special Education" (Stangvik 1998). Individual educational plans may be effective means for high quality in special education, as shown in one study (KUF, 1998a), but Ogden (1999) suggests that teachers—and authorities—were sometimes more concerned about doing the paperwork correctly than doing the teaching well. Are we getting a system where formalities established to secure equality are actually more important than the quality of the content? What have we compromised by underlining the number of special lessons and stressing the way that the IEP is written? Interestingly, when most special schools closed down about 1990 many were renamed "competence centers" to assist local schools with their "SEN" students. When the function of these centers has been evaluated, the main finding is that there is no relationship between the quality of special education as judged by teachers and parents and the services given by the competence centers (Skårbrevik, 1996). Again, questions surface that are not easily answered: Are the systems established in the name of equality failing to meet basic demands of quality? Has the interpretation of equality been reduced to mere formalities?

There are also reports in the national research program concerning education for dyslexia, blindness, and other diagnostic groups; however, given the constraints of space, this will not be addressed here. The leader of the national research program, Peder Haug (1999), admits that the research within this program is mainly a supplement to the existing individually orientated knowledge base, and that much is still lacking in the example of special educational research. Haug has repeatedly noted that surprisingly few projects focus on classroom activities. As well, historical and theoretical investigations and longitudinal studies are scarce. As a consequence, the dominating Norwegian special education research tradition—within or without the national program—remains firmly grounded in the psycho-medical paradigm (Clark et al., 1995).

Language Minority Research

Language minority students have won the right to receive equitable and suitably adapted education in their primary language. More specifically, these students have the right to be taught *in* their native language during the first four years at school or as a new arrival to Norway. This includes the right to be taught *in* the native language for individual subject matter. However, the right to be taught in Norwegian as a *second language,* while specific, is not as explicitly expressed by law as the right to special education. For example, decisions about educational programs for minority students cannot be legally appealed, in contrast to decisions about special education. Only about half of the students are offered lessons in their mother tongue, and about three quarters of the students in question are offered Norwegian as a second language (Aasen and Mønness, 1998). Still, there are accounts of minority students denied access to lessons in Norwegian as a first language, even if they are capable of joining them (Ali 1997). Municipalities vary greatly as to the amount of specially adapted lessons for minority students. For example, Oslo, with the largest school-age population in Norway,[4] does not give much priority to native-language lesssons. On average, the extra financial resources spent on a language minority student is less than a tenth of what is spent on a SEN student (Aasen and Mønness, 1998; Stangvik, 1998). When we turn to the issue of quality versus equality, it seems that adapted educational programmes meant to ensure equitable education are only on occasion followed up for language minority students.

It comes as no surprise that in Norway as well as in other countries, school attainments of students from a minority background are consistently lower when compared to the majority students' results. In one Norwegian study, for instance, 27% of the pupils from language minorities were judged by teachers to have attained very little academic growth in the subjects of natural and social science (Özerk 1992). Such judgment was not ascribed to any native Norwegian student. In a related study, final exam results in Norwegian and mathematics were below average and differences within the group were broad (Engen, Kulbrandstad, and Sand 1996). Although some language groups do better than native Norwegian speakers, these researchers found that students living in the immigrant communities of inner Oslo have average lower attainments than the general population of minority students. Evidence of this kind prompts questions about the quality of lessons provided to language minority students, and signals the need for justifiable standards to be upheld.

Inclusion and the Welfare State Today: Quality versus Equality

Like many readers, I am familiar with the perception that many Norwegians and other Scandinavians hold—that we are world champions of equality and justice. This is certainly the case in the example of the integration of disability in school and society, as Scandinavian countries have a history of democracy, equality of opportunity, and social welfare. The concept of schooling designed for social justice assumes the school will be meaningful for all. Because of this, the size of schools is often kept small, with a 1:10 teacher-pupil ratio (Lauglo, 1998).[5] For nearly a quarter of a century we have had legislation to promote integration; yet many students from a minority background, and those with disabilities, actually participate in a fraction of ordinary school life. How is it that teachers in the

1990s could still respond to researchers' questions in the following way when questioned about students who leave their classrooms for special instruction:

Where is Daniel?
Oh, he is out of class right now. He is integrated, you see . . . but he will come back later.

Such a scenario is so common in Norwegian schools that I turn my attention to two aspects of the current welfare state and suggest possible consequences in light of the quality-equality dimension. My emphasis will focus on people with disabilities.

The Expansion of Traditional Welfare State Ideology

As a result of the weight placed on formal structures and state centralism, the state service systems, like health and education and the tax system, expand in extent and in power. According to Holst (1999), this expansion works as follows:

> These institutions run peoples' lives. They determine the framework of how and where people live. They manage the culture. They regulate the extent to which one may love one's neighbour, without this activity being regarded as salaried work, subject to taxes and dues. The institutions look after people who become social cases, fall ill or simply give up. The institutions manage, people are managed. The institutions of the state help, the citizens receive help. (185)

The welfare state regulates the relationship between state and individual. Where the relation between society and disabled people is concerned, *normalisation* has been a principle for this regulation in many Western countries for the last 20 years or so. Normalisation builds upon the same ideas of equality and justice as the welfare state. The principle mainly applies at the system level, including the legal level, the socioeconomic level, and so forth, with all systems of society assumed to serve all its members (Stangvik 1994). *Farewell to Special Care* (Johnsen, 1982) is a Norwegian book that captures the spirit of the term "normalisation," but it also holds up an individual aspect as well (Stangvik 1994). Such is our history and so must be our culture. But in recent years, normalisation has been challenged with the question, To what normal or ordinary life were people to be normalised? In my own research with disabled people who had recently moved from state institutions to residential flats, I noted that the style of furniture and curtains in the homes of disabled people that I visited was almost identical in all the flats. Even if the residents' family background differed a lot, such differences were not reflected in the choice of sofas or textiles in their homes. What *was* revealed was the taste of the professionals helping them. This raises the question, Is normalisation about fitting into certain prescribed average ways of life, whether in the example of home decoration or daily routines? The hidden message easily becomes, "They know what is best for me, they know what the good life is about; why should I bother to try to find out for myself what I want?" (cf. Holst, op. cit.). The management logic assumed the ability to account for and to plan, control and regulate the economy to the smallest detail. Such decisions were made by highly qualified professionals assumed to know, as a consequence of specialized training, that which was in the best interest of the recipients. Further,

> This management logic has the following characteristics: central planning and regulation; professionally correct decisions; the production of uniform and efficient services, financed by taxes; case orientation, reflecting a specialist-client relationship, between the professional worker and the public. (Bergsöe and Brydensholt, 1986, quoted in Holst, 1999:185)

The "normal" and expected formula for normalisation at the personal level is: low degree of disability = high degree of normalisation, and the reverse. Thus, if the handicap is substantial, the chance of a life similar to the life of an imagined norm will be smaller than if the handicap is a minor one. We have seen from our own research material and from the findings in the national research programme that this is not necessarily so; other factors seem to be equally important. In order to benefit from services meant to increase one's level of normalisation, one must first be perceived as "abnormal." To attain a higher degree of normalisation, one has to have been marked as deviant and falling short of normality in the first place (Nes, 1999). Would it be a stretch of the imagination to hold that an inclusive society implies that diversity is normal and that nobody need then be defined as abnormal? Might then inclusion be another way of thinking, and further that this logic suggest that normalisation is incompatible with inclusive ideology?

A Shift in the Welfare State Ideology

Tjeldvoll (1998) edited a book called *Education and the Scandinavian Welfare State in the Year 2000,* in which he finds that there is an ongoing shift away from considerable political concensus on solidarity and equity. He is primarily concerned about schooling, but his fears are evident in all branches of society. For example, during the 1990s the market absorbed historically public-held interests such as telephone and electricity provision—such interests are now privatized. Income differences increased during this same period in Norway after having diminished during the previous few decades.[6] A more "rugged individualism [emerged] and less concern for collective values and interests are observed in Scandinavia," Tjeldvoll claims (xiii). And further, Norway, once

> characterized by equality of access and financing, by progressive pedagogy and by being almost one hundred percent public [interest], may become more like its European neighbors, more organizationally differentiated by abandoning the principle of comprehensive schooling and more quality oriented in all subjects, be they vocational or academic. Put differently, the progressive in general social policies may be facing an end. (xv)

Quality and knowledge, competence and creativity are favourite claims reflected in the aims of school policy documents during the mid-1990s in Scandinavian countries. At the same time the need for accountability and evaluation is also emphasised, as if no contradiction exists. Not surprisingly we now find that the number of private schools is slowly increasing. Slagstad (1998) argues that the 1980s Thatcher version of "management by objectives"—an agenda adapted from business and public enterprises into schools—was adopted by the social-democratic leadership in Norway. And yet, at the same time the rhetoric of equal access and "suitably adapted education for all" is maintained. There must be "quality in equality," the Norwegian government espoused in 1994—*without irony*—in an attempt to unite traditional social-democratic policy with the new competitive demands of the market. Government leaders expanded compulsory schooling years from nine to ten years and increased enrollment in upper secondary education to ensure that education was accessible for all. In addition, extensive reform targeting learner competence for adult education was planned (KUF 1998b). The expressed objectives, while tied to justice and equality, also stressed the need to ensure increased international competitiveness (KUF, 1997b). Tjeldvoll raises the question of whether market-orientation has taken over Scandinavian school ideology too. In other words, is the demand for quality measures threatening to drown the established ideal of equality? "Functional schooling in modern capitalism seems destined to be unequal," according to Tjeldvoll (op. cit., 21, 1998) who contends that quality is definitely privileged at the expense of equality. Others wonder whether mass schooling as a part of modernisation[7] has served the creation of "a modern basis for legitimating social inequality"? (Lauglo, 1998:48).

Conclusion

In exploring a few aspects of the terms quality and equality, I recognize that Skrtic (1991) applies the more or less corresponding terms of excellence and equity. He argues against the seeming conflict between the two in American schools to suggest that student excellence is not at risk in a classroom for all. Equity and excellence are *not* mutually exclusive. On the contrary he argues that coping with diversity and the ad hoc problem solving that is needed in a complex situation provides the desired experiences and necessary competence for the future. While I cannot argue with such an ideal, clearly the ideal dissolves when one looks closely into actual contexts. The questions I have posed are not intended to be answered by this author, nor are they to be judged as the most essential or most comprehensive. I have posed them as away of looking into a few aspects relative to inclusion in Norway that might easily be overlooked. Unlike the United States, which draws from a long history of segregation of minorities which now informs educational inclusion—Norway has no such history. Increasingly, we are coming to grips with the strains posed by immigration and racial tensions in a country once acclaimed for its welfare state support of succor and security from cradle to grave. Social democracy in an era rocked by the increasing presence of asylum seekers, economic immigrants, and reunified family members has forced a new emphasis on understanding cultural differences in Norway. Although anti-immigration policies are at the core of recent civic debate, we may well find that previous efforts to integrate members of the disability community likewise merit reexamination of policy and practice. What is more likely to prevail is the realization that all we believed we accomplished for disabled citizens through our welfare system in promotion of inclusion and integration will not be fused into policies to benefit minority individuals.

Appendix

About Metaphors

Brantlinger (1997), in her essay on the uses of ideology in special education, explained the frequent use of metaphors found in the literature reflective of war (e.g., battlefield terminology, rallying, marshalling, using tactics, etc.). In Norway these are well-known concepts; however, the bandwagon metaphor as introduced by Brantlinger is quite unfamiliar. As a non-American and non-native English speaker, that particular image was puzzling. My only mental association was a vague picture of a parade with lively musicians playing, seated on a carriage of sorts—bandwagon! The symbolic meaning was unfamiliar to me, as was the expression "bandwagons within bandwagons." I wondered if getting on the bandwagon was good or bad, something done without thinking so that being carried away by the popular music and fun by everybody else was worthy or unworthy? Webster's dictionary gave some support to this idea by its explanation of the metaphorical meaning: "be or jump on a bandwagon: to support an apparently successful candidate, cause, or movement." Further, I initially thought the drumbeat mentioned in the article came from the band on the wagon, too, until informed about the reference to Thoreau!

Metaphors are used with great frequency, and mostly unconsciously in everyday speech, although sometimes in a deliberate fashion, as in the instance of poetry or rhetoric. They are used by politicians, as in the opening example in this chapter of "the peoples' home." Rhetoric has found its way into postmodern science, too—for instance, using metaphors is no longer considered unscientific (cf., the Janus face used to describe aspects of present special education in Norway). Maybe we could find other metaphors to illustrate the challenges we face in the field of inclusion, or stretch the use the metaphors? For instance, the Janus face refers to polarities, double nature, contrasting aspects, but also to a doorway, an entrance, a beginning (cf., the month of January beginning a new year). Other metaphors could be bridges—bridging the gap (although, "to bridge" is not a verb in Norwegian). Bridges are possible to build where waters are not too wide or too wild to cross. What about the gap between the "traditionalists" and the "inclusionists" (Brantlinger, op. cit.), could it be bridged? I wonder.

Another image is the house, specifically the schoolhouse. A recent cover picture in the *Norwegian Journal of Special Education* showed a typical school with an extension named "Department of Integration" added to it on the outside. The alternative to building such extensions or to building separate schools would be to change the interior of the existing building and to maybe widen the entrance so as to include the full range of students. In fact, the enrollment of six-year-old students in compulsory schools in Norway led to discussions about the suitability—the accessibility—of the actual school buildings for smaller bodies. Obviously, even further and more radical changes to the main house are possible if we can imagine the need.

Notes

1. For a discussion of the ideology concept in a Scandinavian context, see my colleague Marit Strømstad's chapter in this book.
2. The percentage of students attending private schools in 1993–94, mostly religious or Waldorf schools, was 1.5%. The number is increasing.
3. The largest language group is Urdu, mainly due to Pakistani work migration in the seventies, followed by Vietnamese, mainly due to refugees after the Vietnam war; and family reunions for both groups (Aasen and Mønness 1998).
4. In Oslo more than 25% of the studens in compulsory school belong to language minorities (KUF 1997 b).
5. When looking at the teacher-student ratio one must take into account the high proportion of small schools in Norway. Most classes have some twenty students though, with a maximum of 28–30.
6. See also Keith Ballard's chapter from New Zealand in this book.
7. Modernisation here meaning urbanisation, division of labour, modern technology, secularisation and the development of science (cf. Lauglo op. cit.).

References

Aasen, J. and Mønness, E. (1998) *Minoritetselever i grunnskolen. Analyse av ressursbehovet til særskilt norsk- og morsmålsopplæring (Minority students in compulsory education. An analysis of funding needed for instruction in mother tongue and in Norwegian as a second language)*. Hamar, Norway: Høgskolen i Hedmark, Avdeling for lærerutdanning.

Ali, M. R. (1997) *Den sure virkeligheten (The bitter reality)*. Oslo, Norway: Tiden.

Booth, T. (1998) From "special education" to "inclusion and exclusion in education": Can we redefine the field? In Haug, P. and Tøssebro, J. (eds.) *Theoretical Perspectives on Special Education*. Kristiansand, Norway: Høyskoleforlaget/ Norwegian Academic Press, pp. 43–60.

Brantlinger, E. (1997) Using Ideology: Cases of Nonrecognition of the Politics of Research and Practice in Special Education. *Review of Educational Research* vol. 67 no. 4 pp. 425–459.

Clark, C., Dyson, A., Millward, A., and Skidmore, D. (1995) Dialectical Analysis, Special Needs and Schools as Organisations. In Clark, C., Dyson, A., and Millward, A. (eds.) *Towards Inclusive Schools?* London: David Fulton Publishers pp. 78–95.

Dalen, M. (1999) Hva vet vi—hva gjør vi? Forholdet mellom kunnskapsstatus og praktisk utforming av tilbud for elever med behov for spesielt tilrettelagt opplæring. (What do we know—and what do we do? The relationship between existing knowledge and actual practice as to educational arrangements for student with special educational needs). Oslo, Norway: *Nordisk tidsskrift for spesialpedagogikk (Nordic Journal of Special Education)* no. 34, pp. 230–240.

Dalen, M. and Skårbrevik, K. J. (1999) Spesialundervisning på grunnskolens område 1975–1998 (Special education in the field of compulsory education 1975–1998). In Haug, P., Tøssebro, J. and Dalen, M. (ed) *Den mangfaldige spesialundervisninga. Status for forsking om spesialundervisning (The diversity of special education. Research on special education: the situation now)*. Oslo, Norway: Universitetsforlaget, pp. 151–191.

Engen, T.O., Kulbrandstad, L.A., and Sand, S. (1996) *Til keiseren hva keiserens er. Om minoritetselevers utdanningsstrategier og skoleprestasjoner (Unto Caesar that which is Caesar's. About minority students' educational strategies and school results)*. Vallset, Norway: Oplandske bokforlag.

Fylling, I. (1999) *Spesialpedagogiske ressurser—individuell rett til kollektivets beste? (Resources for special education—an individual right for the benefit of all?)*. Paper presented at the conference "The Janus-face of special education." Oslo, Norway, May 4.

Gustavsson, A. (1999) Integration in the Changing Scandinavian Welfare State. In Daniels, H. and Garner, P. (eds.) *Inclusive Education,* London and Stirling: World Yearbook of Education, Kogan Page, pp. 92–98.

Haug, P. (1998) Norwegian Special Education: Development and Status. In Haug, P. and Tøssebro, J. (eds.) *Theoretical perspectives on Special Education.* Kristiansand, Norway: Høyskoleforlaget/ Norwegian Academic Press, pp. 15–42.

Haug, P., Tøssebro, J., and Dalen, M. (ed.) (1999) *Den mangfaldige spesialundervisninga. Status for forsking om spesialundervisning (The diversity of special education. Research on special education: the situation now)*. Oslo, Norway: Universitetsforlaget.

Haug, P. (1999) Utvikling og motseiingar i forskingsfeltet (Development and contradictions in the research field). In Haug, P., Tøssebro, J., and Dalen, M. (ed.) (1999) *Den mangfaldige spesialundervisninga. Status for forskning om spesialundervisning (The diversity of special education. Research on special education: the situation now)*. Oslo, Norway: Universitetsforlaget, pp. 14–43.

Holst, J. (1999) The Welfare State and the Individual Freedom. In Daniels, H. and Garner, P. (eds.) *Inclusive Education,* London and Stirling: World Yearbook of Education, Kogan Page, pp. 180–193.

Johnsen, F. (1982) *Farvel til særomsorgen (Farewell to special care)*. Oslo, Norway: Universitetsforlaget.

KUF (1997a) Kirke-, utdannings- og forskningsdepartementet (Ministry of Church, Education and Research) *Læreplanverket for den 10-årige grunnskolen (Core curriculum for primary and secondary education)*. Oslo.

KUF (1997b) Kirke-, utdannings- og forskningsdepartementet (Ministry of Church, Education and Research) *St.meld. 17 (1996–97) Om innvandring og det flerkulturelle Norge (About immigration and the multicultural Norway)*. White Paper, Oslo.

KUF (1998 a) Kirke-, utdannings- og forskningsdepartementet (Ministry of Church, Education and Research) *St.meld. 23 (1997–1998) Education for Children, Adolescents and Adults with Special Needs,* Oslo (White Paper, title translated from Norwegian. An English summary can be obtained from the ministry).

KUF (1998b) Kirke-, utdannings- og forskningsdepartementet (Ministry of Church, Education and Research) *St.meld. 42 (1997–1998) The Competence Reform report*, Oslo (White Paper, title translated from Norwegian. An English summary can be obtained from the ministry).

KUF (1999) Kirke-, utdannings- og forskningsdepartementet (Ministry of Church, Education and Research) *St.meld. 25 (1998–99) Elever fra språklige minoriteter i grunnskolen (Minority students in compulsory education)*. White Paper, Oslo.

Lauglo, J. (1998) Populism and Education in Norway. In Tjeldvoll, A. (ed.) *Education and the Scandinavian Welfare State in the Year 2000. Equality, Policy and Reform*, New York and London: Garland Publishing, pp. 25–55.

Mordal, K. N. and Strømstad, M. (1998) Norway: Adapted education for all? In Booth, T. and Ainscow, M. (eds.) *From Them to Us: An International Study of Inclusion in Education*. London and New York: Routledge, pp. 101–117.

Nes, K. (1999) Three Voices from the First Generation of Integration Students in Norway. In Ballard, K. (ed.) *Inclusive Education: International Voices on Disability and Justice*, London: Falmer Press, pp. 116–128.

Ogden, T. (1999) Individuelle forskjeller som utfordring for enhetsskolen—reformer og resultater (Individual differences as challenge to the unitary school—reforms and results). Oslo, Norway: *Nordisk tidsskrift for spesialpedagogikk (Nordic Journal of Special Education)* no. 34, Oslo, pp. 151–166.

Özerk, K. (1992) *Tospråklige minoriteter. Sirkulær tenkning og pedagogikk (Bilingual minorities. Circular thinking and education)*. Oslo, Norway: Oris forlag.

Pijl, S. J. (1999) *International outlook*. Paper presented at the conference "The Janus-face of special education," Oslo, Norway, May 4.

Skårbrevik, K. J. (1996) *Spesialpedagogikk på dagsorden—en evaluering av prosjektet "Omstrukturering av spesialundervisningen" (Special education on the agenda—an evaluation of the project "Restructuring special education")*. Molde, Norway: Møreforsking, report no 14.

Skrtic, T. M. (1991) The Special Education Paradox: Equity as the Way to Excellence, *Harvard Educational Review*, vol. 61, no. 2, pp. 148–205.

Slagstad, R. (1998) *De nasjonale strateger (The national strategists)*. Oslo, Norway: Pax Forlag A/S.

Slee, R. (1995). Education for all: Arguing principals or pretending agreement? *Australian Disability Review: Journal of Disability Advisory Council*. vol. 2, pp. 3–19.

Söder, M. (1997) Integrering: Utopi, forskning, praktik (Integration: Utopia, research, practice). In Tøssebro, J. (ed.) *Den vanskelige integreringen (The problems of integration)*, Oslo: Universitetsforlaget, pp. 33–57.

Stangvik, G. (1994) *Funksjonshemmede inn i lokalsamfunnet: prinsipper og arbeidsmåter (The disabled into the local communities: principles and methods)*. Oslo: Universitetsforlaget.

Stangvik, G. (1998, November 18) Skolens spesialundervisning som bremse (Special education in school as obstacles). Oslo, Norway: *Aftenposten*, p. 4.

Telhaug, A. O. (1994) *Utdanningspolitikken og enhetsskolen. Studier i 1990-årenes utdanningspolitikk (Educational policy and unitary school. Studies in educational policy of the 1990s)*. Oslo, Norway: Didaktika.

Tjeldvoll, A. (ed.) (1998). *Education and the Scandinavian Welfare State in the Year 2000: Equality, Policy, and Reform*. London and New York: Garland Publishing, pp. 3–23.

Tøssebro, J. (1997) (ed.) *Den vanskelige integreringen (The problems of integration)*. Oslo, Norway: Universitetsforlaget.

Tøssebro, J. (1999) Epilog—refleksjoner over status innen norsk forskning om spesialundervisning (Epilogue—reflections on status within Norwegian research on special education). In Haug, P., Tøssebro, J. and Dalen, M. (ed) *Den mangfaldige spesialundervisninga. Status for forsking om spesialundervisning (The diversity of special education. Research on special education: the situation now)*. Oslo, Norway: Universitetsforlaget, pp. 258–274.

III

RESEARCH TENSIONS: ESPOUSED VERSUS LIVED IDEOLOGY

9   *Lous Heshusius*

SPECIAL EDUCATION KNOWLEDGES: THE INEVITABLE STRUGGLE WITH THE "SELF"

> *If I am not what I've been told I was, then it means that you're not what you thought you were either. . . . And that is the crisis.*
>
> JAMES BALDWIN *(1988, p. 5)*

> *I should let me be us.*
>
> UNIVERSITY STUDENT IN SPECIAL EDUCATION

> *Fear is at the root of all forms of exclusion just as trust is at the root of all forms of inclusion.*
>
> JEAN VANIER *(1998, p. 73)*

A close colleague, teaching a disability studies course to general education students, called to tell me about an episode with her students. Several disabled speakers had related what it was like to live their lives. My colleague had shown several videos, including the documentary *Selling Murder*, the story of Hitler's careful manipulations to get the German people ready to accept "mercy" killing of people with disabilities. It had been the first time that many of the students had been directly confronted with the lives of disabled people and what can happen to them because of their disabilities. The students had become scared.

"Scared of disabled people?" I asked, not understanding. "No," she said, "scared that they would become disabled themselves." An accident perhaps. A disease. Should she try some counseling techniques with them?

I gave a gut-level response and in the next few minutes said more or less the following: No, I would not counsel them on their feelings. If you would do that, they could interpret it as sympathy or empathy, implying agreement that it would be terrible to be disabled. The emphasis would shift toward the comfort level of the abled-bodied again, rather than stay with issues of disability. I would do no more than acknowledge their fears as real, but not as something you have to deal with. Just let them sit there with their fears. They will have to become familiar with them. And they have to do it themselves—by looking their fears straight in the eye.

Afterward, I thought long and hard about my response. To become intimately and relentlessly familiar with our fears might be the only way to integrate them into our "selves" by seeing that what we fear, we fear because it is part of all our possible selves. Rather than having our fears of different others be pacified and receive sympathy—which would dull them, allowing them to stay hidden and thus keep their power over us—we need to see our fears in all their force and clarity. Perhaps that is what freedom is about—to become intimately familiar with our fears of different others that are indicative of what we consciously or unconsciously try to exclude from that which we construct as desirable for our own "selves."[1]

Constructing the Other, Constructing the Self

The attachments to images we hold as desirable for our selves create fears of others who are different in ways that do not fit these images. And there are many, many such others. Most of us don't mind the thought of having a "self" that is more attractive, smarter, richer, healthier, a self that belongs to a group with desirable status, but not one that would, in our view, reduce us and make us inferior to who we think we now are. Most, even possibly all, of us live comparative lives, which is a cause of much misery and harm. While we talk much about diversity, when it comes to making deep connections and deep friendships, the self typically chooses to do so only with people with whom there is enough overlap and commonality. We keep a safe physical distance, if possible, but certainly a psychological, political, and emotional distance from everyone else. The very need to establish and protect a certain kind of desired self imagines a threatening otherness in those whose lives remind the self of what it does not want for its own. This distancing act can take many forms and many guises. Theorists and researchers, from whatever persuasion, are not exempt from these processes.

Perhaps the most important question is whether one can even see this process operating when the self is bent on the act of excluding that which it does not want for its self. Fear and desire blind us from seeing the kind of self we protect, precisely because these processes are not at all necessarily carried out consciously and deliberately. At the center of this chapter's epistemological story is the view that the selves of positivist/empiricist traditions engage in these processes of constructing otherness to protect a certain kind of self in obvious ways, but that alternative approaches to research do not, by definition, make the researcher immune to doing the same. For alternative researchers, too, the act of protecting a certain kind of self is typically hidden from awareness. I further would like to voice the possibility that the very act of seeing oneself as "a researcher" can all too easily, and often does, involve the construction of a certain kind of self that legitimizes to the self and to the world these processes of exclusion in our embodied encounters.

In thinking over the conversation with my colleague about her scared students, I was reminded of another incident that occurred some years ago, when I took a dozen graduate students from York University to the Netherlands, my home country, for a cross-cultural course in special education. We visited the institution De Hartenberg, well known for its embodied approach to being with the severely disabled (Hulsegge & Verheul, 1986). One entire wing of a building is devoted to activities collectively referred to as Snoezelen. This institution is where Snoezelen originated as the brainchild of the artist Ad Verheul. The Dutch word "snoezelen" refers to coziness, to safe snuggling, to being together with someone or something in ways that are soft and pleasant to the senses and to the soul. When one snoezels, there is a total absence of demands, for the need to rank the other or the self for evaluations, or for any other goal-oriented behavior. Snoezelen expresses human warmth, belonging, tenderness, trust, and lots of goodwill.[2]

The Snoezelen wing is an oasis for the senses and for human contact, both physically and emotionally. In the various rooms of the wing, residents and staff can touch soft objects, including walls covered with soft materials, lie on a floor that lights up and warms up when one lies down on it, and smell lovely aromas coming from fancy tubes attached to the wall. In a large room that would be the envy of the well-to-do for its aesthetically inviting and even luxuriously relaxing atmosphere, residents like to linger, following soft lights that move across the walls and ceilings, listening to calming music, being rocked softly by a floor that is essentially a huge, luxurious, leather waterbed that folds into cushionlike forms into which one can cuddle and snoezel, alone or with someone else. Here, the staff lies down with residents, holding them, resting hand in hand or nestled against each other.

The Snoezelen philosophy is revolutionary—that is, revolutionary for those with severe disabilities. For "normal" folks it is straightforwardly human to snoezel with spouses, lovers, one's children, and even one's pets, as a normal expression of good relationships, and most of us reap the emotional and physical benefits from being so together. Typically, people who are disabled or retarded in institutional care are not allowed the expression of this depth of their humanity. In this institution Snoezelen is seen as a profound human right and necessity—never as therapy, never as a measurable "intervention" for academics to focus their research on.

Back in the hotel that evening during our discussion of the day's events, one of the students shared what she had experienced. That morning upon our arrival, one of the handicapped residents had started to touch some of us. This student told us that she had panicked and said to herself, "If he touches me, I'm going to throw up." In her written reflection of the day she wrote:

> I felt this way because I have never experienced a profoundly retarded person as another human being. . . . I was afraid that I myself might look repulsed. . . . The struggle isn't with what I saw/experienced today. *It is with what I have inside* [emphasis added].

She told the class that having seen the staff touch and hold these persons, she could see them for the first time as human beings. They now appeared to her to be more like herself. In her journal she reflected philosophically:

> I should let me be us, and accept us as we have the potential to already be. . . . This may be the weirdest entry you'll ever have to read, but I think I've undergone a break through in a fear block. It's a freeing sensation.

I have always kept a copy of these pages of the student's journal. When I read her words, I knew that her realization that her fear was not with what she saw but instead with something inside of her was a straightforward, yet profound and extremely difficult-to-reach insight. It is not easily reached because of the probably innate human need to maintain the images that create a safe, stable, and socially desirable notion of "self" for ourselves, fearing those selves that threaten those images.

"Scary things not always outside. Most scary things is inside," says a character in Toni Morrison's (1997, p. 39) novel *Paradise*. In speaking about the "Dragon–Princess," the poet Rainer Maria Rilke (in Mood, 1975, p. 99) says, "Has it [the world] terrors, they are our terrors; has it abysses, those abysses belong to us." Only someone who is ready for everything, Rilke (p. 98) says, someone who excludes nothing, will live the relation to another as something alive and will draw exhaustively from his or her own existence.

Ralph Waldo Emerson (in McQuade, 1981, p. 183) speaks of an old man who says to his boys scared by a figure in the dark: "My children, you will never see anything worse than yourselves." Emerson goes on to say about the human being, "He (sic) cleaves to one person and avoids another, according to their likeness or unlikeness to himself." No doubt many more wise thinkers could be found who have spoken of this fear inside, a fear of that, which, in its shadow form, is already part of one's actual or potential self, is what the self does not want and therefore pushes away.

Constructing Separativeness, Entering Trust

Contemporary social inquiry acknowledges that the self is involved in its historical and ideological formations, but rarely do researchers acknowledge—if they are at all aware of this—that the images of what they desire for their own self (solidified into a stable notion of self) can function significantly during the actual embodied interaction with the "researched" other. Elsewhere (Heshusius, 1994), I wrote of my work as a researcher many years ago, when I was doing a participant-observation study in a group home for "retarded citizens" and became aware of my own need to distance myself, a distancing act that definitely stood in the way of genuine listening and attending. I wrote:

> I remember distinctly being confronted early on with power and status differences that stood in the way of fully attending. I was forced to recognize my upbringing, values, and related emotions until I finally came to pose the question of merging: Could I imagine such a life for myself? Only when I could start seeing their lives as worthy for myself, or for my children . . . forget the ego concerns that constitute the self, and be fully attentive. . . . I had to completely and non-evaluatively observe my personal reactions and in that attentiveness, dissolve . . . them, which opened up a mode of access that was not there before. (p. 19)

This personal reflection became an illustration for my discussion of the differences between an alienated and alienating mode of consciousness, which keeps the other at a distance, and a more participatory mode of consciousness within which the constructed separation between other and self begins to blur, as the self begins to consciously lower its boundaries that were constructed to exclude. Then other and self can merge, however briefly, into a mode of attending in which the need to be separative is temporarily dissolved. As the student reflected on her fear of being touched by a severely disabled other: "I should let me be us and accept us as we have the potential to already be."

I use the word "separative" to signal that at the core of exclusionary processes, which erect what appear as distinct boundaries between self and other, lies not a nominal construct, not something that already exists, such as "separation" or "separativeness," but, rather, an agential construct that achieves separation each time again. It is not the case that sharp separations and boundaries already exist before our arrival but, rather, that the need to be separative from that which threatens the desired images for the self constructs them each time anew. This process becomes habitual, and it seems that the boundaries between self and other are "real," are already there. But at the deepest level of consciousness, the separation is constructed time and time again, however rapidly this occurs. When attention to this process as it happens is deliberately slowed down and experienced in slow motion—which can happen only if one is completely attentive and observant and wants to see— the habitualness of perceiving boundaries-as-already-existing (instead of realizing that one constructs them anew, again and again) can be broken.

To enter a more participatory, inclusionary mode of awareness, trust, says Vanier (1999, p. 73), rather than fear, must guide the self. In my case, trust took the form of finally finding peace with the notion that if I myself, or my children, would be living a life as theirs, that would be worthy of life nonetheless. Then, and only then, could I enter a mode of awareness and of listening and being with them that was much less guided by exclusionary fears. My reflection also goes to show how deliberately entering a less exclusionary mode of consciousness presents a serious struggle for the self. It shows how the self must be willing, at least potentially, to let go of the images that brings it security (or so it thinks). In my case, to come to that point involved a long struggle with my own attachments to the idea of "normalcy," to desirable status of intelligence, to what appears as attractive, as worthwhile—in short, with a whole array of ego needs. The struggle, as my student wrote, was not in the first instance with what I saw and heard but instead with what I carried inside.

Accepting the possibility of a very different life for oneself as worthwhile, and the related ability to deeply connect with those who are so "other" that the self instinctively wants to exclude them, may well be one of the criteria against which to check the depth of today's discussions about diversity and inclusion. Jean Vanier (1999), co-founder of the now more than 100 L'Arche communities in 30 countries, where intellectually disabled and nondisabled people choose to live together, has this to say about such deeper connections. Using the story of Lazarus as an analogy, he states:

> It is dangerous to enter into a relationship with the Lazaruses of our world. If we do, we risk our lives being changed. All of us are, more or less, locked up in our cultures, in our habits, even in our friendships and places of belonging. If I become the friend of a beggar, I rock the boat. Friends may feel uncomfortable, even threatened. . . . They may become aggressive. . . . I am beginning to discover how fear (of those who are different) is a terrible motivating force in all our lives. . . . Fear is at the root of all forms of exclusion just as trust is at the root of all forms of inclusion. . . . We are all so frightened of losing what is important for us, the things that give us life, security, and status. (pp. 71, 73)

"Where do you want special education to go?" was the question our editor asked us to address. In short, my response is: more and more into a participatory mode of consciousness, in its research, its theorizing, and its pedagogy. Her second question was more difficult to respond to: "What do you see as necessary to get us there?" I would have to say that, if we ever get "there," it will demand hard work in regard to something we are not at all used to focusing on: those inner images that give the self security, safety, and stability but that block participatory attentiveness and, therefore, block participatory knowing and being.

Alternatives to positivist/empiricist traditions acknowledge the power of gender, class, sexual orientation, and race in the making and unmaking of knowledges. These alternatives include the current emphasis on deconstructionist methods that speak of "death of the self." This particular death, this dying of a certain notion of self in deconstructionist thought, however, does not occur in the embodied present. However well theorized, theoretical and historical deaths are not directly at stake in what I am pursuing here. Deconstruction's deaths are not immediately personal enough. They are not embodied, lived deaths. What is needed is an actual lived death to the desired self-images the self harbors, while one is in an actual encounter, so one can be free to fully attend. The postmodern deconstructionist theorized "death of the self" does not accomplish this. It is not the case, I believe, that postmodern deconstruction has gone too far, as some critics would have it, but instead that it has not gone far enough. It does not foster an actual ability to die to self-protecting images and desires that are at work in actual embodied moments, and that separate and distance.

I think of the students' fears, in my colleague's class, of becoming disabled themselves, which in the first instance had to do with fearing the loss of the desired images for the self they were attached to (of being competent, able-bodied, strong, and healthy). They could not imagine the death of that self while trying to listen to the disabled other. The very confrontation with the possibility that they, too, might have to give up the desired images for themselves someday blocked an ability to fully attend to the different other who possessed characteristics that were undesired and feared for their own selves. I think of the student who felt nauseous at the thought of being touched by one whose life she could not possibly imagine for her self. I think of my own blockages in my actual interactions with residents of a group home for "the retarded," because of my own ego-shaped desired self that I had a hard time dying too.

All these fears were operative in the present moment of these actual encounters, not in theoretical reflexivity about representation, language, and power—an important reflexivity, to be sure, but a reflexivity within which one does not necessarily have to feel and live one's disgust, fear, jealousy, or whatever, toward another. It is a reflexivity that does not call attention to the feelings, fears, and images of one's own self-in-action. To see the historical and structural unfolding of hidden inner exclusionary fears, to see how class, race, gender, disability, sexual orientation, and so forth can be the channel for their materialization and externalization, and to demystify the outcomes of these processes, is extremely important. Doing so, however, should not be equated with a focus on the self in embodied encounters that exist only in the actual present. The scholarly engagements in deconstructing relations of power do not necessarily help to recognize the exclusionary fears within that are operative in actual, embodied moments, fears that construct a threatening otherness. The two modes of knowing involved do not necessarily overlap in one's conscious awareness and can stand in a number of different relations to each other.

The foregoing leads to the view that, in special education theorizing and research, what is at stake in the first instance is not disability, not the "other" in the study of exceptionality, but instead the particular needs of the researching and theorizing self, which in turn decides the parameters by which the other will come to be known or unknown, included or excluded. "Special education" is a process that decides who is "in" and who is "out," who is "regular" and who is "special," who is "abled" and who is "disabled." As many have said, this process is never politically and ideologically free. But neither is it ever an ego-less process from which the embodied self, its life always in the present, is excluded. "There is an endless list of those whom we may exclude," says Vanier (1999, p. 71), and "every one of us, we may be sure, *is on someone's list*" (emphasis mine). All of us are vulnerable to be excluded so that some other self can feel safe and privileged, and all of us are vulnerable to needing to exclude others so we can feel the self of ourselves to be a safe and stable one.

The Refusing Other

When the other refuses to be the "other" the way we need him or her to be so we can be the self we want to be, we are faced with a profound confrontation. As James Baldwin (1988, p. 5) said to the self of the white master: "If I am not what I've been told I was, then it means that you're not what you thought you were either. . . . And that is the crisis." I believe Baldwin's insight holds up for all relationships. When another thinks he or she knows who I am, it is because he or she needs to be a certain self. When I think I know a person, it is because I need to be a certain kind of self when facing that person.

Many groups that have been forced into being known by the selves of researchers are objecting. They refuse to participate in the self–other construction that serves to maintain the researchers' selves. They have taken in their own hands whatever research they deem necessary. This has given rise to much feminist revisionism in epistemology and methodology (Reinhartz, 1992); to post-colonial voices (Sadaawi, 1996); to disability studies (Campbell & Oliver, 1996); to indigenous reappropriations of research methodology into proper indigenous cultural protocols (Bishop, 1998); and to bicultural bilingual research by the deaf community (Lane, 1996). These groups, along with others, have claimed their full right to their own epistemological and methodological story. This poly-voiced chorus of epistemological voices is not always harmonious, and not everyone listens to each other, but it constitutes nothing less than an epistemological civil rights movement.

It therefore is more than disconcerting to still hear positivist/behaviorist voices in major special education journals claim that there is only one way to valid knowledge: theirs (see, e.g., Brigham & Polsgrove, 1998; Kauffman, 1999; Kauffman & Brigham, 1999; Sasso, 2001; Walker et al., 1998). But the easy days in which positivism reigned in special education as the only legitimate voice will not come back. Complex processes, such as the evolution of human knowledges, are not reversible. Time evolves and cannot be reduced to the past (see, e.g., Prigogine & Stengers, 1984). I personally believe that at least some of the positivists in our field who, by virtue of the past still hold political power, know that their privileged status is slipping and giving way to more complex views. But complexity always threatens those who need stable, secure, continuous selves. Their writings have a tone not just of anger but also of despair. Just as important, as noted in Chapter 2, when I listen to graduate students or to new Ph.D.s in special education, I often notice a great appetite for literature in other areas and an excitement to bring differing epistemologies back to their understandings of special education as a social construct.

But it is the self-advocacy movements among the retarded, the deaf, the disabled, the deaf power and disability power movements that most powerfully challenge the traditional world of special education by refusing its academic ownership over them. Special education knows itself now confronted with demands by those it previously did not consider to be competent enough to do what they now do — demanding that their voices count in the deepest epistemological sense possible. For instance, Charlton's (1998) book, a powerful account of the "disability-based consciousness and organization" (p. ix) by independent disability groups worldwide, contests any knowledge constructed about them by others. I mention this book because its title says it all: *Nothing about Us without Us*.

The contemporary poly-voiced nature of scholarship further challenges the self-assigned superiority of positivism and empiricism by blurring the traditional separations between what traditionally have been considered very different and incompatible ways of knowing. Theoretical knowledge becomes a partner with personal experience; storytelling functions as both deconstruction and reconstruction; advocacy work is written up as dissertations; art forms serve for data presentation of formal research; and self-reflexivity has gained the status of formal knowledge. Years ago, in special education, the Blatts, Bogdans, Biklens, and Fergusons of the world started blurring the lines between theory, photography, stories, narrative, and personal experience. Increasingly, others are engaging this blurring of different ways of knowing in creative and often insightful ways, raising new questions, offering more complex pictures of the behavior of all humans involved in this enterprise we still call special education. In another book about the rapidly growing disabled people's movement in Britain, the authors, Campbell and Oliver (1996), state:

> This book is a mixture of social theory, political history, action research, individual biography, and personal experience. We have resisted the temptation (and some academic advice) to separate out these things and treat them as analytically distinct, because we do not regard them as separable. All of the people in this book are, in our own ways, social theorists, political historians, action researchers and personal autobiographers trying to understand our own experiences. To present this in separate academic categories is to fly in the face of reality and to distort our own experiences. (p. 1)

Though I personally believe that academic categories have a place for certain purposes, the blurring of genres surely is a most significant development that emerges from an awareness of the embodied complexity of all of our lives. It is a complexity and an embodiment that the positivist traditions fear, because complexity and real life cannot be controlled and control is what positivist researchers need above all else to maintain their stable, safe, inner, detached sense of self. As exceptional others refuse to stay in the restricted places that we, as a field of education, needed them to be in so we could be the kind of "selves" we wanted to be, we are not who we thought we were either (expertly in charge, with privileged intellectual status and privileged ways of knowing). And that is, I think, at least one major reason for the tone of despair in today's positivists' defenses of their own position. As the deaf, the retarded, the disabled—by increasingly forming their own organizations and in speaking out on their own—refuse to stay in the places assigned to them by traditional researchers and theorists, the latter no longer can be who they thought they were either. When impairment, disability, deafness, and retardation show their faces as dissent, as action, and as voice, any traditional research approach to those so identified takes on a serious sense of the suspect.

It is in part because of these dynamics, I believe, that the full-inclusion movement is so threatening to traditional special educators, as Brantlinger (1997) has commented on incisively. The "regular" selves—which constructed themselves as "regular" when perceiving differences that were too different for comfort and in doing so constructed the "special needs other" who needed to be excluded from places where the "regular" selves wanted to be alone (physically, emotionally, socially)—now are asked to change who they thought they were, and they do not want to do so. But as the other refuses to occupy the place of the special-needs segregated other, the regular self can't very well stay regular.

The fact remains, however, that many of those placed in segregated settings do not have the freedom to refuse. Elsewhere (Heshusius, 1996, p. 626), I imagine a scenario where special education youngsters take epistemological ownership over the knowledge they construct. They are taking the whole matter of inquiry in their own young hands. What might be the focus of their investigations? Whom would they turn into "subjects" for their studies? Their teachers? Their psychologists? Their researchers? Which settings would they research? Which aspects of curriculum, pedagogy, and instruction would they see as needing to be researched by them? Which outsiders would they invite to be involved in their studies, if any? What approaches to research would they take? Would they even see the need for research? And if not, what kind of actions would take the place of research?

It is relatively easy to continue a critique of positivist and empiricist traditions in the light of my comments so far regarding the need to protect a stable image of the inner self. The measuring and ranking self of the positivist researcher is perhaps the most isolating, insulating, distancing, distanced, and dissociated self the social sciences have known. When we asked 11 educational researchers who had been trained within the positivist/empiricist framework, and who had made a paradigmatic transition to interpretive and qualitative perspectives, to tell the personal story of their changing beliefs, they wrote in a strikingly similar way of the estranged self of their positivist period (Heshusius & Ballard, 1996). At the time of their writing, 6 of the 11 contributors had been, or still were, involved in special education. They told of the frustration they experienced, the discomfort, the stress, and even paralysis, and the physical feelings of resistance, fatigue, and nausea they had felt when forced to make their selves invisible, having to repress everything they knew from their own lives, having to deny their emotive, somatic, and real-life knowledges by adopting the measuring and ranking exercises of positivist traditions.

Measuring and ranking are the same movement in one's consciousness. They call each other into being. One necessitates and is implicated in the other. Although positivist thinkers may not explicitly link the two at the level of ideas, the idea that one has the obligation to measure in order to know, seen in positivist traditions as the core obligation, is identical to the idea of needing to rank in order to know, for measurement makes the idea of failure concrete. To have the need to rank other folks, one first must construct and adopt the idea of failure. Measuring then, is simply the concretization of this idea.

This is not to say that only positivist researchers rank. Youngsters are referred to by teachers who measure and rank all the time. The school system demands they do so, and so does most of society, and so do we all, in many—I am sure, far too many—aspects of our lives. When researchers measure and rank, however, the ranking act has a extra painful edge to it because they claim that their methods are privileged and render an objective, uncontaminated truth. This hides the reality that the need to measure and rank the other is deeply embedded in the "habits of the heart." Some positivist thinkers who are influential in editorial decision making keep insisting that these measuring and ranking practices are, first and foremost, the most fundamental activity of our field. "We must," says Sugai (1998, p. 171), "assume responsibility for measuring and owning the impact of our actions and decisions."

I read Sugai in a literal sense of actual proprietorship. The other is literally owned in an epistemological sense: When one owns the only correct way to know, what results from that process is, by extension, one's epistemological possession. The object of the measuring act becomes epistemologically known precisely, and only (positivists believe) because of having been put through the measuring/ranking act. No other ways of knowing (personal, political, cultural, sociological, descriptive, narrative, and knowing through close interactions in day-to-day living), however interesting perhaps, and possibly informative for informal purposes, are acceptable as formal knowledge claims. (Obviously, I am not eschewing accountability for what we do. I am breaking the particular equation of accountability = measuring/ranking.)

The deepest flaw in the logic of justification that informs this view is a threefold denial:

1. The denial that the self of a human being is deeply involved in these measuring and ranking acts.
2. The denial that such self is shaped by forces of history in all its ideological manifestations.
3. The denial that this self also is fundamentally shaped by self-protecting inner needs and images in actual interactions.

The sadness of the measuring and ranking dictates is that diversity, which the field of education increasingly says it values, does not thrive on ranking. It thrives on being engaged and lived with.

Special Education for Tomorrow: The Continued Struggle with the Self

Researchers engaging in alternative epistemologies and methodologies are not immune from distancing and separative modes of consciousness when they do their work. The inner self of the alternative researcher does not necessarily give up on the need to separate and distance, which, one might argue, constitutes the measuring/ranking act in a different guise. Few, if any, of the alternative approaches to date ask of the researcher to enter the kind of relationship in which the self of the researcher is asked to deliberately attend to, and then try to gently set aside, her or his inner protective and separative inner needs that operate in any given actual encounter.

In setting aside positivist dogmas, and by engaging in research in which we interact with and listen to the other in real-life settings, we have made our "knowing selves" certainly somewhat less safe, less stable, and less secure. This helps to create more open and democratic notions of inquiry. We work directly with research participants, face to face, with no instruments between us. Our research encounters become human encounters. A rationality of method has become a human rationality that makes it impossible to play a game of ventriloquism and makes it more difficult to hide our own lives from the impact the contact with the other will have on the self.

Nevertheless, the entire story of the human race illuminates the extraordinary need we have to construct superior, stable, distancing, and safe selves. Changing epistemologies and research methodologies does not release us so easily from this need. As Fine (1994) states, qualitative researchers, too, "speak 'of' and 'for' Others while occluding ourselves and our own investments . . . protecting privilege, securing distance" (pp. 70, 73). Alternative approaches to research ask of researchers to make the self more visible as a location and an agent in the construction of knowledge. This self-positioning typically refers to one's class, race, gender, and any other historically evolved power relation in which one possibly could be found.

However much such reflexivity is needed, I suggest here that its engagement does not necessarily mean that the researcher is free from the need to be separative during the actual research encounter, free from the need to "other" the other because he or she poses a threat to the desired images of the self. That is, there is no necessary relationship between what happens in thinking and writing, however reflexively engaged in, and what happens in one's consciousness in any given present vis-à-vis an actual embodied other. It is possible, of course, that scholarly theorizing does create greater awareness of the self's own distancing act during the research encounter. But it would seem equally possible that scholarship can be used, however unconsciously, as a substitute for witnessing one's self engaging in precisely that which one later problematizes in theorizing.

The need of the ego to establish the self as separate, safe, and secure is so great that we find ingenious ways of doing so, even when we set out trying not to. Most researchers (positivist, qualitative, interpretive, ethnographic, action-oriented, deconstuctive, narrative, reflexive, and emancipatory alike) continue to position their researcher's self in some kind of separative manner, in terms of the actual desires, fears, likes, dislikes, judgments, and other such preoccupations that dwell in our consciousness and attentiveness while we are in the actual research encounter, despite a sincere desire to be collaborative. These inner—often subtle—desires, fears, judgments, and preoccupations go well beyond those typically dealt with in the literature (those of race, gender, ethnicity, class, sexual orientation, ability) to include appearance in its many expressions: mannerisms, dress, speech patterns, and so forth. Anything other than what our selves see as desirable can bring about the distancing trick. Or, alternatively, anything that we are embarrassed about or feel guilty about in relation to the "researched other" can do the same.

How do you collaborate equally with those who are many steps down or many steps up the ladder in social status and material well-being? What are the many emotions that present themselves in the presence of research participants who are not nearly as healthy, wealthy, competent, and attractive as we consider ourselves to be? As a friend and colleague who is doing collaborative research with refugee women in Toronto told me, in what was not a detached voice: "Lous, they don't even have money to take the bus, or to buy diapers! I make tons by comparison. . . ."

We did not pursue the anguish that informed the comparison she inevitably had to draw between herself, the researcher, and the refugee women with whom she set out to do collaborative work. I did not ask what, at a deeper level, she did with her comparison, or how her embodied reaction to the poverty of her research participants quite possibly affected the nature of the collaboration in perhaps subtle, but nonetheless important, ways. The very differences that she observed, and that caused her existential guilt, which I am quite certain most of us carry within us, surely must have colored in some way the notion of collaboration and the notion of equality in knowledge construction and created a site of emotional conflict that could be handled only by the distancing impulse.

I am not assigning a moral story to any of this. I am pointing to the inherent contradictions we construct between what we say about collaboration and the need to demystify power relations in our research and theorizing on the one hand and what plays itself out in the embodied encounters at deep personal levels on the other hand, involving contradictions that we don't know how to reconcile.

Research with the "special need others," whose lives we likely would not choose for ourselves or for our children, must be filled for many with deeply personal reactions of all kinds, repressed as soon as they arise, for they call up contradictions with what we say we want our research approach to be like. How does one separate "doing the research" from these gut-level personal reactions to those different others whose lives may shock us at these deeper, self–other constructing levels? By what mechanisms does one do so? Can it be done? And would it not be possible that the very definition of oneself as "a researcher" or "a theorist" actually might continue to facilitate and legitimatize this distancing act, protecting desirable images for the self while pushing away the other, even within what we think of as collaborative and equal research relations? What would my colleague do if she were in a friendship relation with one or more of these refugee women? Knowing her, she would buy them tons of diapers and lots of other things.

The research role does not mean being friends. But what, exactly, does collaboration and equality in the research relationship mean, given the impossibility of separating the researcher from the person?[4] How does one draw the line between equality and collaboration in research and buying badly needed diapers, if we take seriously the notion that researcher and person cannot be separated, and that research can be nothing more than just one other voice alongside others in the conversation of humankind? How do I separate the voice of research from the voice of care, friendship, fear, likes and dislikes? Can that really be done in the first place? What does being "a researcher" still privilege us to do or be, or not to do or not to be? What is still the source of such power? I often remind my students: Just because you have taken (or taught, for that matter) course 101 or 201 or whatever in research methods, that does not give you any epistemological or other privileges at all.

It would make for quite a study if someone were to collect the honest feelings—such as my colleague's—of a large number of researchers working with those of both much lower and much higher statuses (of various kinds) in life and trace how the deepest personal reactions to those others might differ from the relationship stipulated by the research in its epistemological and methodological commitments, and, further, to try to understand how the researchers deal with conflicts thus produced. Such a study would address Fine's (1994) "Working the Hyphens" in relation to the inner separative acts, which, too, stand between researcher and researched and keep reproducing power relations.

Can our minds and attentiveness be "uncluttered," asks Vanier (1999, p. 124), of inner needs to feel separate, to be in charge of the self, to feel stable, to feel secure? Uncluttered of the need to protect the desired self? These inner needs, which Vanier (1999, p. 106) refers to as "compulsions deep within us," stand in the way of completely attending to and being with the other, blocking the creation of more inclusive living and learning communities, which we say we want to have. And when our minds and hearts cannot be uncluttered from such needs, when our gaze does not want to go, as my student said, to what is inside, what does that mean for the research we do with "special needs others"?

To be sure, I am not referring to writing audit trails, and to personal reflective journals of one's feelings and emotions during the research process, however helpful these after-the-fact reflections might be in some cases. Rather, what is at stake is the question whether there can be clarity of attention in the moment that focuses directly on becoming aware of what, exactly, the self tries to protect as this act of protecting, and therefore of distancing, is occurring. Because the problem is that one can't protect the needs of the self and listen, and be with another, at the same time.

Toward an Epistemologically Listening Self

To do the work required to set aside the separative impulse that has characterized epistemologies and methodologies of social science research, a stance of complete attentiveness and listening, both to the self and to the other, is necessary. Complete attentiveness and listening are difficult for anyone.[5] In special education, positivist researchers, convinced of their duty to measure and rank the other into being, cannot afford to attend and listen in that complete manner, for to do so would threaten the images of the researcher's self as epistemologically and methodologically superior. The positivist self listens in relation to what it has decided it must measure, but it does not listen.

The narrative, action, qualitative, ethnographic, emancipatory, reflective researcher typically is asked to listen carefully, but there is no guarantee that what epistemological and methodological values say should be done, is done. The inner self cannot be told what to do. There is no guarantee at all that adhering to any set of formal values assures that the listening and attention are not shaped by a host of other directives, including those inner needs that want a self that is superior, stable, and safe.

To listen completely, the mind must be silent (as distinct from silenced). And to be thus silent is so difficult, says Corradi (1990), that we are hardly prepared for it. In her influential (and I think brilliant) book *The Other Side of Language,* Corradi addresses the history and philosophy of the place of silence and listening, which she says are integral to language and to knowledge. But in the development of Western epistemologies, silence has come to be associated with powerlessness.

Within educational research, Scheurich (1997), commenting on the race-based epistemologies in which educational research is grounded, recognizes our inability, as a field of inquiry, to listen. After discussing the "imperial violence" that colors all our notions of validity, Scheurich (1997, p. 90) states that perhaps we ought to be "stunned into silence," into a space that "appropriates no one or no thing to its sameness." But we either fail or fear that space, Scheurich says. The best we can do, he states, is to enter a "polyphonic, tumultuous conversation."

If that, indeed, is all we can do, I must picture a scenario in which everyone speaks but no one listens. For where there is a lack of ability to voluntarily enter a state of silence in which one does not appropriate someone or something else to its sameness—that is, a state in which the desired images for the self are temporarily forgotten—the self may hear but cannot listen, can only translate hearing into speaking, and will exclude from attentiveness all that falls outside of the range of its own assertions. The dynamics of fear of that which we do not want for ourselves make our listening not quite listening and keep our politics externalized. There is a world of difference between being "stunned into silence" (which instantly brings about an impulse toward closure, if not a certain kind of paralysis) and being voluntarily silent. Not to be able to self-forget, be voluntarily silent and completely attend is to let "the compulsions deep within us" do their work.

What would it do to our notions of research if all courses in research methodology were to attend to this fundamental need to be completely silent and attentive in the construction of knowledge, and in that silence to learn to see what the self is doing? To see what mischief it is up to?[6] What if an entire course would be devoted to that attentive listening to both self and other, to listening as "the other side of language," to borrow Corradi's (1990) phrase, as an integral part of language and knowledge, the way research courses are now devoted to the practice of measuring and ranking the other, the generation of codes and categories about the other, or to the telling of stories about the other?

Researchers, especially from female and feminist perspectives, have written about the shocks, surprises, and confrontations in relation to their understanding of the self during their research activities, surprises, and confrontations that to various degrees bear on the habitual self–other construction discussed in this chapter (see, e.g., Ely, 1991; Reinhartz, 1992). This is difficult, as self-disclosure is inherently involved. Writing publicly what I learned when directing my attentiveness to what I had inside while trying to be a researcher of "retarded citizens," notwithstanding that the recounting was only a few short sentences, I experienced the conflicted emotions that occurred when doing so in a formal publication: Can I really do that? I am not supposed to be that personal. What is the reader going to think? But I came to conclude that it had to be done to stay true to what actually happened in the construction of the knowledge I shared with the reader.

Jean Vanier's work (1999) may well be among the most explicit writings available that illustrate what I am suggesting lies at the core of the politics of ex/inclusion: the need of the inner self to defend its images of what it finds desirable for the self, and thus exclude from participation those who threaten these images. He openly addresses the tremendous difficulties involved in witnessing this process in himself. In January of 2000, the Canadian Broadcast Corporation broadcasted the Massey Lectures of 1999 given by Vanier. Himself a privileged son of Georges Vanier, a former governor general of Canada, Jean Vanier was a philosopher and university scholar before he joined others in living with disabled and retarded people. The CBC program describes Vanier as a social and political thinker. With astonishing honesty, he speaks in these lectures of often wanting to stay distanced from those (the poor, the retarded, the homeless) who threaten his own safe sense of self. Recounting his running away from a woman who had asked him for money as he realized, once he started to talk with her, that she had immense needs, Vanier says, "I was frightened of being swallowed up by her pain and her need." We are frightened, he says, that our hearts will be touched if we enter into a relationship with an other who threatens our own self-safety, for then we have to let the self go. Fear about the safety of the self always seeks, and finds, an object (p. 73). He speaks of his anger and violence at times because of the difficulty in being faced with the intellectual disabilities of those he has chosen to live with. He then says something very important for the entire struggle around the politics of special education:

> In a world of constant, and often quite intense, relationships, you quickly sense your inner limits, fears, and blockages. You can feel the anger rising up in you. When I was tired or preoccupied, my inner pain and anguish rose more quickly to the surface. . . . I have often come head-to-head with my own handicaps, limits, and inner poverty. (pp. 100, 101)

Inclusion in education asks for constant and close relationships, between students and teacher, students and students, and teachers and parents. It does not help to deny or gloss over the idea that the inner selves of many are threatened that they now have to enter into close encounters with those whose lives they would not want for themselves or for their children, which, as I suggest here, triggers the need to distance the other into a threatening otherness—unless one is vigilant and intent enough to want to witness this deep compulsion, also within research and theorizing activities, and is capable to look the associated fears straight in the eye, so they might perhaps be set aside.

Another telling account of the self–other construction in the area of disabilities is Beck's (1999) autobiographical story of her initial horror when she discovered that she was pregnant with a Down syndrome child. Beck, too, tells with brutal honesty about her inner needs to protect a desired sense of self, which was all tied up with what others would say about the child, but also about her. Her sudden understanding of the inner fear of a hospital doctor who, accompanied by three medical students, tries to talk her into an abortion, portraying his own images of his desired self, is illuminating of what I have tried to sketch out in this chapter. His fear, she understands, is fear about his own need to avoid being seen, ever, as a failure, and therefore needing to reject and exclude (literally from life) anything that reminds him of the very possibility of failure. As she is struggling with her confusions when this doctor is spending an unusual amount of time and effort trying to gravely convince her to do the "sensible" thing, she suddenly hears the question in her own mind: Why is he doing this?

> I looked at Grendel closely, suddenly feeling like an observer rather than a patient . . . this man always made a great show of being too busy even to look at his patients. Why was he spending this inordinate amount of time trying to convince me to abort a child he would probably never even see? . . . I looked at Grendel's face, and there, just behind the tight-stretched skin, I seemed to see another face appear. . . . This face was terrified. . . . Why should this be? I relaxed and looked frankly at the second face. . . . The fear in it spoke to me of a lifetime spent desperately avoiding the stigma of stupidity, of failure, of not measuring up. (pp. 221–222)

Broun (Broun & Heshusius, 2004) provides a deeply striking story of the self–other construction that goes on in the deep levels where the images we hold as desirable for the self have taken root. This account is particularly powerful because, in this case, the self–other construction regards a self and an other that live in the same body. Broun tells a tale of rejection of disability by a normally walking self that in fact has its home in a body that is disabled. It was the imaged, normally walking self that pictured her disabled self into the status of other. Broun had focused her research on the question of educational achievement by disabled women. She chose a life-history approach to her study and included herself as a participant. She was not prepared for what happened. She could not get through an analysis of the stories because, as she states:

> I did not want to analyze the data because I did not want to analyze myself. . . . It was with effort and self-reminders that I wrote "we" instead of "they." Although including

myself as a participant had seemed such a natural thing to do. . . . I thought of my participants as other and did not identify myself with them, though I assumed that I had. . . . I had been attempting to discuss a group to which I often felt I belonged only as a pretender. . . . I had always pictured myself as walking without a limp. While I knew that it was not true, it was easier for me to get on with my life if I perceived myself as walking normally . . . but now, in the video of my mind, I walk with a limp and I can't get back my limpless self. . . . I wanted to choose the time when I would allow myself to make the switch. I didn't want it to come unbidden. I had anticipated that I would make the shift to my limping self when I was older. . . . Actually I had planned that this shift would occur at the time of menopause, having found Greer's (1991) description of the freedom of the invisibility of later middle age quite enticing. . . . Now, as a result of my deep engagement with my research participants, the limp is there and I am no longer beautiful to myself. . . . For me, this research has resulted in praxis; however, it has been unwelcome and involuntary.

Broun ends by expressing the hope that she will, in the end, emerge more at peace with herself, no longer having to struggle "to keep the image of the false (but desired) limpless me at the forefront of my imagination."

Turning one's attentiveness inward to the images that the self holds as desirable while the self is active in relationship, and witnessing how the images stand in the way of relating, has not to do with confessional tales, or with engagement in subjectivity. Nor is it, in the first instance, a moral story. Rather, it points to human impulses that forcefully participate in the construction of knowledge. The important goal of such inward witnessing is not to judge, not to eradicate, but, rather, to become familiar with these forces so one can actually see them operate. Otherwise their power cannot be recognized. What is needed to be able to see in that way is a complete, vigilant nonjudging attention to the precise nature of these images as they operate in an actual moment of relation. Only then can they perhaps be gently set aside.[7]

All this was more or less implied when I responded to my colleague who called me to tell that her students had become scared, as recounted at the beginning of this chapter. Through her course, she wanted them to temporarily self-forget—that is, to forget the images they held about their selves as healthy and invulnerable, as able and able-bodied, so they could fully listen to the disabled other, but they were not able to do so. Their fears about their own potential disabled and undesired self kept them from the ability to self-forget and listen.

The Vaniers of the world, who collapse ontology and epistemology—who live as they speak—are intense social and political thinkers. In collapsing their thinking and their living, they engage the most demanding of political undertakings. In doing so, they critique existing conditions of power relations from the inside out. Vanier is not suggesting that we all must sell everything we have and live our day-to-day lives in communities with very different others, though doing so would surely change the face of (special) education overnight. Rather, he is saying, I believe, that at any given moment, wherever we happen to be, also as researchers, we must attend to this self–other constructing process and learn to pay vigilant attention to that which, as my student said, we have inside. To engage in such seeing of the inside is a prerequisite for understanding that the inner and outer are one, deeply continuous movement (see also Krishnamurti, 1972, 1993) and, therefore, that inclusion "implies a shift in consciousness" (Vanier, 1999, p. 82).

If we were to imagine that no one in society would get scared at the thought of being disabled, that no one would feel nauseous at the thought of being touched by a severely disabled person, that no one would feel superior in the embodied presence of "retarded citizens," that no one would shy away from forming genuine friendships with them, that no one would have wanted to see herself or himself (and wanted to be seen) as a "regular" learner (which, by definition, requires others who fail in being "regular") — in short, if we were to imagine that no one in society would have any inner fears for those who are very different — social relations would be unrecognizable and a book such as this one would not exist. Power relations in institutions and other established structures must be demystified, but the inner embodied life cannot be exempted from the process. They surely are deeply intertwined. Established structures and institutions that are separative are made by and made up of separative selves.

One might argue that this view is naive and romantic — that every civilization, every culture has its exclusionary practices, that the human self is innately self-protective, that ego needs are part and parcel of being human. It seems clear that this has been the case. But we are evolutionary creatures. Might it thus be that, as Vanier implies, we are not quite human but really are in the process of "becoming human" (the title of his CBC lectures)? Might it be that seeing this very process of other construction within one's self, and doing even the smallest thing toward lessening this distancing act, is at the heart of the evolutionary processes of humankind, which, Vanier seems to suggest, is not yet a humankind?

The past few years, when teaching courses in qualitative research methodology, which included students in departments of special education, I make the gist of what I have tried to say here the central principle for the course. I tell the students, and remind them often, that any and every methodological decision they make is first and foremost a decision about the kind of relationship they want to enter into with the other, which is determined consciously or — likely far more often — unconsciously by the images they hold for what constitutes a desirable self. Before any research decision is a decision of method, it is a decision about a certain kind of other–self construction. And before that, it is a decision about the kind of self we desire to be.

The message is not that we should no longer do research, as it is, after all, only about the self. The message is that research is in the first instance a construction of an other–self relationship, and precisely in being that, it is a construction of knowledge. Research, and every decision that we make about the process of research, from conceiving the question to the manner in which we write up the study, is in the first instance about the images of the self we want to maintain before it is about the other. These images of the self in research will determine what the other is allowed, or is not allowed, to be.

Turning to one of my cherished writers, I open up Ralph Waldo Emerson's essays (in Gilman, 1965, p. 154) and read:

> Do you see that kitten chasing so prettily her own tail? If you could look with her eyes you might see her surrounded with hundreds of figures performing complex dramas . . . long conversations . . . many characters . . . and meantime it is only puss and her tail. How long before our masquerade will end its noise of tambourines, laughter and shouting, and we shall find it was a solitary performance?

As researchers and theorists, we, too, are like this kitten. We think we catch someone else's tail, but in the first instance it is invariably our own. Everything we say is about this chase. But perhaps we can learn to enter more deliberately into a state where we can tend this process and make the chase less and less self-protective, lessening inner ego needs and entering larger forms of awareness and, therefore, of knowing, both of self and other. "To attend means to be present," says Bateson (1994, p. 109); it means to give heed, to be vigilant. The root word of attention means to stretch the mind toward something (Bohm & Edwards, 1991, p. 139). As Bohm and Edwards note, "attention" and "intention" are directly and intimately related; where one's attention goes, one's intention goes, and vice versa. What one attends to, and the quality of such attending, will decide where one's intentions go and to what one's actions are directed. One, therefore, must be careful where one's attention goes.

Even though the many research alternatives we now engage in have opened up in scholarship at least the possibilities to attend to these mirroring processes within ourselves of fear/exclusion, of self/other, of trust/inclusion, much hard work remains to be done. Perhaps this is another way of saying what I hope for the future of education: a stretching of awareness that makes possible a more complete attentiveness to the self-protecting needs of the self as it is engaged with the different other in all matters that relate to what we still refer to as "special education," in its pedagogy, social policy, legislation, research, and theorizing. We must not forget in all of this that self–other constructions, and the morality that such constructions engender, are themselves evolutionary processes. It is precisely in this that hope for the possibility for further emergence of genuine participatory communities lies.

Berube (1996), a scholar in literary theory and father of a Down syndrome son, concludes his insightful—in many ways both deconstructive and embodied—story about being the parent of Jamie, his son, by saying that a crucial question is how we will represent the range of human variation to ourselves. In this chapter I add what I believe is the more primary question of how we represent our desired self to ourselves. The question that follows, then, is whether we dare to witness that desired self splashed all over the other in our embodied encounters. The need to develop a more focused attention and vigilance regarding the intensely private site of the self, where exclusionary impulses linger, may well be in the end, and therefore in the beginning, the most intense political dimension that humans face in the difficult struggle around the tensions between exclusion and inclusion.

Notes

1. A previous version of this chapter was presented at the International Colloquium on Inclusive Education: Ideology and the Politics of Inclusion, University of Rochester, New York, June, 1999. In my introductory comments I stressed that I was not suggesting, by choosing my topic, that I considered myself an "inclusive self." To the contrary, I said, this paper had emerged from an ever deepening realization of just how difficult inclusion is. Most of us write not about what we have absorbed but instead about what we are struggling with. In responding to a question from the audience, asking for an example from day-to-day life, I shared a recent incident as one of many I could have provided, of what I mean by separative and distancing self–other construction based on desired images the self holds for its self.

   I recounted how, when strolling leisurely in a city I visited, I noticed a woman who was exotically but poorly dressed, who radiated something that pulled me toward her. I could not make out if she was a homeless person or a mentally ill one, or perhaps both. As I passed, our eyes met and I said, "Hello." We were across from a fancy restaurant, where elegantly dressed people were entering.

   She started to talk about the neighborhood, including the museum next to the restaurant, which she obviously had visited and knew a lot about. Then she said about the restaurant, "They have excellent food." I was surprised, as her dress and appearance would not suggest she would eat there. Hesitantly, I asked, "Have you eaten there?" "No," she said, "but they feed me in the kitchen." I told the audience that, had the restaurant been a McDonald's or some other cheap place, I undoubtedly would have invited her for a meal, as I needed a meal myself and was interested in talking with her further. But now I suddenly saw an uncomfortable picture of the two of us sitting amidst elegantly dressed folks.

   I easily could have rationalized, I said in my presentation, that I did not invite her because she would have been uncomfortable. But the true observation of my "self" at that moment was that it was my own self, my image of who this self is, what I look like, with whom I socialize, and so forth, that would have been uncomfortable. What would the folks in the restaurant think of me?

   There it was. Exclusion followed. My decision not to invite the woman was in the first instance not because of her but, rather, because of the images about the self I carried inside. I believe this is a clear example of the separative and exclusionary actions that occur routinely in our day-to-day self-in-action—typically outside of our direct awareness—in regard to those whose lives we do not want for ourselves, including those we place in special education settings.

2. A video in English (1988) of the Hartenbergs' approach to Snoezelen is available through Rompa, De Hartenberg, Ede, P.B. 75, 6710 BB, The Netherlands.

3. "Snoezelen" has been transported to North America, and, in the process, unfortunately has been rendered, in all cases I am familiar with, as a "set of pleasant activities" to do for disabled youngsters. Items for a "Snoezelen room" now can be ordered from a catalog, regardless of the originators' legal action to prevent the commercialization of their philosophy. I have nothing against such activities as pleasant activities, but the point is that a philosophy of relations and human intimacy that honored the depth of humanness has been reduced to a set of activities to be scheduled, monitored, programmed, and even IEPed.

4. See Smith (1988, 1989) for excellent discussions on the inseparability of the person as researcher and the researcher as person.

5. This difficulty must be the reason why Deborah Tannen's (1986, 1990) books have been on best-seller lists for years.

6. Eastern spiritual traditions have focused for centuries on the importance of silence and of attentive observation of the self-in-action as integral to coming to knowledge. Some Western scholars who address the importance of these states of being, drawing directly from Eastern understandings, include Kalamaras, 1994, and Varela, Thomson, and Rosch, 1993.

7. Krishnamurti (1972, 1993) has been particularly lucid about the paradoxically strengthening effect that the acts of evaluating and judging that which one wants to stop doing has on one's ability to let go of the undesired behavior.

References

Baldwin, J. (1988). A talk to teachers. In R. Simonsen & S. Walker (Eds.). *The Graywolf annual five: Multicultural literacy* (pp. 3–12). St. Paul, MN: Graywolf Press.

Bateson, M. C. (1994). *Peripheral visions. Learning along the way.* New York: HarperCollins.

Beck, M. (1999). *Expecting Adam.* New York: Random Books.

Berube, M. (1996). *Life as we know it: A father, a family, and an exceptional child.* New York: Panatheon Books.

Bishop, R. (1998). Freeing ourselves from neo-colonial domination in research: A Maori approach to creating knowledge. *Qualitative Studies in Education, 11*(2), 199–219.

Brantlinger, E. (1997). Using ideology: Cases of nonrecognition of the politics of research and practice in special education. *Review of Educational Research, 67*(4), 425–459.

Brigham, F., & Polsgrove, L. (1998). A rumor of paradigm shift in the field of children's emotional and behavioral disorders. *Behavioral Disorders, 23*(3), 166–170.

Broun, L., & Heshusius, L. *Disability Studies Quarterly,* Spring 2004, V24 (2) www.dsq-sds.org. *Unexpected encounters in participatory research.*

Bohm, D., & Edwards, M. (1991). *Changing consciousness: Exploring the hidden source of the social, political, and environmental crisis facing our world.* San Francisco: HarperCollins.

Campbell, J., & Oliver, M. (1996). *Disability politics: Understanding our past, changing our future.* New York: Routledge.

Charlton, J. I. (1998). *Nothing about us without us: Disability oppression and empowerment.* Berkeley: University of California Press.

Corradi, F. G. (1990). *The other side of language: A philosophy of listening.* London: Routledge.

Ely, M. (1991). *Doing qualitative research: Circles within circles.* London: Falmer Press.

Fine, M. (1994). *Working the hyphens: Reinventing self and other in qualitative research.* In N. K. Denzin & Y. S. Lincoln (Eds.), Handbook of qualitative research (pp. 361–376). Newbury Park, CA: Sage.

Gilman, W. H. (Ed.). (1965). *Selected writings of Ralph Waldo Emerson.* New York: New American Library.

Greer, G. (1991). *The change: Women, aging, and the menopause.* New York: Fawcett Columbine.

Heshusius, L. (1994). *Freeing ourselves from objectivity: Managing subjectivity or turning toward a participatory mode of consciousness?* Educational Researcher, 23(3), 15–22.

Heshusius, L. (1996). *Modes of consciousness and the self in learning disabilities research: Considering past and future.* In D. K. Reid, W. P. Hresko, & H. L. Swanson (Eds.), A cognitive approach to learning disabilities. Houston: Pro-Ed.

Heshusius, L., & Ballard, K. (Eds). (1996). *From positivism to interpretivism and beyond. Tales of transformation in educational and social research. (The mind-body connection).* New York: Teachers College Press.

Hulsegge, J., & Verheul, A. (1986). *Snoezelen. Een andere wereld. Nijkerk,* The Netherlands: Intro.

Kalamaras, G. (1994). *Reclaiming the tacit dimension: Symbolic form in the rhetoric of silence.* Albany, NY: State University of New York Press.

Kauffman, J. M. (1999). Commentary: Today's special education and its messages for tomorrow. *Journal of Special Education, 32*(4), 244–254.

Kauffman, J. M., & Brigham, F. J. (1999). *Editorial. Behavioral Disorders, 25*(1), 5–8.

Krishnamurti, J. (1972). *You are the world.* San Francisco: HarperCollins.

Krishnamurti, J. (1993). *On mind and thought.* San Francisco: HarperCollins.

Lane, H. (1996). *A journey into the deaf-world.* San Diego: Dawn Sign Press.

MacMillan, D., Gresham, F., & Forness, S. R. (1996). Full inclusion: An empirical perspective. *Behavioral Disorders, 21*(2), 145–159.

McQuade, D. (Ed.). (1981). *Selected writings of Emerson.* New York: Modern Library.

Mood, J. J. L. (1975). *Rilke on love and other difficulties: Translations and considerations of Rainer Maria Rilke.* New York: W. W. Norton.

Morrison, T. (1997). *Paradise.* New York: Penguin Plume.

Prigogine, I., & Stengers, I. (1984). *Order out of chaos: Man's new dialogue with nature.* New York: Bantam Books.

Reinhartz, S. (1992). *Feminist methods in social research.* New York: Oxford University Press.

Sadaawi, N. E. (1996). Dissidence and creativity. In C. Miller (Ed.), *The dissident word: The Oxford Amnesty Lectures.* New York: Basic Books.

Sasso, G. M. (2001). The retreat from inquiry and knowledge in special education. *Journal of Special Education, 34*(4), 78–193.

Scheurich, J. J. (1997). *Research method in the postmodern.* London: Falmer Press.

Smith, J. K. (1988). The evaluator/researcher as person versus the person as evaluator/researcher. *Educational Researcher, 17*(2), 18–23.

Smith, J. K. (1989). *The nature of social and educational inquiry: Empiricism versus interpretation.* Norwood, NJ: Ablex.

Sugai, G. (1998). Postmodernism and emotional and behavioral disorders: Distraction or advancement? *Behavioral Disorders, 23*(3), 171–177.

Tannen, D. (1986). *That's not what I meant! How conversational style makes or breaks relationships.* New York: Ballantine Books.

Tannen, D. (1990) *You just don't understand: Women and men in conversation.* New York: Ballantine Books.

Vanier, J. (1999). *Becoming human.* Toronto: Anansi.

Varela, F. J., Thompson, E., & Rosch, E. (1993). *The embodied mind: Cognitive science and human experience.* Cambridge, MA: The MIT Press.

Walker, H. M., Forness, S. R., Kauffman, J. M., Epstein, M. H., Gresham, F. M., Nelson, C. M., & Strain, P. S. (1998). Macro-social validation: Referencing outcomes in behavioral disorders to societal issues and problems. *Behavioral Disorders, 24*(1), 7–18.

10

Jude MacArthur

TENSIONS AND CONFLICTS: EXPERIENCES IN PARENT AND PROFESSIONAL WORLDS

I'm speaking here as a parent and as a professional . . .

The difference I've seen between professionals is that some recognize that they are not the expert, the good one comes in and says, I'm not the expert, I'm the expert at accessing resources, but I'm not the expert on this child. The other comes in and says I am the expert, this is what I'm doing, this is what she should be doing, wee Annie should be drawing eyes on faces because this checklist says so.

Inclusive education involves the full participation of children with disabilities and children from other minority groups in all aspects of the ordinary curriculum and activities of regular education settings. In the New Zealand context, this means "[E]very child has the right to access the culturally valued curriculum of their society as a full-time member of an early childhood setting or school classroom alongside the other children of similar chronological age" (Ballard, 1998, p. 307).

When children with disabilities are included in ordinary early childhood centers and schools, support from other professionals who have a "specialist" focus may be needed to support the child's development in the center. This implies a need for teamwork between parents, early childhood teachers, and other professionals such as early intervention workers, physiotherapists, occupational therapists, and speech-language therapists (Twiss, Stewart, & Corby, 1997; O'Connor, 1997; Giangreco, Edelman, Luiselli, & MacFarland, 1996). Ideally, such teamwork is underscored by principles of role-release and role expansion that recognize the role of itinerant professionals as resource people with both information and skills from their own discipline to share, rather than as experts who deal with children on the occasion of their visit (Rainforth, 1998). This approach has been found to strengthen the ability of teams to provide cohesion and reduce confusion (Doyle, 1997). While teamwork may involve additional time and effort, proponents of transdisciplinary teamwork recognize that this is far outweighed by the advantage of collective knowledge at work (O'Connor, 1997; Rainforth, 1998).

While this is the ideal, there may be some way to go before this is achieved in practice. Some early childhood professionals in New Zealand have described difficulties accommodating itinerant professionals who do not fully understand the philosophical, pedagogical, and curriculum context of the early childhood center (Purdue, MacArthur, & Ballard, 1998). Where "expert" individual knowledge takes over, some teachers have identified barriers to achieving inclusion in their centers:

> It is really the itinerant teachers who come in that sometimes can cause the problems with inclusion. Depending on how qualified they are . . . they quite often don't understand early childhood and our practices . . . anybody in that role when they start should meet with the staff of the center to work all this out and find out what her role is and what our policies are, what strategies we use. (Purdue et al., 1998, p. 22)

The Research Context and Process

The research for this chapter was motivated by a comment from Kate to me, following the confusing process of diagnosis for her four-year-old-daughter, Annie. Kate is a teacher with senior responsibilities in an early childhood center for children under five years of age. Included in this center are three children who currently receive itinerant support from a number of professionals who focus on various aspects of the children's cognitive, social, and physical development. One is her four-year-old daughter Annie, recently diagnosed with a rare syndrome. Kate and the other staff in the center had been struggling for several months with the actions of some itinerant professionals employed to provide early intervention support to children with disabilities, including Annie. In particular, they were experiencing tensions and conflicts between their own beliefs and actions as teachers, and those of other professionals. For Kate, these tensions were magnified further as she began questioning the actions of these professionals as Annie's mother. During our ongoing discussions about the content and focus of this chapter, Kate recognized that her recent experience as a parent had in fact contributed to her understanding as a teacher:

> Now I'm a parent, I feel it more. Being a parent highlights the issues, I wouldn't have talked about it otherwise. You pay more attention when it's your child. It's not that I don't see progress for Annie, I do, it's just the way (itinerant support) is done. There's

a gut reaction, I felt disempowered, frustrated. I realize now that for other children, we would see the progress and we might not have noticed (how inappropriate the itinerant support was), we might have just let it happen.

Kate and I would snatch moments in the hallway to talk about inclusion, to throw around ideas about the roles and responsibilities of itinerant professionals, and what might be done to create change in an environment that Kate identified as "not being good for kids." Working as a university lecturer involved in teaching early childhood, primary, and secondary teachers about inclusive education meant that I had some understanding of the critical contextual issues involved in creating inclusive education settings. In the end, talking wasn't enough, and together we began thinking about ways in which itinerant professionals, parents, and early childhood teachers can work together to support the development of all children. Kate's concern that "something be done" about establishing protocols and procedures for early childhood teachers to use when working with itinerant professionals was the incentive for the research. Almost without realizing it, we had entered into a collaborative relationship with a shared goal to open up critical debate over issues of expertism and explore, through practitioner-focused publications, the elements that make up productive and supportive professional relationships.

A Critical Exploration of Professional Values

This study looks critically at the values and actions of itinerant professionals and the messages conveyed through these actions, through Kate's eyes as a parent and professional. It is based on an understanding that "more stories of parents are needed because parents live the experience of their child's disability in ways that many professionals cannot know, despite their good intentions otherwise. This is what parents can teach" (Ware, 1999, p. 64). As such, this chapter aims to serve as "an instrument of criticism that borrows from the voice of the parent in the study" (Ballard, 1999, p. 175). The project was motivated by "the idea that there is value in an understanding of personal experiences and meanings, those of participants and researchers" and that "the reality of personal accounts may cause us to care about what happens to another person and thus move us to action" (Ballard, 1999, p. 175). My task as researcher in this context was one of informing discourse on and practice in inclusion by emphasizing the inherent value of the parent's experience and perspective (Ware, 1999). As speaker and listener, Kate and I became what Ferguson and Ferguson (1995) describe as "implicit collaborators" involved in a process of giving meaning to that which is told (p. 105). Kate told her own story, in her own voice, in her own words. Story telling is underpinned by an interpretivist paradigm in which meaning is socially constructed, and where the goal of research becomes that of "describe, interpret and understand" (Ferguson & Ferguson, 1995, p. 112). The value of telling stories lies in their ability to be reformative:

"Letting parents describe their experiences and perspectives about raising children with severe disabilities in the community, in the local school, with other children, has been one of the primary forces toward . . . [achieving] inclusive education . . . It begins with the individual." (Ferguson & Ferguson, 1995, p. 118)

The data were collected through two semistructured, in-depth interviews with Kate (Patton, 1990). The questions I asked were framed collaboratively. I knew before the interview that she had given considerable thought to the role of itinerant professionals in early childhood centers, and I was aware from our informal discussions that Kate would need few prompts to tell her story. In this sense, we negotiated the form and content of the study from the outset, and this negotiation continued as we collaborated over the account of our discussions, and my attempts at conceptualizing, analyzing, and writing about her experience (Tripp, 1983). The data were analyzed using analytic induction as described by Bogdan & Biklen (1982) in which concepts were derived from the data and formed into conceptual interpretations and definitions relating to the roles, responsibilities, beliefs, and actions of itinerant professionals as Kate had experienced them. To preserve anonymity, no real names are used in this chapter.

Expertism

Roles and Responsibilities

She sees herself as an expert, definitely. This is the way we'll do it, this is the right way to do it because I've been doing it for years and years. . . . it's just her approach. She comes in as a professional, acts like a professional, but doesn't act professionally.

The values and actions of some itinerant professionals prompted Kate to reexamine the philosophy, curriculum, and practice of the early childhood teachers in Annie's childcare center. In her fused identities as an early childhood teacher with senior responsibilities in the center, and as Annie's mother experienced considerable tensions in her interactions with these professionals. In particular, the actions of Annie's "itinerant teacher," Mary, had had a profoundly negative impact on the center.

A fundamental question related to the roles and responsibilities of the itinerant teacher in terms of the support she provided to Annie. When asked what she saw the itinerant teacher doing, Kate said:

Sometimes she does a checklist, sometimes she needs to catch up with Annie before we have an IEP (Individual Education Plan), or fill out some forms that she hasn't filled out yet, so she comes in and does that for half an hour, sometimes an hour. There's no set time, I never know. I see her ticking boxes and carrying folders around. And she decides when there should be an IEP and she coordinates the IEP for Annie and she liaises too with Sue (speech/language therapist) and me and Jane (the ESW) and Ros (Annie's key teacher in the center). So she liaises, and I say liaises, but it's all on her terms.

The staff in the center, including Kate, was unsure about the various roles and responsibilities of itinerant professionals where much confusion followed. "People were coming and going at one stage and we didn't know who was supposed to be doing what." In part this uncertainty appears to have been fuelled by a lack of communication from the outset about the roles and responsibilities of other professionals, and about the implications for center teachers. Routines, as well as the power that routine authorizes, were disrupted.

Interactions with Annie

A fundamental theme of *Te Whariki,* the New Zealand early childhood curriculum, involves getting to know individual children and their strengths, interests, and challenges; and uses this information to direct planning and teaching decisions. Kate felt that the itinerant teacher did not know her daughter, and that some of her interactions were insensitive and highlighted Annie's disability:

> She calls her "Wee Annie." Now here's a child that's in the bottom 3% of the population for height for her age and she says, "So how is wee Annie?" Really patronizing stuff, you know, and that really, really bothered me and I should have said something but I didn't. I mean that's just the first rule of working with families and children with special needs, you watch your language.

The other side of the language issue was equally troubling, as Kate felt that the itinerant teacher was more interested in the label given to Annie's disability following a long period of searching for a diagnosis. The meaning of the label took on profound meaning as she now "had something to work on." Although the label assigned to Annie's condition was useful to Kate, I had had lots of doubts, and it was like, " 'phew' that's all right now." Kate viewed these contrasting perspectives and other actions to a deficit model perspective, which, as a parent, she found disturbing: "She comes in and monitors Annie, just Annie, she doesn't look at Annie within the environment of the center." Kate assessed these visits as excluding Annie, "she doesn't come in and look at the good things. . . . it makes me feel that I don't want her to know Annie any more because she might find more things wrong."

Although she was concerned that Annie had not developed a rapport with Mary, it was against the view of what constitutes a "good professional." That is, "the good professionals talk to Annie. They involve her. Mary talks to me, but she never gets on Annie's level, never . . . and that's very inappropriate."

Interactions with Kate as Parent

On occasion, Kate and Mary met in Kate's home, but most of their interactions were in the early childhood center. In this setting, Kate felt the expectation to stay in her role as Center Supervisor remained with some frequency, "Because you're a trained teacher." It seemed that Kate's fused roles were troubling, "She doesn't talk to me as a parent, I don't think [or when] she does it's very patronizing." Annie's father had a similar response and was quickly put off by meetings, in time, leaving this process to Kate alone. Although the family was excited about Annie's development and learning, Mary persistently reminded them of that which Annie could not do—or challenged her accomplishments relative to age-appropriate scales. "She's really good on the computer and that's a great thing in our family. She has great eye-hand movements and she's *better* than some other four-year-olds, and it gives us time out because she will sit for a long time, so we're really excited about that." In the everyday context Kate valued Annie's explorations on the computer. However, Mary worried about what "sorts of things she would be matching on the computer. Activities would be linked back to cognition and what she can't do. That's it you see, we get excited, but she doesn't share our passion about it."

In the end, Kate persisted with the relationship because she saw it as a key to accessing resources for Annie and for the center. She wanted to create change both for herself and for other parents. However, the process also clarified for Kate the value of a lifestyle assessment process initially described to her by the speech-language therapist. With a positive focus on the needs of the whole family, it stood in sharp contrast with the deficit-based and individual focus of "special ed":

> I'm always in conflict with what she's telling me. She'll say. "Oh, she's doing this really well now, but she's not doing that and we need to work on it," and I don't agree with a lot of it. I've tried to say that to her, but she just doesn't listen. She asks me questions, but it's things like, "Does she draw eyes when she draws circles?" For me that's totally irrelevant. I don't care, she's enjoying drawing, that's what I'm interested in. But she'll say, "Well, she really should be doing this by now." She'll say inappropriate things like that to me, so I really don't listen much to her because I don't respect a lot of what she says. I don't believe that she has good knowledge of Annie to make good judgments about Annie. I believe she judges Annie from the point of view of her own values and objectives. And I've seen other itinerant professionals doing the same thing. You have a box and the child has to fit into that box.

Kate's comments are sufficiently nuanced, and perhaps suggest benign exchanges, but taken together, they reveal how parents commonly experience professional judgment. According to Kate,

> Professionals' values have a huge impact. Mary has judged me as a scatty (unfocused) person who can't pull herself together and is disorganized. But she makes me feel like that. I don't know when she's coming, what's she's doing, where she's going, what the next step is. I'm always on the back foot (one step behind) with her.

Kate further felt that the interactions between the itinerant teacher and the family had rendered her husband powerless, and could have had the same impact on her had she not relied upon her own professional experience. She was quick to remind that many parents lack such experience, and are therefore likely to be more vulnerable to professional expertism that would silence or discourage participation, as it had for her husband. Kate began to realize the value of wearing the two caps of professional and parent, which prompted increased reflection:

As a parent I would say think about who is really the expert of these children. Think about who knows them best. It's not you. You have knowledge of things but not of this child. Get to know early childhood, the philosophy, and aspirations for children. For children to develop there needs to be three-way relationship with the parent, the professional and the child. Special ed. coming into it involves the teacherprofessional corner of the triangle; it's not about replacing the parent and their input, it all has to be equal. I want to say "Wake up. Get into the real world." They live in a world where they set unachievable goals, really.

Interactions with Teachers

The role of the itinerant teacher in New Zealand involves working in a team. The team comprises specialists such as educational psychologists, itinerant teachers, education support workers (teacher aides), speech-language therapists, and specialist advisors. The "team" does not include early childhood teachers. Rather, it is assumed that the team will work in conjunction with early childhood teachers to meet the needs of children with disabilities and their families (Twiss et al., 1997). The teachers in Annie's early childhood center did not feel involved. The itinerant teacher rarely interacted with teachers in the center, and Kate interpreted this as a failure to recognize that teachers have an important contribution to make. The teachers were routinely dismissed even though they had an equal share in the discussions. In her view, the professionals were at the top of the hierarchy, "because we've sat back and let them be the professionals." Curiously, Mary's professional interactions with Annie actually made little difference to the center teachers:

I think she intimidates the teachers to a certain extent. They can't be bothered with her now. Some will say, well, she's the expert, with maybe a sense of relief, "I'm glad I don't have to deal with Annie." But they don't ask her questions, because she comes in and tells us! "This is what we're doing with Annie." Staff are puzzled about what these people do with Annie but they just go on their merry way. And that's fine, because in a way, I want Annie to be like the other kids, you treat her like everyone else.

Knowledge of *Te Whariki* and Early Childhood Education

Itinerant professionals who were not valued in this center were, according to Kate, in touch with the principles, philosophies, curriculum, and practices of ordinary early childhood education. New Zealand required teachers to have a qualifications and experience in early childhood education before undertaking training for an early intervention diploma (Twiss et al., 1997). In some cases, this background may be in the distant past. Kate concluded that professional development should be ongoing for professionals working in this area, and that such development should include a focus on ordinary early childhood philosophy, curriculum, and practice. For example, Mary's suggestions for "time-out" were dismissed by staff as inconsistent with the curriculum document *Te Whariki*, and further,

Goals for children are about getting boxes ticked on checklists versus *Te Whariki* which is about looking at the child first and extending. Mary works from *Te Whariki* as a checklist and the goals aren't based on what children *can* do, it's what they *should* be doing. She's got that ingrained in her as a value and belief so that's the message she gives other people in centers.

Professionals who understood ordinary early childhood education had a leading edge in Kate's view. She expected itinerant professionals working in the center to interact equally well with the children and the teachers, "*Te Whariki* is about our aspirations for children and how we will get there." Kate advised,

> I would observe Annie first and get to know her first. Spend time with her, get to know Annie as a person. I would talk to the other teachers so that I have a varied perspective on Annie, not just my own observations. I'd talk to Annie's parents, talk to Annie as much as possible, and then look at *Te Whariki*. Look at the things that we aspire to for children. And then have a look at the things that she already does to extend that [skills set] using *Te Whariki*. *Te Whariki* can be used as a checklist, but that is to make sure that you are covering everything, not as a checklist to say, she's not doing that, we need to get there, OK?

Two other professionals supporting Annie's physical development now only saw her every six months. While not sharing a background in early childhood education, they seemed nonetheless to understand the culture of the center, and worked in ways that were consistent with early childhood philosophy and practice. Not all itinerant professionals working in early childhood centers have a background in early childhood education, although all itinerant teachers should have. For those who do not, Kate suggested that an acknowledgment on their part that they do not fully understand the context, would pave the way toward establishing a productive, collaborative relationship. As an example, she offered,

> I recently spoke with a new itinerant teacher who has just come from early childhood teaching. She considers herself a resource person. She invited me to one of the meetings before a new child came to the center to informally discuss some strategies for settling in this little boy. I didn't know him from a bar of soap, but she involved me right from the very word go. She now comes in, makes appointments, considers herself the resource person. She says, "I can't fill out these things that they want me to fill out, only you as the teachers and the mother can do this." With a completely different attitude, she goes and talks to the staff working with the child about filling out these things.

Impact on Planning and Teaching

According to Kate, "good" professionals recognized that they were not experts. . . . the good one comes in and says, "I'm not the expert. I'm the expert at accessing resources, but I'm not the expert on this child." While discussing another child with a disability in the center, Kate stressed that the other itinerant teacher who provided support to the center was able to make a positive contribution to the planning and teaching for this child:

> The other itinerant teacher has made a difference for all of us. We've got common goals for this boy, we're all very clear about who does what and she makes appointments. We work with her as a team.

This teacher began with a "Me chart," an informal assessment chart filled in for all center children by parents and teachers together. This first step fit perfectly with the beliefs and actions of the center teachers:

> The other itinerant teacher started with a "Me chart," which is just how we start our planning for any child. We can use that Me chart and we have a copy of it. She did a test sort of thing that she had to do, but we got a copy of it. She said you might see something different so let me know. Lots of accountability, but she said to me that there are some things that she refuses to do. She knows that it's not OK, what's the point and what's the purpose?

Creating Change: Whose Responsibility?

Although Kate often expressed the desire to swap teachers, she instead committed herself to creating change. She aimed to look past the personal reaction she felt as a parent, and hoped to get the support of her teachers in her role as an administrator. Kate knew from the actions of supportive itinerant professionals that successful collaborative relationships could develop. Her dual perspective contributed to an understanding of the need for teamwork that involves parents and professionals on an equal basis. Thus, her advice to itinerant professionals working in early childhood center began quite simply as, "Get to know the center. Look around, talk to people, read the policies. Work *with* the team, the parent, staff, the child, don't work *for* them. Their role is to make sure that everyone has equal partnership and to know where you're going with the child.

Knowledge Is Power: A Collaborative Effort

Kate realized the shortsightedness of the initial response to the challenges she and her staff faced: default to the authority of the professional only made resentment grow. She states: "I think it has been a case of lethargy in the past, not enough time, not enough funding. But now I believe that decisions should be center driven." She also realized that taking back the power they willingly abandoned would not be easy. "I see no coordination, I see us being angry. That's not doing the child any good at all." On a personal note Kate accepted that working from the framework of what every mother might prefer for her child might prove useful, not only for herself but also for the center: "I know what I want for my child, that's me the mother, and me the teacher says these children are ultimately my responsibility." Kate also requested staff development strategies to improve collaboration from a graduate student and myself.

Tensions and Conflicts: A Clash of Ideologies

It's a good title. It's not just me. It's tensions and conflicts for all the staff, you know? Tension definitely, because when they come in no one knows what they are doing. They feel it's not their place to ask. And conflict between what we are trying to achieve and what they are trying to achieve in our center. It doesn't fit with our philosophy.

Kate's experiences and perspectives on the roles played by some itinerant professionals with her child in an early childhood center may be conceptualized as involving conflicts and tensions between the ideology of the itinerant teacher as "expert" and the ideology of center staff as trained and experienced early childhood teachers. The actions of these professionals may be understood as coming from a diagnostic-prescriptive-remedial paradigm in which children with disabilities are perceived as broken and in need of being fixed (Ballard, 1997; Guess & Thompson, 1991; Meyer, 1991; Skrtic, 1986; Tomlinson, 1987; Wood & Shears, 1986). This approach fails to recognize that learning for all children involves a complex, interactive and socially mediated process between children and children, and adults and children (Vygotsky, 1978); yet for early childhood teachers in New Zealand this concept is basic to their understanding of how children learn. The scene, then, is set for conflict.

The diagnostic-prescriptive paradigm has readily accommodated the behavioral model as a model for teaching children with disabilities, and has had a significant impact on the way in which students with intellectual disabilities in particular have been taught. The assumptions and practices of behavioral teaching, however, including their exclusive focus on the individual child, do not fit readily with the curriculum and teaching approaches found in ordinary mainstream education settings, contributing themselves to exclusion in both education and community environments (Guess & Thompson, 1991; MacArthur, 1993). In the present study, Kate worried that the actions of some professionals in isolation from the other children, teachers, and wider context of the early childhood center excluded Annie and made her look different. She even wondered if the center teachers themselves might be negatively influenced by the actions of the itinerant teacher, such that they felt "glad I don't have to deal with Annie" and thus exempted from caring. The itinerant teacher assumes the role of the person who "does the inclusion" (Purdue, MacArthur, & Ballard, 1998).

The field of early intervention has often involved multidisciplinary teams of health, education, and welfare professionals, an enterprise that has been strongly associated with both the notion of rehabilitation and special education (Mitchell & Brown, 1991). Kate suggested that some professionals have lost touch with what ordinary early childhood teachers do in their centers, perhaps because their professional development has focused on special education rather than on developments in regular education. As a consequence they begin to view children as an amalgam of deficits in which assumptions of pathology and normative differences limit full knowledge of the child (Purdue, MacArthur & Ballard, 1998; Skrtic, 1991, 1995).

Further, an ideology of expertism urges the belief that it is specialist knowledge alone that counts, so that the knowledge and experience of ordinary early childhood teachers in this case is not valued by some itinerant professionals. Yet this view of the expert as "all-knowing" is challenged, since "Specialists may have expertise within their discipline, it is the people who spend most time with the student on an ongoing basis who have the most experience-based expertise about the person" (Kunc, 1992, cited in Giangreco, Edelman, MacFarland, & Luiselli, 1997, p. 330). Kate's sense of alienation as a parent in the process of receiving some itinerant support, and her concerns about the interactions between Mary on the one hand, and Annie and her teachers on the other, may be seen as examples of such exclusion. Giangreco, Dennis, Cloninger, Edelman, and Shattman (1993) described such difficulties with what they saw as a "specialist reliant" approach, including specialists having separate goals and different agendas from classroom teachers; specialists disrupting class routines; and specialists using approaches that were overly technical and stigmatizing to children. Parents, too, have raised concerns about working with a range of professionals, being overwhelmed and confused about roles; deficiencies in communication; and feeling excluded and experiencing fragmented services (Giangreco et al., 1997).

At the same time, inclusive education, on the other hand, has brought a renewed focus to the beliefs, philosophies, and practices of regular classroom and early childhood teachers. Research has become more concerned with "an examination of the mainstream itself . . . [with] an interest in values and ideology as determining features of school and community contexts" (Ballard, 1997, p. 244). Murray (1991) and Giangreco (1997), for example, have argued that it is the task of regular teachers to commit themselves to the value of inclusion for all children, to take responsibility for teaching the children in their class who have disabilities, and to call upon and use their skills and knowledge to teach all children. The tensions suggested by inclusion will continue to merit close examination.

Expertism: A Service Model or a State of Mind?

In New Zealand, early intervention services are provided to children and their families in early childhood centers through early intervention teams made up of a range of professionals with education, health, and welfare backgrounds. The itinerant teacher's role is to coordinate supports and services for the child and family while also playing an itinerant teaching role in early childhood centers. These teachers are required to have a background in ordinary early childhood education while receiving ongoing professional development. This grounding would seem to be important, particularly in light of Kate's experiences with professionals perceived not to have a sound recent knowledge of early childhood education, and such an emphasis may become increasingly important as more children with disabilities receive their "early intervention" in regular early childhood settings (Purdue et al., 1998).

Early intervention is based on assumptions that children with disabilities differ in some way from their normally developing peers and may therefore be in need of services and supports that are not normally found in ordinary early childhood settings (Bailey, McWilliam, Buysse, & Wesley, 1998). Leaders in the inclusive schools movement have been criticized by some for trying to deconstruct special education both as a construct and as a structure" for fear it will rid the education landscape of professionals called 'special educators'" (Fuchs & Fuchs, 1994, p. 301), with "specialists" following children into the mainstream. Yet this is exactly what needs to happen. Some early childhood teachers committed to inclusive education *have* felt a need for support to assist with modifying curriculum and instructional strategies to address the unique needs presented by an individual child with disabilities (Lieber, Capell, Sandall, Wolfberg, Horn, & Beckman, 1998). In this context the spotlight falls on the processes involving "specialists" and regularly trained teachers working together effectively in teams (O'Connor, 1997), and guided by common goals and a shared framework of "ever-evolving beliefs, values, and assumptions about education, children, families, and professionals to which all team members agree" (Giangreco, 1997, p. 195).

The present study suggests that these beliefs, values, and assumptions need to be grounded in the everyday experiences of regular early childhood education, and not in the expert-focused ideology of special education. Further, the present study suggests that some professionals were able to transcend the limitations of the model in which they found themselves working, through their beliefs and actions as they conveyed them to Kate and to the center teachers. These itinerant professionals were highly valued. What set them apart from their "expert-oriented" peers was an understanding of the early childhood context and a desire to work collaboratively with staff—which involved them fully in discussions and decision-making. Kate described them as "experts of resources, not experts of children" and had a strong sense that all of these people "really care about Annie." These professionals may be seen as superseding a working model based on expertism by adopting a perspective on collaboration which is rooted in ordinary early childhood education philosophy and pedagogy, and which recognizes that all participants (parents, teachers, and children) have knowledge to share as well as shared goals for children (Giangreco et al., 1997).

Supportive itinerant professionals may be viewed as working from a valued ideological perspective that creates inclusive learning environments. These professionals began with the regular early childhood context, thus rejecting the diagnostic-prescriptive-remedial paradigm that has been so widely embraced in the special education field (Slee, 1993). They understood Kate as parent, and the center teachers, to be the "experts" on Annie's strengths, interests, and challenges. They therefore took time to talk with and listen to the center teachers. They worked in ways that were consistent with the philosophies and practices of the center, recognizing and responding to the interests of other children and checking out their practices with the teachers. Kate described as "so refreshing" one itinerant teacher's decision to begin the assessment process with a "Me chart," a typical starting point for any child in an early childhood center. This professional's strength may lie in her recent teaching experience in regular early childhood education, and in an empathetic perspective gained through her "induction" (Skrtic, 1995) into regular, rather than special, education.

In Annie's center, however, other valued itinerant professionals did not share this same background in early childhood education. When asked about how she might account for this, Kate concluded that they were nonetheless able to work in their own specialist area *within the context of the center*. This suggests that a background or induction into early childhood education may not be a necessary prerequisite for those professionals whose "expertise" is in areas other than teaching and education. In this case, professionals' own understanding, attitudes, and beliefs about their role in relation to Kate, the center, and center teachers was critical, with valued professionals adopting a position reminiscent of Giangreco's (1997) "shared framework." Professionals who worked with the teachers, rather than with Annie; who recognized their own limitations in terms of their knowledge of early childhood; who checked out their plans and actions with staff; and who learned about Annie by talking with the teachers, would, in Kate's words, "have so much support from all the staff because the message is that we are working together to achieve that goal."

Research as a Partnership

This chapter began as a joint concern between myself as a researcher, and Kate, the mother of a child with a disability, and a trained and experienced early childhood teacher. It evolved into a working partnership on many levels with multiple reciprocal gains. Clough and Barton (1996) remind us that research is not a neutral activity and that as researchers we should consider the extent to which we, as researchers and teacher-researchers, put our skills and knowledge at the service of the researched. Our work should involve discussions with research participants about the topic of investigation and the use to which our findings are put. A collaborative approach goes some way toward redressing past imbalances where the researcher as expert has contributed to the oppression of people with disabilities:

> Disability research should not be seen as a set of technical objective procedures carried out by experts but part of a struggle by disabled people to challenge the oppression they currently experience in their daily lives . . . the major issues on the research agenda for the 1990s should be, do researchers wish to join with disabled people and use their expertise and skills in the struggle against oppression or do they wish to continue to use these skills and expertise in ways in which disabled people find oppressive? (Oliver, 1992a, p. 102)

Debates in the literature about who should have authority to speak about disability issues, or even do disability research (e.g., Oliver, 1992(b); Reindal, 1995; Shakespeare, 1993) has raised important questions about power relations in disability research, including its ultimate impact on disabling practices. My personal response to Kate's experience as she has struggled to understand the actions of specialist professionals with her child, are as much those of a parent and teacher as those of someone who knows about some aspects of disability but does not personally experience disability. This is our common ground. It is a position not to be apologized for, but rather one to be valued—for it is this relationship that gives Kate the power to say what she needs to say. Such a relationship may be conceptualized as involving a participatory mode of consciousness (Heshusius, 1994, and Chapter 9, this volume) in which a regulated distance between the self and other is both undesirable and unachievable. We have never viewed our relationship as that of researcher and participant, where the researcher as objective expert is in control of the participant. Rather, we see ourselves as colleagues, sharing skills and perspectives on an issue of concern to both of us. This relationship forms a supportive context in which personal views and experiences are readily shared and explored.

I locate my own position in this research as a teacher and a parent as well as a researcher interested in inclusive education and disability issues. In doing so, the research itself may be understood to be about teaching and education, as much as it is about disability and discrimination (Ballard, 1997). Being a parent and a teacher is an added bonus in the research process. Issues become personalized, and the actions and attitudes of others were challenged because as a mother and as teacher, I know they are not right. While I do not share Kate's experience as a mother of a child with a disability, the shared personal experiences we do have as trained and experienced teachers and mothers might be seen as the cement for a collaborative relationship in which both participant and researcher share a concern for what is studied and what becomes of the results (Barton, 1996; Clough & Barton, 1995, Tripp, 1983). Understanding disability research in this way means that those with a personal experience of disability can join with others who have an ethical commitment to social problems that they have not personally experienced, to seek an end to discrimination and oppression (Reindal, 1995).

Conclusion

The approach to research taken in this chapter mirrors one of the key themes in the study of parent-professional and professional-professional relationships. That is, that in the area of inclusive education, professionals (or researchers) and parents (or people with disabilities) need to form collaborative relationships and alliances in order to create the kinds of changes needed to make the world a better place for people with disabilities and their families. Kate's story makes complex issues meaningful in a way that we can use as intuitive, reflective, and complex human beings (Ballard, 1994). Her response to her story as she read through this chapter, was, "I didn't realize I was such an angry woman!" On reflection, she agreed that the chapter accurately described the way she had been made to feel through the attitudes and actions of some itinerant professionals. Professionals motivated by an ideology of expertism can create exclusionary pressures that are damaging to inclusion. Poor professional practice should be open to critique, exclusionary pressures need to be identified and resisted (Booth, 1996), and ideologies that challenge inclusion need to be identified and eradicated (Brantlinger, 1997). It is equally important to highlight supportive professional practice and to celebrate ideologies that promote the participation of children with disabilities within the culture and curriculum of ordinary education settings. Our joint task, then, is to publish material that is accessible to practitioners who might learn and benefit from Kate's experiences and insights.

References

Bailey, D., McWilliam, R., Buysse, V., & Wesley, P. (1998). Inclusion in the context of competing values in early childhood education. *Early Childhood Research Quarterly, 13*(1), 27–47.

Ballard, K. D. (1994). Inclusion, paradigms, power and participation. In A. Dyson, C. Clark, & A. Milward (Eds.), *Organisational change and special needs: School improvement or dilemma management?* London: David Fulton Publishers.

Ballard, K. D. (1997). Researching disability and inclusive education: participation, construction and interpretation. *International Journal of Inclusive Education, 1*(3), 243–256.

Ballard, K. D. (1998). Disability and development. In A. Smith, *Understanding children's development: A New Zealand perspective*. Wellington, New Zealand: Bridget Williams Books.

Ballard, K. D. (1999). Concluding thoughts. In K. Ballard (Ed.), *Inclusive education: International voices on disability and justice*. London: Falmer Press.

Barton, L. (1996). Sociology and disability: Some emerging issues. In L. Barton (Ed.), *Disability and society: Emerging issues and insights*. London: Longacre.

Bogdan, R. & Biklen, S. K. (1982). *Qualitative research for educators: An introduction to theory and methods*. Beverly Hills, CA : Sage Publications.

Booth, T. (1996). Stories of inclusion: Natural and unnatural selection. In E. Blyth & J. Milner (Eds.), *Exclusion from school: Inter-professional issues for policy and practice*. London: Routledge.

Brantlinger, E. (1997). Using ideology: Cases of nonrecognition of the politics of research and practice in special education. *Review of Educational Research, 67*(4), 425–429.

Clough, P. & Barton, L. (1995). Introduction: self and the research act. In P. Clough, & L. Barton (Eds.), *Making difficulties: Research and the construction of SEN*. London: Paul Chapman.

Doyle, B. (1997). Transdisciplinary approaches to working with families. In B. Carpenter, *Emerging trends in family support and early intervention*. London: David Fulton Publishers.

Ferguson, P. M., & Ferguson, D. L. (1995). The interpretivist view of special education and disability: The value of telling stories. In T. M. Skrtic (Ed.), *Disability and democracy*. New York: Teachers College Press.

Fuchs, D, & Fuchs, L. (1994). Inclusive schools movement and the radicalization of special education reform. *Exceptional Children, 60*(4), 294–309.

Giangreco, M. (1997). Key lessons learned about inclusive education: Summary of the 1996 Schonell Memorial Lecture. *International Journal of Disability, Development and Education, 44*(3), 193–206.

Giangreco, M., Edelman, S., Luiselli, T., & MacFarland, S. (1996). Support service decision making for students with multiple service needs: Evaluating data. *Journal of the Association for Persons with Severe Handicaps, 21* (3), 135–144.

Giangreco, M., Dennis, R., Cloninger, C., Edelman, S., & Shattman, R. (1993). "I've counted Jon": Transformational experiences of teachers educating students with disabilities. *Exceptional Children, 59*, 359–372.

Giangreco, M., Edelman,S., Luiselli, T., & MacFarland, S. (1996). Support service decision making for students with multiple service needs; evaluative data. *Journal of the Association for Persons with Severe Handicaps, 21*(3), 135–144.

Guess, D. & Thompson, B. (1991). Preparation of personnel to educate students with severe and multiple disabilities: A time for change? In L. Meyer, C. Peck, & L. Brown (Eds.), *Critical issues in the lives of people with severe disabilities*. Baltimore: Paul H. Brookes.

Heshusius, L. (1994). Freeing ourselves from objectivity: Managing subjectivity or turning toward a participatory consciousness? *Educational Researcher, 23*(3), 15–22.

Lieber, J., Capell, K., Sandall, S., Wolfberg, P., Horn, E., & Beckman, P. (1998). Inclusive preschool programs: Teachers' beliefs and practices. *Early Childhood Research Quarterly, 13*(1), 87–105.

MacArthur, J. (1993). *Teaching students with severe disabilities*. Unpublished Doctoral Thesis, University of Otago, Dunedin, New Zealand.

Meyer, L. H. (1991). Advocacy, research and typical practices: A call for the reduction of discrepancies between what is and what ought to be? In L. Meyer, C. Peck, & L. Brown (Eds.), *Critical issues in the lives of people with severe disabilities*. Baltimore: Paul H. Brookes.

Mitchell, D. & Brown, R. I. (Eds.) (1991). *Early intervention studies for young children with special needs*. London: Croom Helm.

Murray, M. (1991). The role of the classroom teacher. In G. Porter, & D. Richler (Eds.), *Changing Canadian schools: Perspectives on disability and inclusion*. Toronto: The G. Allan Roeher Institute.

New Zealand Council for Educational Research (NZCER) (1996). *Te Whariki*-Early Childhood Curriculum, Wellington, New Zealand: Ministry of Education.

O'Connor, B. (1997). *Interprofessional teamwork and interagency collaboration supporting a young child with severe disabilities*. Unpublished Ph.D. thesis: University of Queensland, Australia.

Oliver, M. (1992a). Changing the social relations of research production? *Disability, Handicap and Society, 7*(2), 101–114.

Oliver, M. (1992b). Intellectual masturbation: A rejoinder to Soder and Booth. *European Journal of Special Needs Education, 7*(1), 20–27.

Patton, M. Q. (1990). *Qualitative evaluation and research methods*. Newbury Park, CA: Sage Publications.

Purdue, K., MacArthur, J., & Ballard, K. (1998, 35 September). *Inclusion in early childhood education as early intervention*. Proceedings of the Australian Early Intervention Third Biennial Conference, AJC Convention Centtre, Randwick, Sydney, Australia.

Rainforth, B. (1998, 30 September–1 October). *Special education teams; putting knowledge of collaboration into practice*. Keynote address to the Specialist Education Services

Conference "Knowledge into Practice: Education for success in the community. Auckland, New Zealand.

Reindal, S. M. (1995). Discussing disability—an investigation into theories of disability. *European Journal of Special Needs, 10*(1), 58–69.

Skrtic, T. M. (1986). The crisis in special education knolwedge; A perspective on perspective. *Focus on Exceptional Children, 18*(7), 1–16.

Skrtic, T. M. (1991). *Behind special education: A critical analysis of professional culture and school organization.* Denver, CO: Love Publishing.

Skrtic, T. M. (1995). *Disability and democracy: Restructuring [special] education for postmodernity.* New York: Teachers College Press.

Shakespeare, T. (1993). Disabled people's self-organisation: A new social movement? *Disability, Handicap and Society, 8*(3), 249–265.

Slee, R. (1993). The politics of integration—new sites for old practices? *Disability, Handicap, and Society, 8*(4), 351–360.

Tomlinson, S. (1987). *A sociology of special education.* London: Routledge & Kegan Paul.

Tripp, D. (1983). Co-authorship and negotiation: The interview as act of creation. *Interchange, 14*(3), 32–45.

Twiss, D., Stewart, B., & Corby, M. (1997). Early intervention education services in Aotearoa/ New Zealand: Inclusion of infants and young children in regular early childhood settings—current provisions, issues and challenges. In B. Carpenter, *Emerging trends in family support and early intervention.* London: David Fulton Publishers.

Vygotsky, L. (1978). *Mind in society: The development of higher mental processes.* Cambridge, MA: Harvard University Press.

Ware, L. (1999). My kid, and kids kinda like him. In K. Ballard (Ed.), *Inclusive education: International voices on disability and justice.* London: Falmer Press.

Wood, S. & Shears, B. (1986). *Teaching children with severe learning difficulties: A radical reappraisal.* London: Croom Helm.

11

Linda Ware

THE POLITICS OF IDEOLOGY: A PEDAGOGY OF CRITICAL HOPE

Wouldn't it be better to end on a more hopeful note?
RESPONSE TO THIS CHAPTER BY DISTRICT ADMINISTRATOR

Seems that the book ends on a sort of "depressing" note—I'd want people to walk away feeling at least somewhat hopeful, seeing possibilities for change and increasingly inclusive schools and society.
RESPONSE TO THIS CHAPTER BY AN ANONYMOUS REVIEWER

We need critical hope the way a fish needs unpolluted water.
PAULO FREIRE, *Pedagogy of Hope*

In this chapter I provide a brief glimpse into a yearlong effort by a five-person team comprised of three high school teachers, two building administrators, and this researcher as we planned for school-based, state-mandated inclusion. I borrow from the case study I prepared for the Redding City School District that documented the efforts of these individuals as they struggled with the politics of ideology in pursuit of a pedagogy of critical hope. Both the progress and failure that accompanied their efforts to draft an inclusion implementation proposal to district administration are included here. As such, this chapter veers from the tradition among special education researchers who author a continuous progress narrative of policy and practice that minimizes the complexity of the field as a whole and inclusion in particular. That said, the chapter provides a hopeful account of the real-time efforts of three teachers in one high school as they attempted to respond to state- and district-mandated inclusion. Their efforts were informed by hope, when defined as more than "mere stubbornness" and refusal to contend with the material conditions of struggle (Freire, 1992:8). It is suggested that struggle is both a given and a goal informed by hope in the process of transformation, according to Freire. That is,

> I do not mean that, because I am hopeful, I attribute to this hope of mine the power to transform reality all by itself, so that I set out for the fray without taking account of concrete, material data. Declaring, "My hope is enough!" No, my hope is necessary, but it is not enough. Alone, it does not win. But without it, my struggle will be weak and wobbly. We need critical hope the way a fish needs unpolluted water.

Making the Leap to Inclusion

Making the Leap to Inclusion, a case study prepared as an evaluation component for the Redding City School District (hereafter, the district) describes research conducted with a team that included three teachers, the district's inclusion facilitator, two building administrators, and myself as we attempted the leap to inclusion at Wellington High School.[1] My involvement with the district and Wellington followed my appointment to the district's Task Force on Inclusion, an "oversight" committee that included district administrators, teachers, a parent, university faculty, and one of the attorneys who filed the class action suit. The task force was convened in the mid-1980s as part of a consent decree that mandated greater inclusion in general education of identified special education students.

The Wellington teachers, like many with whom I have previously supported in the development of school-based inclusion, were deployed as front-line workers who attempted to challenge, if not to transform, the culture and structure of their schools. They often carry the burden of critical reform on their backs, and as a consequence, these foot soldiers have much to lose in the process. As key informants in the ongoing struggle for social justice in education, they are too often silenced by the very policy mandates they aimed to use as tools for change. It is important to acknowledge that as an educational researcher, I bring to this work a clear bias informed by a cultural perspective reflecting my experiences as a teacher, parent, administrator, and advocate of inclusion. Consistent with the view outlined by Corbett and Slee (2000), I view educational inclusion aligned with deep cultural transformation. In their three-tier model of inclusion, the first level is led by policy and notions of school effectiveness; the second reflects structural modifications to the school environment and to the curriculum, and the third level, that of deep culture, is characterized by

> the hidden curriculum of fundamental value systems, rituals and routines, initiations and acceptance which forms the fabric of daily life. It is at this degree of inclusion

that real quality of life issues reside. This can be an intangible process whereby students are taught to see themselves as either valued or de-valued group members. (pp. 140–141)

Although Corbett and Slee view this level as the most "satisfying" type of educational inclusion, they are quick to remind that this depth of inclusion is very hard to "monitor or even to fully define" (ibid). My own research underscores the belief that inclusion will demand nothing short of deep cultural reform in the school, across the district, and throughout society. Elsewhere I have suggested the necessity for school-based inclusion reform that explicitly engages cultural awareness of disability located outside of K12 schools (Ware 2001, 2002, 2003a). Public attitudes are shifting from the historic view of disability as individual pathology to one that reckons with disability as a social category akin to race, class, and gender. Were school-based inclusion reform efforts more widely informed by a cultural/historical perspective on disability, the complexity of inclusion initiatives might prove less threatening for educators. What remains too often true is that for those who attempt this reform matrix in the absence of grappling with its social political dimensions, few are satisfied, many are sacrificed, and others simply surrender just short of rewriting the fundamental value systems that drive everyday exclusionary practice in schools. Despite the obvious combustibility of interrogating school systems to expose values, rituals, routines, and initiations as the explicit mechanisms that underwrite exclusion, my research inevitably returns to exploration of the moral challenges that inclusion presents (2002, 2003b). I view teaching as a "moral craft" (Tom, 1984) and thus cannot but wonder if educators, in their efforts to promote inclusion reform, are ready for what promises to dismantle much of what we have constructed and come to rely upon as "the system." Here I document one such struggle and the unflinching self-critique and openness to contradiction, discontinuity, and the difficulty of attempting reform that, *by design*, is nonlinear, untidy, and unfinished.

Setting the District Context

This research was conducted during a period when the Redding City School District was under a consent decree (1983–1984) and enforcement order (1993–1994) to create more inclusive schools[2] as the result of 1981 a class action suit. The Inclusion Task Force was chaired by the then-acting director of special education instruction (hereafter, the chair). Monthly meetings were consistently well attended and the interactions were positive and seemingly supportive. On occasion, critical issues were raised, including the overrepresentation of minority youth in special education, the lack of administrative leadership in the example of inclusion, ineffective or inconsistent instructional opportunities, nonsystemic training to support inclusion, et cetera. However, when our discussion veered too close to "ideological" concerns, the chair reminded us that "moral issues" fell outside the charge of the committee.

His censure passed without comment as he hastily returned to the monthly agenda, ticking off items with efficiency, and thus ended our meetings on time.

The city of Redding and the district are congruent with demographics and national trends reported for large urban areas where steady growth by low-income families and recent arrivals for whom English is not their first language impacts schooling (Feagin, 1998; Hodgkinson, 1999). Towler (1998) reported that in 1997, 90% of students in the city schools received free or reduced lunch, a figure contrasted with 22% in 1980. For every 100 students who were freshman in the city schools in the fall of 1993, only 68 were in the 1994 sophomore class, only 46 were in the 1995 junior class, and only 27 graduated in the spring of 1997. Of this number, 5 received a Regents diploma (discussed below), and 15 went on to college. In contrast, the neighboring 17 suburbs in the county reported that for every 100 freshman, 95 moved to the next grade level and 84 graduated with their class. Rates of poverty in the suburban districts vary from an average of 30% for schools in the inner ring of suburbs to less than 10% in the outer rings (those farther away from the city). Similar to other urban cities in the United States, the suburbs emerged as a consequence of "white flight" from urban areas dating back to the 1960s, a phenomenon Feagin (1998) describes as "urban apartheid."

Another significant influence that came to bear on this research was standards-driven reform in New York State prompted by the New York Board of Regents. This reform was initiated in an effort to raise academic standards, phasing in more stringent graduation requirements for the class of 2000, and eliminating the lower track diploma known as the "local diploma." Although the new standards would impact many students, that was particularly the case for students in special education, many of whom previously graduated with a local diploma (a modified IEP diploma, Individualized Educational Plan). The mass relocation of students from separate self-contained settings into general education settings occurred by fiat, resulting in abrupt and radical changes in the daily context.

Warning: Do Not Read Me!

Much effort has been exhausted among education researchers to either provide a universal definition of inclusion or to concede to the necessary ambiguity about terms, and focus instead on exclusion. Words are often strung together to suggest that those in pursuit of inclusion know just what we are after and how we might get there—*wherever there is*! In contrast, Julie Allan (2003b) borrows from Derrida to explain that "inclusion is like the piece of grafitti which reads, 'do not read me' (1979, 145)—an order that has to be transgressed in order to be obeyed" (141). The likelihood of this graffiti appearing on school district Web sites or hallway banners is slim, as the goal in most educational settings remains focused on reform efforts inscribed by structural modifications and service delivery models—as was the case in Redding. According to a document provided by the chair at an early Inclusion Task Force meeting for the 1998–99 school year:

Inclusion began in the 1988–89 school year when the district received approval from the State Education Department to serve students with disabilities in Blended classrooms. Inclusion continues to grow through the School Based Planning Team (SBPT) process of developing and implementing innovative models for the delivery of special education services. (District Document, 1998, p. 2)

The district developed three models of inclusion identified as the blended classroom, the modified blended classroom, and the individual placement. The relocation of students into these new settings was determined on a case-by-case basis. In an early task force meeting I attempted to encourage a discussion of the problems associated with an "individual focus" as a disincentive to systemic reform. The chair replied, "On the contrary, our data show that some classrooms were inclusive prior to the mandate for inclusion, although few would view themselves as 'fully inclusive.'" He was quick to explain, "People don't like that terminology." Confused by his response, I elaborated on my point to explain that if we viewed inclusion through a civil rights lens, the limitations of a "case-by-case" approach might be more apparent. "Yes," he replied, and moved on to the next agenda item. Following the meeting, other task force members remarked on my comments and welcomed my "fresh" perspective. In time, it became clear that the monthly meetings were convened to document compliance outlined by the court order for inclusion and that the committee exerted little influence otherwise.

Inclusion in Redding remained at the first level led by policy and notions of school effectiveness authored by the state, and it was launching the second tier of structural modifications that was authored by the district. The expectation for schools amounted to little more than relocating students for purposes of compliance.

Taking Note

Although the task force required little more than my attendance, I agreed to serve as an unpaid consultant to provide "technical" support to the district's "mini-grant" schools. This initiative was an attempt to accelerate schools' inclusion efforts in anticipation of the inclusion mandate in 2000. One of the two inclusion facilitators who worked under the direction of the chair invited me to accompany her on weekly site visits. In my role as consultant I was afforded great latitude to support any of the targeted schools (seven elementary, two middle schools, two high schools) that applied for and received mini grants ($3,000–5,000). The mini grants were made to schools with few strings attached other than the expectation they keep informal documentation of their efforts to be reported at the end of the school year.

Informal conversation with the schools confirmed the chair's earlier assessment that the schools viewed themselves as "mostly inclusive" following the initiative of one or two teachers who took the "lead" to promote inclusion. None described their school as "fully inclusive." In dialogue with teachers one-on-one, or in meetings mandated by the district, I asked for a paraphrasing of the district's goals for inclusion. Teachers and administrators were quick to cite district policy documents and the pressure mandated by the state. School effectiveness was not mentioned as a stated goal despite the state's efforts to advance that claim. In fact, many voiced just the opposite and predicted increased school failure. A sample of the comments made in my initial visits to various schools included the following:

> Between the new standards and six-hour-long Regents Exams—it will be hard enough to get my own students to pass—I can't even imagine what the Sped kids will do.

> When the district gets cited for increased school failure because of this inclusion idea—what new plan will they roll out?

> There's pretty much a consensus that inclusion is bound to fail along with the sped students they place in our classes. It's a losing game all around.

> These kids can take the test again and again, but they'll never pass. We know that much already.

> So remind me—just what exactly are we including them in anyway? If my kid was in special education I, for sure, wouldn't go along with this. I'd want some protections in place.

When I heard the teachers' remarks I sensed their frustration and noted concern for the students. Later when I transcribed my notes it seemed that more pressing concerns emanated from disruption of the existing system. The long established mechanisms that supported exclusion served to maintain the myth of smooth operations. That is, although the reauthorization of the Individuals with Disabilities Act (IDEA) in 1997 mandated student placement in the least restrictive setting, failure among these students did not reflect upon the status of the school. The existing system assumed certain safeguards were in place to ensure that those who passed were as deserving as those who failed. In other words, the students for whom passing mattered were counted and those who did not matter were not counted. Taking note of what was said and what was not said, it bears mentioning that neither teachers nor administrators suggested inclusion might provoke the possibility of revising fundamental value systems, the need for curriculum reform, or the opportunity to reexamine the rituals, routines, and initiations that sanction acceptance and/or authorize rejection on a daily basis in schools.

Morgan and Wellington

Within six weeks I committed to both of the high schools that received mini grants. My participation was loosely structured between the poles of educational resource and critical friend. Morgan and Wellington were quite distinct settings, as evidenced by their response to the needs assessment required by the district—an instrument served to inventory technical needs across 11 items:

1. Instructional issues/approaches (planning/adaptations, assessment and evaluation, curriculum modifications, cooperative learning, multiple intelligences, learning styles, computer assisted instruction).
2. District curriculum, standards, and expectations (for compensatory students, modified IEP students, functional IEP students).
3. Classroom management.
4. Models of inclusion (blended classrooms, modified blends, individual placement).
5. Site visits (in district, out of district).
6. Disability awareness for all staff, including clerical and lunchroom.
7. Collaborative/communication.
8. Roles and responsibilities (general educators, special educators, paraprofessionals, building administrators, related service providers, school-services-support team).
9. Scheduling issues.
10. Parental/family involvement.
11. Other.

Morgan identified a singular and urgent need—that of classroom management (circled in red and highlighted). In contrast, Wellington sought assistance in two areas: roles and responsibilities and site visits.

Morgan teachers who teamed up for math instruction began the school year with large class sizes ($n = 40$) prompting their concerns for classroom management. One team seized upon my offer to observe their classes and to problem-solve various behavioral management approaches. In contrast, teachers at Wellington requested evidence-based research to inform their nascent efforts to increase faculty involvement to support inclusion. Wellington had nearly ten years of team-teaching experience that afforded them recognition as one of the more "inclusive" schools in the district. The three teachers on the team included Michael, who taught science; and two special educators, Marianne and Mary, each with considerable coteaching experience. Ten years earlier, Michael had completed his student teaching at the school that developed the initial "models of inclusion" prototype. He now joked that as the first generation offspring of the district's coteaching experts, his DNA inscribed him as a lifelong inclusion advocate. On a serious note, he added, "I've been coteaching ever since and while it's not exactly rocket science, I would never bother without support from administration."

For the most part, the teachers at Wellington viewed their administrators as more supportive than not, although the principal received mixed reviews relative to inclusion. For this reason both the building principal and the house administrator responsible for special education students were included on the team. Meanwhile administrative leadership at Morgan was nonexistent, as the assistant principal assigned to the team was pulled in many directions and never attended a meeting. I was surprised to learn that Morgan once led the district's early efforts at inclusion and that several teachers there were responsible for the development of the models of inclusion prototype on which Michael was trained. At the time, a special education teacher (now the district inclusion facilitator) and a science teacher teamed in a blended classroom for science instruction. National and international visitors trekked to upstate New York to observe the first blended classroom in the district. The science teacher was still on the Morgan faculty, but no one mentioned him as a possible resource in support of the mini grant. Within weeks following my observations at Morgan, the inclusion planning team fell apart. Although no formal reason was provided, it was clear that leadership was sorely lacking, and as a consequence, interest in planning for inclusion was far from enthusiastic.

Although the Wellington principal agreed to participate on the team, her energies were consumed by the schools' efforts to launch a prestigious International Baccalaureate program. Midway through the year she had yet to attend a meeting, although she stayed informed via e-mail. Only Michael raised concerns about the principal's absence, but like Marianne and Mary, he felt confident that their autonomy was authorized—if only by e-mail. Lesley, the house administrator, maintained a steady presence at the monthly meetings and sometimes joined our weekly sessions.

Looking into Wellington

High schools in Redding are organized as magnet schools that focus on a particular program of study (i.e., the arts, law and business, science and technology, etc.). Students can attend their neighborhood school or any other district high school of their choosing. Wellington, with a student population of 1,100 and 120 faculty, was well regarded in the district for its long-standing history of academic excellence. The school was organized into a three-house structure comprised of Science/Technology (third floor), Academy of Excellence (second floor), and Transition Tech (basement). This structure was premised on the belief that creating smaller clusters of students and faculty would promote a more intimate and caring community. Special education services were provided at all schools, but only Wellington coined new terminology for their program—"Transitional Tech" (TT)—and isolated these students in a separate house. When I questioned the motivation behind this the team cited "spin" and a desire to emphasize that the status of the school's higher levels of attainment-special education fell outside the perception of high achievement. Over time TT had become a synonym for special education not only at Wellington; students at other schools used the term to taunt their peers. When I pointed out the usage of this term during a Morgan visit, the inclusion facilitator dismissed my observation, citing its use as typical of the teasing, and likely not linked to Wellington at all. The team believed otherwise, although they were surprised that an otherwise "insignificant" label would find its way outside the school. Michael concurred that its use was likely pejorative, but Marianne challenged him. She argued that Wellington students never used the term to insult. "They know it's just a way to distinguish the third house."

The stigma and objectification associated with the language of special needs is often overlooked in schools as if the eugenic impulse that assigns individuals to a hierarchy of worth was merely a benign tradition. On a previous occasion I noted the use of replacement terminology when the inclusion facilitator spent forty-five minutes explaining the different models of inclusion (blended, modified, and individual placement). This amounted to little more than calculations fed by body count (e.g., number of teachers, paraprofessionals, and students—both general and special). And yet the inclusion coordinator was highly invested in drilling the teachers on the appropriate use of terminology. In a self-congratulatory tone she later explained that the usual state distinctions of 15:1:1, 12:1:1 and 6:1:1 (similar to the 20% formula Slee considered in Chapter 3, in this example New York state casts the subset of students by the "degree of need"). Classrooms with 15 students, one teacher, and one paraprofessional suggest fewer needs, classroom with 12 students, one teacher, and one paraprofessional suggest increased needs, and classrooms with 6 students, one teacher, and one paraprofessional represent the greatest needs. It was now suggested that such calculus would be deemphasized in a move to standardize new language relative to classroom structures. "That's interesting," I exclaimed! "Renaming the site of intervention from the student's body to the classroom?" Somewhat tentatively, she explained, "We're back to thinking about classroom needs. Now our structures allow us to make funding decisions to support everyone in the classroom and not just those identified students with disabilities."

Emerging Critical Insights

As a new arrival in Reddington, my lack of local historical/institutional knowledge about the district and the state left me feeling more like a learner than a consultant. I aimed to focus on listening, gathering relevant information from the professional literature, accompanying the team on area site visits, and on occasion, raising questions to seek clarification. It was increasingly clear that understanding inclusion relative to its moral or critical dimensions was of little interest to district administrators. And despite their willingness to conform to the district's technicist impulse, the teachers could be drawn into reflection on the moral implications of the task before them. The literature I provided was broad in scope, including those who approach inclusion as a "new-skills-set" training event (e.g., Friend, Reising, & Cook, 1993; Villa & Thousand, 1995); those who offer a larger critique of foundational special education knowledge (e.g., Biklen, 1992; Brantlinger, 1997; Heshusius, 1982; Skrtic, 1991, 1995; Tomlinson, 1995); and those who view inclusion as a complex and transformative social project (e.g., Allan, 1999; Ballard, 1999; Barton, 1997; Bernstein, 1996; Corbett, 1996). This scholarship was excerpted to avoid saturation and in hopes of initiating conversations rather than lectures as the team began to point out critical contradictions at Wellington.

For example, when Michael voiced doubts about the perception of inclusivity and community at Wellington, he cited both structural and cultural barriers unique their program. He noted that since the disabled students were housed in the basement, the majority of Wellington teachers could move through the day and the year with little or no interaction with these students. Not surprisingly, these "exempted" teachers could ignore both the recent mandate for inclusion and shared responsibility for all students. "So, who *really,* who cares about 'our' kids?" Michael asked in mocked bewilderment. On the hunch that he might be interested in *Geographies of Exclusion* (Sibley, 1995), I excerpted a few pages, in particular the theoretical insights of Basil Bernstein and Anthony Giddens. Given that each house occupied a separate floor and provided discrete curriculum exclusive to the identified students they served, Bernstein's analysis of open and closed curriculum organization seemed useful (see Table 11.1 below).

Bernstein identifies the very same exclusionary structures Michael cited as barriers to the implementation of inclusion at Wellington. His discussion of the inherent hierarchy in schools pointed to a more focused understanding of the structures that merit reexamination. Sibley's (1995) discussion of "purified space" was also a powerful concept for the team. After reading these excerpts Michael opened the next meeting by reading several key phrases: "A hierarchical structure does not like ambiguity"; "when the curriculum is strongly classified, new ideas on pedagogy or academic content are seen to be threatening" (80). I had previously urged the necessity of ambiguity in the process of planning more inclusive schools, now after considering Bernstein's causal connections to "exclusion" ambiguity was a less troublesome notion. Building on Michael's initial observations, it was now logical to probe the relationship between the structure of social space by both the built environment and organization schemas sanctioned by the institution.

These insights would slowly inform the team's critical analysis over time. My earlier "abstract" assessment of schools as sites for containment and control of student bodies, disciplined not only through policies and practices but within physical space and real boundaries was now underscored by their own examples. When Mary wondered aloud why interest in teaming had decreased—Michael was quick to reason that too few directives or incentives from the principal urged against internal norms that viewed teaming as the responsibility of some, but not all

TABLE 11.1. Characteristics of Open and Closed Curriculum Organization

Open	Closed
Ritual order celebrates participation and cooperation	Ritual order celebrates hierarchy and dominance
Boundary relationships with outside blurred	Opportunities for self-government
Boundary relationships with outside sharply drawn	Very limited opportunities for self-government
Mixing of categories	Purity of categories

teachers. He further speculated that increased segregation and elitism would likely accompany Wellington's move to become the first International Baccalaureate (IB) school in the district. Although Michael welcomed the program per se, he recognized that it signaled greater exclusion due to the prestige associated with IB schools and the creation of new hierarchies for students and teachers—both imagined and real.

Marianne and Mary voiced greater anxiety about the threat of standards and mandated Regents Exams for their students than was suggested by the IB program. In contrast to district administrators who joined the state-led chorus about the merit of standards, they were struck by the timing of two such obviously incompatible reforms. The standards pressure erupted throughout the school and across the state, prompting new waves of advocacy by teachers, parents, students, and a few brave administrators—but no one on the team joined this campaign. Interestingly, Marianne had since followed up with her students in discussion of the impact, if any, of the TT label. Following a few informal conversations, she structured more formal interviews with her students, and Mary did the same with her students. When we met as a team, Marianne announced with near horror, "These kids even call themselves TTs!" Michael was quick to respond, "Well, yeah, why shouldn't they? That's what we call them." When I asked if the students might be attempting to reclaim the word—to be 'in-your-face' about it" (as Jenny Corbett suggests), the team looked perplexed. Briefly, I explained Corbett's somewhat wicked analysis of "teaching the dumb to speak," which she outlines in "Bad Mouthing: The Language of Special Needs" (1996), and her directive that disabled people subvert the language that has oppressed them. Originally I opted against including this work in their readings, but the teachers seemed intrigued now and wanted to see the book for themselves. Soon after, Marianne made copies for her special education colleagues of Corbett's suggestion that the language used to bad-mouth disabled students cuts both ways. That is,

> the sentimental language of "special need" that is embodied in the imagery of protection, care, tenderness and love. I dislike and suspect sentimentality. I think it is a sham emotion and one which tends to mask cold, callous indifference. (xi)

For Corbett, both the "sugar-coated poison" of special needs terminology and the flip side are equally problematic given the historical use of words and images that foster "fear, mistrust, loathing and hostility" (ibid). She goes on to explain how terms of abuse such as "idiot," "imbecile," and "moron" are similar to slurs such as "nigger," "queer," and "spastic," which have recently been appropriated for use by other marginalized and now activist communities. For Corbett, it is "essential to disengage 'special needs' from its 'educational' base and place it in a wider social and cultural context in order to appreciate how pervasive and damaging these dual elements are (ibid). Although Marianne's colleagues were mostly unresponsive to her efforts to engage them on the language issue, Mary and Michael were eager to grapple with the numerous limitations of how special education has been conceptualized. This prompted a timely introduction to Doug Biklen's multi-layered account of creating inclusive schools and society in *Schooling without Labels* (1992).

In the instance of Wellington students and their use of TT documented in Marianne's interviews, it was clearly a dehumanizing term, whether its use was official or otherwise. For purposes of this research, this realization marked a significant turning point for Marianne and Mary, who until the students made this knowledge known to them, accepted the term "TT" as a mostly insignificant term. It was incredibly difficult for Marianne and Mary, as special educators, to relinquish the normative view ascribed to their practice as founded upon useful, objective knowledge that benefits children. This dogma is so ingrained in both teacher preparation and everyday practice, that to interrogate it is nothing short of sacrilege. Perhaps it was their growing confidence in the task before them, the authority to develop a proposal to reinvent a more equitable system, or perhaps it was the collegial interactions with Michael, myself, and the readings we discussed that enabled Marianne and Mary to challenge special education policy and practice. Clearly, they had begun the process of unraveling the threads woven so tightly over time to hold special education mythology intact. The challenge became where this new knowledge, that which Bernstein describes as "dangerous knowledge," might best be utilized within the system. Would it be rejected? Suppressed? How might it inform the system and the team as they continued to develop plans for inclusion with increasing recognition of the complexity of the task before them?

Shifting Discourses

Despite the seeming progress of the team's slowly shifting discourse from technical solutions to a rights discourse, the proposal they drafted focused on increasing the number of team-teaching partnerships. A workshop series was scheduled to address teaching strategies to promote better educational delivery to all students, and as such, reference to the 2000 mandate for inclusion could be deemphasized. In this way, the team would downplay the "special education" thrust of the initiative for inclusion. Since the proposal required the approval of the school-based planning team (SBPT), the team decided a PowerPoint presentation would be an effective way to present their proposal. Michael was one of a handful of Wellington teachers recognized for his technology expertise, and naturally he jumped at the opportunity to help storyboard the proposal. Initially the team agreed to focus on establishing the need for inclusion, stressing the mandate from the state and cajoling their peers through compliance. But in discussion about their preferred take-home message they ultimately decided against arm-twisting and opted to inspiration: to promote the belief that inclusion was the *right* thing to do for all kids, and hence, all teachers. Actually, their discussion was influenced more by technology than by ideology. Because the PowerPoint presentation integrated dynamic content that included teacher and student testimony relative to the positive aspects of inclusion at Wellington, the presentation promised to literally sell inclusion to the faculty. Or so hoped the team.

However, the team was more than surprised by the insights of their TT students, who offered an incredibly sophisticated analysis of the real workings of the "hidden curriculum of fundamental value systems, rituals, routines, initiations and acceptance that forms the fabric of daily life" (Corbett & Slee, 2000, p. 136). The students revisited events throughout the semester to explain the numerous ways their difference is isolated and marked. For example, TT students are singled out from their friends for separate pre-enrollment procedures, they are issued books after general enrollment concludes to ensure availability to those who actually use the books, SC (special classification) is stamped in bold red ink across their student identification cards and other student forms to denote their "special" status, and later, their report cards are similarly marked. When relating this list to the team, Marianne observed, "It reminds me of how we treated Jewish people in Nazi Germany. Really! I mean they didn't say that exactly, but I could tell that they really feel ostracized." Mary winced in response, saying, "I think the comparison is a bit strong for our purposes." But Michael was quick to add, "It's okay by me. I think the analogy holds. Maybe you should ask them—it's worth pursuing, don't you agree, Linda?" Michael was not seeking permission when posing his question; rather, it was very much in the spirit of support.

Mary felt her students had provided key insights about the unexamined practice of exclusion, having learned from her students why many were reluctant to participate in the formal graduation ceremony. She said, "Have you ever stopped to think about our tradition here where each house administrator hands out diplomas to their respective students during the graduation ceremony?" Mary paused just long enough for Marianne and Michael to respond. Both drew a blank. "Our kids are singled out the moment they walk across the stage and receive their diploma from Lesley, right?" Mary continued, "The TT house administrator bestows those diplomas to their own students. All at once this ritual of celebration becomes public humiliation!" Struck by this insight, Marianne remarked, "No wonder they don't come. I just figured graduation didn't matter that much to them."

The Wellington team was clearly invested in exploring the subtle trappings of ideology as Ellen Brantlinger explained in chapter 1. Particularly in that "ideologies operate largely at an unconscious level, they go unnoticed, especially the ideologies that are the most common and widespread." Teachers at Wellington made assumptions about language use, physical space, and institutionally sanctioned procedures that segregated students in clearly dehumanizing ways. Until they heard otherwise from their students, most of these artifacts were routinely overlooked. It is not that the faculty were either unthinking or noncaring—quite the opposite. But as evidenced here, it was easy to proceed with the belief that objective protocols insure morally-free technical choices in schools. More importantly, institutionally sanctioned routine practices and placements at Wellington minimized the need to explore the overrepresentation of African-American students in the TT house. Although the school had engineered new language and the myth of high standards and high achievement, this clearly applied to some, but not all students.

Taking the Risk

Somewhere between the time the team came to hear what the students knew and to recognize their own unwitting complicity in propping up institutional processes that stigmatize and devalue students, they revised their proposal. The result was nothing short of a call to action inspired by outrage similar to their own, solidarity informed by the experiences their students recounted, and critical hope inspired by recognition of shared responsibility to interrupt the subtle workings of schoolwide exclusion. They would still address teaming concerns and instructional strategies as originally planned, but these components would be interspersed with various philosophical perspectives about inclusion with excerpts from both general and special education students in discussion of the meaning of inclusion. They ended their PowerPoint presentation with the recommendation that the TT house be eliminated. The final slide listed the following bulleted items:

- Having Transition Tech as a third house, specifically for students with disabilities, negatively impacts self-esteem and the perception of how we treat individuals who are different from us.
- The location of special education classes and offices in the basement is not only unfair, but perpetuates the stigma associated with disabled students as being less worthy individuals.
- It is our position that the place called Transition Tech has been a model that promotes ignorance, stereotypes, and poor social skills in most students and staff.

The team was confident that the quality of their work would hold great appeal. As the last item on the agenda they promised the SBPT chair they would require no more than the 15 minutes they were allocated. Once their presentation began, a noticeable discomfort erupted across the SBPT audience signaled by sighs, squirming bodies, and snickering in hushed commentary. Despite its technical polish, the PowerPoint failed to inspire the SBPT with the same degree of solidarity now enjoyed by the team. Following the presentation the team received a curt thanks and the reminder that SBPT protocol dictated they return in a month to answer questions. Emotions ran high as the team pushed the cart of computer equipment back to Michael's room. "What was all that about?" Michael snapped. Marianne, visibly shaken, stammered, "I thought I was going to cry . . . I just hoped I wouldn't . . . I had to tell myself, don't cry Marianne, not now." She held her composure even after Mary leaned forward with a hug, as we boarded the elevator. Once inside, we stood in silence like strangers. Back in Michael's room for our debriefing we were at a loss to explain what might have provoked the negativity that pervaded room during the presentation. Was the presentation too long? Too corny? Too honest? Had prior SBPT business compromised their colleagues' attention? The silence returned, and with so little to make sense of, everyone headed home.

A few days later, the team repeated the presentation for the inclusion facilitator and the chair, both who were unable to attend the SBPT meeting. Both were enthusiastic about the presentation and urged that it be viewed throughout the district. Finally, the team seemed to have won appropriate approval for their efforts. But at that same moment, in the few minutes that remained, the Wellington principal joined the meeting and declared that the proposal lacked her endorsement. Further, until the SBPT took action, the issue would remain an internal issue at Wellington. She added that the team had overstepped its bounds by suggesting the elimination of the TT house without her in advance approval. Her words extinguished the enthusiasm that just moments before had filled the room. Her demeanor stunned the two district administrators, who sat in frozen silence. When it became apparent that no one would respond I reminded everyone that the proposal had been in the making over the course of numerous meetings. I recounted the diligent efforts made by the team, their site visits, their readings, their debates, and their struggle with issues that surfaced in our weekly meetings—each of which crystallized in their final proposal. I insisted that theirs was the most progressive work underway in the district. Michael then added, "I started this project with the belief that it was the principal that made inclusion a reality. While that's still true, I've since learned how important it is to ensure that faculty first clarify their own beliefs about inclusion." He added that Wellington needed to come to terms with how exclusion really works in their everyday business. On his words, the bell rang, the teachers rushed back to their classrooms, and the principal directed the chair to her office.

Later, the chair explained that the principal needed some time to come to understand and accept the proposal to eliminate the TT house as the team suggested. He urged that it was best to avoid further conversation on the topic unless she initiated it. Although the chair realized that the principal had usurped the purpose of the SBPT as well as the district's initiative to "accelerate" school-based inclusion, he was powerless to do anything until contacted by the principal. His response evoked his comments, months before, when the Morgan team dissolved without much fanfare.

Risking Imagination

Following the SBPT meeting the team's synergy markedly deteriorated. With the knowledge that no action would be taken until the June SBPT meeting, the weekly meetings were canceled due to increasing demands on teachers' time as the school year came to an end. One week prior to the meeting, the team received a memo from the SBPT listing 47 questions for which they were to prepare a response. Questions of mechanics, mandates, and legal obligation were prevalent throughout the list. For example:

How can we ensure this will not make instruction even more difficult?

What subject area classes are really possible for inclusion?

Who determines whether the rights of regular education students are infringed upon?

Who will change parenting styles?

Who is responsible?

How will students in each house be informed?

How do special education teachers feel about this?

How do our parents feel about this?

Upon receiving these questions the team felt wholly misunderstood, defeated, and insulted by the clear hostility targeted at their plan, and by default, at them. They had expected some questions about the mechanics of scheduling students, specifics about the coordination of teacher teams, maybe some more facts about the mandate. On the whole, they felt quite unprepared for the challenge this list signaled. In a meeting with the team to review the memo, I attempted to raise their spirits by noting that the list read like lines from the chorus of a Greek tragedy—a combination or foreboding danger and obvious despair. They smiled in weak response. Levity was futile given that in every sense, the team faced a community bound by shared fear and resentment rather than shared responsibilities and regard for all students. Although Michael had critiqued this very phenomenon months before, the team felt "exposed" by their ideologies and ridiculed for their efforts to take leadership on this project. The tone of the document was offensive and difficult to overlook. As a consequence, the team made little effort to disguise their "attitude" when, in one afternoon, they drafted their response. In contrast to previous efforts, they became reactionary, issuing answers that were neither generous nor generative. They delivered their memo in advance of the June meeting, at which time the SBPT decided they would take no action until the next school year.

Sacrifice or Surrender

If we begin with the assumption that inclusive education is a distinctly political, "in-your-face" activity, nothing short of tremendous courage will be required for those who work inside systems to challenge the long-standing mechanisms that underwrite exclusion. The starting point must be framed through the lens of civil rights and social justice since *all* else reduces appreciation for the complexity that is likely to follow. The Wellington team found themselves doing political work that at the outset they did not know was necessary. Their actions positioned them against a long history of status quo beliefs and practices common to most schools that signal the necessity of routinized actions that clearly legitimize inequality by individualizing failure. More importantly, listening to the students challenged the teachers once they saw reality from their students' eyes, and *because* they listened, the team was motivated to challenge the system. They could no longer refuse to hear nor refuse to see the intangible processes in schools whereby students are taught to judge themselves as either "valued or de-valued group members" (Corbett & Slee, 2000, p. 134).

At the conclusion of the school year, Marianne and Mary joined the SBPT team for a two-year appointment. They hoped that their presence would ensure that inclusion remain on the table. Ultimately it took two years to move their proposal forward, but in 2003, the TT house was finally eliminated and special education students were reassigned throughout the building. However, by that point in time, Marianne assumed an administrative position in a neighboring school district where she began the struggle anew in support of inclusion in a context she viewed as far more progressive and open to change. She continued to explore the impact of self-production among youth in schools and inclusion initiatives as the topic for her Ed.D. research requirements. Her initial interviews with students were reworked into more in-depth, structured interviews for her research, which in turn served as a tool for the students to authenticate their experiences. Throughout the process of gathering and analyzing her data, Marianne was struck by how "articulate" her students were—a somewhat bittersweet lesson after years of teaching in the absence of a critical consciousness.

Michael opted for what he referred to as a "temporary retreat" from further political battles in the school relative to inclusion. The following year he joined the faculty of the IB program where greater demands for curriculum development were anticipated as the program was launched. However, Michael continued to engage social justice issues in his pedagogy in a manner that was more akin to the politics of hope offered by Giroux (1997, 2003), rather than Freiere. Now drawn to issues of power as his students experienced it in schools, Michael was willing to grapple with the language of critical understanding to make sense of the *school voice,* the *student voice,* and the *teacher voice* (italics in the original, Giroux, 1997: 141). He enrolled in one of my university courses in which we undertook curriculum development informed by a disability studies perspective as the vehicle to challenge taken-for-granted assumptions about disability in schools and society (see Ware, 2003a; 2003b). In fulfillment of the course objectives, he designed a unit for his Theory of Knowledge class wherein students deconstructed the use of labels in educational contexts that mark intelligence. In my observation of his instruction the students treated me to a range of powerful interpretations on this theme. One group recounted the recent history of segregated classrooms at Wellington when students with different and unique learning needs were "housed in the basement" and "out of sight and out of mind." Outrage informed their insights as they segued into a discussion of knowledge as a social construct and the obvious links to the scientific impulse to purify the species.

Conclusion

This chapter captures in real-time the messiness and the "in-betweenness" of educational inclusion with all of its attendant compromises, adjustments, and individual preferences (Corbett, 1997: 55). Once the goal in schools becomes awareness that learners merit inclusion in an "accessible and accommodating community where they are valued for themselves. . . . [t]his emphasis tends to override issues of appropriate teaching and learning contexts" (ibid, 61). It is this rationale, whether in K12 or postsecondary settings, that "paves the way for a long-lasting social inclusion which determines quality of life and social status" (ibid). To understand that inclusion is about more than the issues of special education, of schooling in general, and of reinventing systems is to appreciate the struggle for changing attitudes about disability/ability and locating this initiative within a campaign for basic human rights. To do otherwise by minimizing the social-political and moral implications of educational inclusion all but ensures the worst form of naivete. Finally, to approach inclusion through the application of skills and the implementation of prescriptive models greatly undermines the power of human players to engage complexity and to challenge ideas that inform solidarity so as to *enact change upon their worlds*.

Educating Hope

> Hope, as it happens, is so important for our existence, individual and social, that we must take every care not to experience it in a mistaken form, and thereby allow it to slip toward hopelessness and despair: Hopelessness and despair are both the consequence and the cause of inaction or immobilization. (Freire, 1992: 9)

Despite decades of research that point to uninterruptible hierarchical patterns and well-sedimented structures in society that are readily reproduced in schools, teachers on the Wellington team took the necessary risks to engage the politics of ideology. They did not set out to develop a critical pedagogy of hope, nor did they launch the efforts described here to support my research interests. Instead, they acted, informed by both critical hope and a desire to engage in struggle, one that remains ongoing in their lives and anchored in their practice. It is important to remember that neither the teachers nor I ever welcomed this struggle, even though it greatly informed their lives and this research. Thus, to recount this experience in the absence of the clear challenges it posed suggests nothing short of deceit. Much more could be included here to detail the painful confrontation that often follows rigorous critical encounters with understanding how disability is constructed in schools (Ware, 2001, 2002, 2003a). However, a Freirean lens allows for recognizing the importance of both hope and struggle in an interdependent fashion, and as such, it provides one way to problematize overly romantic approaches to educational reform which Len Barton views as consistently implicating teachers as "scapegoats for factors over which they have little control" (see Chapter 4).

When hope serves as an ontological need, it follows that in the struggle a "kind of education in hope" can serve to counter the tragic despair that often results in inaction and immobilization. The teachers on the Wellington team realized the importance of building a community inspired by shared beliefs, whether it was with their colleagues or with their students, and each moved into distinct communities to accomplish just that. Their hope was neither naïve and superficially sanctioned nor fully realized as it continues to fuel their efforts.

In contrast to the administrators who chose the route of least resistance, some readers might shrug this behavior off as less than surprising. I argue otherwise. Earlier in this book, Len Barton suggests that policy-making always involves "alliances, tactics, and negotiations." Certainly, this case study underscores his arguments relative to the teachers. However, in the example of the administrators, it is their absence, inaction, and silences that merit attention. Throughout the year, disinterest of all things political by administrators—both in the district office and at Wellington high school—was difficult to overlook. There was no alliance, none shared in the strategizing of tactics; and in the end, it was the building principal who relied on inherited power to usurp the very tools of the SBPT processes and procedures sanctioned by the district. When she cited the team for failure to seek her approval in advance, hers was the typical default to power. Similarly, the district administrator who demanded a different version of the Wellington case study— one that minimized the actual events and highlighted the district's generous "support" of the mini-grant schools—was only mildy disappointed by my noncompliance. In the end, there was very little for which he was held accountable in the district's scheme of "inclusion as a procedural compliance." That the teachers could recognize the impact of the symbolic violence on the lives of their students, made all the difference—really, the only difference.

Notes

1. Consistent with ethnographic research, pseudonyms for the individuals and their school are utilized.
2. The Consent Decree specifically pertained to timely evaluation, program recommendations and placements; full involvement in meetings of the Committee on Special Education (CSE) and in other aspects of their children's special education; education in the least restrictive environment and a reduction in the number of students with disabilities placed on home instruction; equal access by students with disabilities to the

District's special schools and programs, curriculum and extracurricular activities, and school facilities, equipment and supplies; and a self-monitoring system in which the District could monitor and maintain compliance.

References

Allan, J. (1999). *Actively seeking inclusion: Pupils with special needs in mainstream schools.* London: Falmer Press.

Allan, J. (Ed.) (2003a). *Inclusion, Participation and Democracy: What is the purpose?* The Netherlands: Kluwer Academic Press.

Allan, J. (2003b). Inclusion and exclusion in the university. In T. Booth, K. Nes, and M. Stromstad (Eds.), *Developing inclusive teacher education,* 130–145. London: Falmer Press.

Ballard, K. (ed.). (1999). *Inclusive education. International voices on disability and justice.* London: Falmer Press.

Barton, L. (1997). Inclusive education: Romantic, subversive or realistic? *International Journal of Inclusive Education, 1*(3), 231–242.

Bernstein, B. (1967, September). Open schools, open society. *New Society, 14,* 351–353.

Bernstein, B. (1996). *Pedagogy: Symbolic control and identity, theory, research, critique.* London: Taylor and Francis.

Biklen, D. (1992). *Schooling without labels.* Philadelphia: Temple University Press.

Biklen, D. (2000). Constructing inclusion: Lessons from critical, disability narratives. *International Journal of Inclusive Education, 4*(4), 337–353.

Brantlinger, E. A. (1997). Using ideology: Cases of nonrecognition of the politics of research and practice in special education. *Review of Educational Research, 67*(4), 425–459.

Brantlinger, E. A. (2003). *Dividing class: How the middle class negotiates and justifies school advantage.* London: Routledge Falmer Press.

Corbett, J. (1996). *Bad mouthing: The language of special needs.* London: Falmer Press.

Corbett, J. (1997). Include/Exclude: Redefining the boundaries. *International Journal of Inclusive Education, 1*(1), 55–64.

Corbett, J., and Slee, R. (2000). "An international conversation on inclusive education." In Armstrong, F., Armstrong, D., and Barton, L. (Eds.), *Inclusive education: Policy, contexts and comparative perspectives,* 133–146. London: David Fulton Publisher.

Council for Exceptional Children. *Creating schools for all of our students: What 12 schools have to say.* (1994). Reston, VA: Council for Exceptional Children.

Democrat and Chronicle, June, 3, 1999, "School standards called too stressful." Rochester, New York.

Derrida, J. (1979). "Border lines." In Bloom et al. (Eds.), *Deconstruction and criticism.* New York: Seabury Presss.

District Document (1998, April). Inclusion Committee Report. Redding City School District, Redding, New York.

Feagin, D. (1998). *The new urban paradigm: Critical perspectives on the city.* Langham, MD: Rowman & Littlefield Publishers.

Friend, M. Reising, M., & Cook, L. (1993). Co-teaching: An overview of the past, a glimpse at the present and considerations for the future. *Preventing School Failure, 37*(4), 6–10.

Freire, P. (1992). *Pedagogy of hope.* New York: Continuum.

Giangreco, M. F. (1996). What do I do now? A teacher's guide to including students with disabilities. *Educational Leadership, 55*(5), 56–59.

Giroux, H. A. (1997). *Pedagogy and the politics of hope.* Boulder, CO: Westview Press.

Giroux, H. A. (2003). *The abandoned generation: Democracy beyond culture and fear.* New York: Palgrave Macmillan.

Heshusius, L. (1982). At the heart of the advocacy dilemma: A mechanistic worldview, *Exceptional Children, 49,* 6–13.

Hodgkinson, H. (1999, May). "The new demographics and its impact on urban schooling." An address to the State of New York Association of School Superintendents, Redding, New York.

Redding City School District, Inclusive Schools. (1998, April). Task Force Committee Report, document, p. 2.

Sibley, D. (1995). *Geographies of exclusion: Societies and difference in the west.* London and New York: Routledge.

Skrtic, T. M. (1991). *Behind special education: A critical analysis of professional culture and school organization.* Denver, CO: Love Publishing.

Skrtic, T. M. (ed) (1995). *Disability and democracy.* New York: Teachers College Press.

Tom, A. R. (1984). *Teaching as a moral craft.* New York: Longman.

Tomlinson, S. (1995). The radical structuralist view of special education and disability: Unpopular perspectives on their origins and development. In T. M. Skrtic (Ed.), *Disability and democracy.* New York: Teachers College Press.

Towler, M. A. (1998, December 915). "Failing our children: The class of 97." *City,* pp. 5–10. Redding, New York.

Villa, R., and Thousand, J. (1995). *Creating an inclusive school.* Alexandria, VA: Association for Supervision and Curriculum Development.

Ware, L. (2000). Inclusive education. In Gabbard, D. A. (Ed.), *Education in the global economy: Politics and the rhetoric of school reform,* 111–120. Mahwah, New Jersey: Lawrence Erlbaum Publishers.

Ware, L. (2001, March/April). Writing, identity, and other: Dare we do disability studies? *Journal of Teacher Education, 52*(2), 107–123.

Ware, L. (2002). A moral conversation on disability: Risking the personal in educational contexts. *Hypatia: A Journal of Feminist Philosophy, 17*(3), 143–171.

Ware, L. (2003a). Working past pity: What we make of disability in schools. In J. Allan (Ed.), *Inclusion, Participation and Democracy: What is the purpose?,* 117–137. The Netherlands: Kluwer Academic Press.

Ware, L. (2003b). Understanding disability and transforming schools. In T. Booth, K. Nes, and M. Stromstad (Eds.), *Developing inclusive teacher education,* 146–165. London: Routledge Falmer Press.

CONTRIBUTORS

Julie Allan is professor of education in the Institute of Education, University of Stirling, Scotland, and director of the Participation, Inclusion and Equity Research (PIER) Network. She is involved in teacher education and was recently adviser to the Scottish Parliament Inquiry on Special Educational Needs. She is the author of *Actively Seeking Inclusion* and most recently, *Inclusion, Participation and Democracy: What is the Purpose?*

Keith Ballard is professor and dean of the School of Education at the University of Otago, Dunedin, New Zealand. His research interests are inclusive education, action research with families of disabled children, and qualitative methodologies. Most recently, he edited *Inclusive Education: International Voices on Disability and Justice.*

Len Barton is dean of professional development, Institute of Education, University of London. He is the Founder and Editor of Disability & Society and is coeditor of a new book series with Kluwer Academic Books entitled *Inclusive Education: Cross Cultural Perspectives 2003.* His numerous publications address education policy and practice informed by a social justice perspective.

Ellen Brantlinger is a professor in the special education program area in the Department of Curriculum and Instruction at Indiana University in Bloomington, Indiana. Her scholarly interests are in the ideologies that interfere with inclusive, democratic school practices and in the influence of social class status on schooling. She recently published, *Dividing Classes: How the Middle Class Negotiates and Rationalizes School Advantage*.

Lous Heshusius is a professor emeritus at York University, Canada. She has published numerous articles in *Exceptional Children, Journal of Learning Disabilities, Educational Researcher*, and *Journal of Education*. She wrote the book *Meaning in Life as Experienced by Persons Labeled Retarded* and coedited *From Positivism to Interpretivism and Beyond*.

Jude MacArthur is senior researcher at the Donald Beasley Institute, an independent research institute dedicated to research and education relating to intellectual disability. Her work focuses particularly on methodologies that support the voices of children and young people with disabilities and their families to impact on school change.

Kari Nes is associate professor of education at Hedmark College, Hamar, Norway. She is involved in international collaboration on inclusion research and on the development of European master studies in inclusive education. She is presently engaged in the national research program for evaluation of the school reform "Reform 97," evaluating inclusion. She is coeditor of the book *Developing Inclusive Teacher Education*.

Roger Slee is dean of education at McGill University, Montreal, Quebec. Most recently he served as the deputy director-general of education at the Queensland Ministry of Education in Australia; dean of the Faculty of Education and foundation chair of Teaching and Learning at The University of Western Australia; professor of Education Studies and head of Department of Education Studies at Goldsmiths College, University of London. He is the founding editor of the International Journal of Inclusive Education.

Marit Stromstad is associate professor in the Department of Teacher Education, Hedmark College, Hamar, Norway. She supports teachers in the development of inclusive education. She is coeditor of the book *Developing Inclusive Teacher Education*.

Sally Tomlinson is professor of educational studies at the University of Oxford, England. She has written and researched extensively in the areas of educational policy, school effectiveness and special education, and the education of ethnic minorities in the UK and globally. Her recent book, *Education in a Post-Welfare Society* won international recognition.

Linda Ware is associate professor and head of the special education program at City College/City University of New York. Her specialties include inclusive education and disability in education studies in both national and international contexts.

INDEX

Studies in the Postmodern Theory of Education

General Editors
Joe L. Kincheloe & Shirley R. Steinberg

Counterpoints publishes the most compelling and imaginative books being written in education today. Grounded on the theoretical advances in criticalism, feminism, and postmodernism in the last two decades of the twentieth century, Counterpoints engages the meaning of these innovations in various forms of educational expression. Committed to the proposition that theoretical literature should be accessible to a variety of audiences, the series insists that its authors avoid esoteric and jargonistic languages that transform educational scholarship into an elite discourse for the initiated. Scholarly work matters only to the degree it affects consciousness and practice at multiple sites. Counterpoints' editorial policy is based on these principles and the ability of scholars to break new ground, to open new conversations, to go where educators have never gone before.

For additional information about this series or for the submission of manuscripts, please contact:

> Joe L. Kincheloe & Shirley R. Steinberg
> c/o Peter Lang Publishing, Inc.
> 275 Seventh Avenue, 28th floor
> New York, New York 10001

To order other books in this series, please contact our Customer Service Department:

> (800) 770-LANG (within the U.S.)
> (212) 647-7706 (outside the U.S.)
> (212) 647-7707 FAX

Or browse online by series:

> www.peterlangusa.com